The
MEDITEF~~~~~~~

Its Storied Citie
Ru

By
T. G. Bonney, E. A. R. Ball,
H. D. Traill, Grant Allen,
Arthur Griffiths, and Robert Brown

I

THE PILLARS OF HERCULES

Portals of the ancient world—Bay of Tangier at sunrise—Tarifa—The Rock of Gibraltar—Wonders of its fortifications—Afternoon promenade in the Alameda Gardens—Ascending the Rock—View from the highest point—The Great Siege—Ceuta, the principal Spanish stronghold on the Moorish coast—The rock of many names.

THE "Pillars of Hercules!" The portals of the Ancient World! To how many a traveller just beginning to tire of his week on the Atlantic, or but slowly recovering, it may be, in his tranquil voyage along the coasts of Portugal and Southern Spain, from the effects of thirty unquiet hours in the Bay of Biscay, has the nearing view of this mighty landmark of history brought a message of new life! That distant point ahead, at which the narrowing waters of the Strait that bears him disappear entirely within the clasp of the embracing shores, is for many such a traveller the beginning of romance. He gazes upon it from the westward with some dim reflection of that mysterious awe with which antiquity looked upon it from the East. The 2] progress of the ages has, in fact, transposed the center of human interest and the human point of view. Now, as in the Homeric era, the Pillars of Hercules form the gateway of a world of wonder; but for us of to-day it is within and not without those portals that that world of wonder lies. To the eye of modern poetry the Atlantic and Mediterranean have changed places. In the waste of waters stretching westward from the rock of Calpe and its sister headland, the Greek of the age of Homer found his region of immemorial poetic legend and venerable religious myth, and peopled it with the gods and heroes of his traditional creed. Here, on the bosom of the wide-winding river Oceanus, lay the Islands of the Blest—that abode of eternal beauty and calm, where "the life of mortals is most easy," where "there is neither snow nor winter nor much rain, but ocean is ever sending up the shrilly breezes of Zephyrus to refresh man." But for us moderns who have explored this mighty "river Oceanus," this unknown and mysterious Atlantic to its farthest recesses, the glamor of its mystery has passed away for ever; and it is eastward and not westward, through the "Pillars of Hercules," that we now set our sails in search of the region of romance. It is to the basin of the Mediterranean—fringed with storied cities and venerable ruins, with the crumbling sanctuaries of a creed which has passed away, and the monuments of an art which is imperishable—that man turns to-day. The genius of civilization has journeyed far to the westward, and has passed through strange experiences; it returns with new reverence and a deeper awe to that enclave of mid-Europe which contains its birthplace, and which is hallowed with the memories of its glorious youth. The grand cliff-portal 3] which we are approaching is the entrance, the thoughtful traveller will always feel, to a region eternally sacred in the history of man; to lands which gave birth to immortal models of literature and unerring canons of philosophic truth; to shrines and temples which guard the ashes of those "dead but sceptered sovereigns" who "rule our spirits from their urns."

As our vessel steams onward through the rapidly narrowing Straits, the eye falls upon a picturesque irregular cluster of buildings on the Spanish shore, wherefrom juts forth a rocky tongue of land surmounted by a tower. It is the Pharos of Tarifa, and in another half hour we are close enough to distinguish the exact outlines of the ancient and famous city named of Tarif Ibn Malek, the first Berber sheikh who landed in Spain, and itself, it is said—though some etymologists look askance at the derivation—the name-mother of a word which is little less terrible to the modern trader than was this pirate's nest itself to his predecessor of old times. The arms of Tarifa are a castle on waves, with a key at the window, and the device is not unaptly symbolical of her mediæval history, when her possessors played janitors of the Strait, and merrily levied blackmail—the irregular tariff of those days—upon any vessel which desired to pass. The little town itself is picturesquely situated in the deepest embrace of the curving Strait, and the view looking westward—with the lighthouse rising sharp and sheer against the sky, from the jutting cluster of rock and building about its base, while dimly to the left in the farther distance lie the mountains of the African coast, descending there so cunningly behind the curve that the two continents seem to touch and connect the channel into a lake—is well worth attentive study. An 4] interesting spot, too, is Tarifa, as well as a picturesque—interesting at least to all who are interested either in the earlier or the later fortunes of post-Roman Europe. It played its part, as did most other places, on this common battle-ground of Aryan and Semite, in the secular struggle between European Christendom and the Mohammedan East. And again, centuries later, it was heard of in the briefer but more catastrophic struggle of the Napoleonic wars. From the day when Alonzo Perez de Guzman threw his dagger down from its battlements in disdainful defiance of the threat to murder his son, dragged bound before him beneath its walls by traitors, it is a "far cry" to the day when Colonel Gough of the 87th (the "Eagle-Catchers") beat off Marshal Victor's besieging army of 1,800 strong, and relieved General Campbell and his gallant little garrison; but Tarifa has seen them both, and it is worth a visit not only for the sake of the ride from it over the mountains to Algeciras and Gibraltar, but for its historical associations also, and for its old-world charm.

We have taken it, as we propose also to take Tangier, a little out of its turn; for the voyaging visitor to Gibraltar is not very likely to take either of these two places on his way. It is more probable that he will visit them, the one by land and the other by sea, from the Rock itself. But Tangier in particular it is impossible to pass without a strong desire to make its acquaintance straightway; so many are the attractions which draw the traveller to this some-time appanage of the British Crown, this African pied à terre, which but for the insensate feuds and factions of the Restoration period might be England's to-day. There are few more enchanting sights than that of the Bay of Tangier as it appears at 5]sunrise to the traveller whose steamer has dropped down the Straits in the afternoon and evening hours of the previous day and cast anchor after nightfall at the nearest point off shore to which a vessel of any draught can approach. Nowhere in the world does a nook of such sweet tranquillity receive, and for a season, quiet, the hurrying waters of so restless a sea. Half a mile or so out towards the center of the Strait, a steamer from Gibraltar has to plough its way through the surface currents which speed continually from the Atlantic towards the Pillars of Hercules and the Mediterranean beyond. Here, under the reddening daybreak, all is calm. The blue waters of the bay, now softly flushing at the approach of sunrise, break lazily in mimic waves and "tender curving lines of creamy spray" upon the shining beach. To the right lies the city, spectral in the dawn, save where the delicate pale ivory of some of its higher houses is warming into faintest rose; while over all, over sea and shore and city, is the immersing crystal atmosphere of Africa, in which every rock, every ripple, every housetop, stands out as sharp and clear as the filigree work of winter on a frosted pane.

2

Nothing in Tangier, it must be honestly admitted, will compare with the approach to it by its incomparable bay. In another sense, too, there is nothing here or elsewhere which exactly resembles this "approach," since its last stage of all has to be performed alike for man and woman—unless man is prepared to wade knee-deep in the clear blue water—on the back of a sturdy Moor. Once landed, he will find that the picturesqueness of Tangier, like that of most Eastern cities, diminishes rather than increases on a nearer view. A walk through its main street yields nothing particularly worthy of 6] note, unless it be the minaret of the Djama-el-Kebir, the principal mosque of the city. The point to which every visitor to Tangier directs his steps, or has them directed for him, is the Bab-el-Sok, the gate of the market place, where the scene to be witnessed at early morning presents an unequaled picture of Oriental life. Crouching camels with their loads of dates, chaffering traders, chattering women, sly and servile looking Jews from the city, fierce-eyed, heavily armed children of the desert, rough-coated horses, and the lank-sided mules, withered crones squatting in groups by the wayside, tripping damsels ogling over the yashmak as they pass, and the whole enveloped in a blinding, bewildering, choking cloud of such dust as only Africa, "arida nutrix," can produce—such dust as would make the pulverulent particles of the dryest of turnpikes in the hottest of summers, and under the most parching of east winds, appear by comparison moist and cool, and no more than pleasingly titillatory of the mouth and nostrils—let the reader picture to himself such a scene with such accessories, and he will know what spectacle awaits him at early morning at the Bab-el-Sok of Tangier.

But we must resume our journey eastward towards the famous "Rock." There at last it is! There "dawns Gibraltar grand and gray," though Mr. Browning strains poetic license very hard in making it visible even "in the dimmest north-east distance," to a poet who was at that moment observing how "sunset ran one glorious blood-red recking into Cadiz Bay." We, at any rate, are far enough away from Cadiz before it dawns upon us in all its Titanic majesty of outline; grand, of course, with the grandeur of Nature, and yet with a certain strange air of human menace as of some piece of 7]Atlantean ordnance planted and pointed by the hand of man. This "armamental" appearance of the Rock—a look visible, or at any rate imaginable in it, long before we have approached it closely enough to discern its actual fortifications, still less its artillery—is much enhanced by the dead flatness of the land from which its western wall arises sheer, and with which by consequence it seems to have no closer physical connection than has a gun-carriage with the parade ground on which it stands. As we draw nearer this effect increases in intensity. The surrounding country seems to sink and recede around it, and the Rock appears to tower ever higher and higher, and to survey the Strait and the two continents, divided by it with a more and more formidable frown. As we approach the port, however, this impression gives place to another, and the Rock, losing somewhat of its "natural-fortress" air, begins to assume that resemblance to a couchant lion which has been so often noticed in it. Yet alas! for the so-called famous "leonine aspect" of the famous height, or alas! at least for the capricious workings of the human imagination! For while to the compiler of one well-reputed guidebook, the outlines of Gibraltar seem "like those of a lion asleep, and whose head, somewhat truncated, is turned towards Africa as if with a dreamy and steadfast deep attention;" to another and later observer the lion appears to have "his kingly head turned towards Spain, as if in defiance of his former master, every feature having the character of leonine majesty and power!" The truth is, of course, that the Rock assumes entirely different aspects, according as it is looked at from different points of view. There is certainly a point from which Gibraltar may be made, by the exercise of a

3

little of Polonius's imagination, to 8] resemble some couchant animal with its head turned towards Africa—though "a head somewhat truncated," is as odd a phrase as a "body somewhat decapitated"—and contemplating that continent with what we may fancy, if we choose, to be "dreamy and steadfast attention." But the resemblance is, at best, but a slender one, and a far-fetched. The really and strikingly leonine aspect of Gibraltar is undoubtedly that which it presents to the observer as he is steaming towards the Rock from the west, but has not yet come into full view of the slope on which the town is situated. No one can possibly mistake the lion then. His head is distinctly turned towards Spain, and what is more, he has a foot stretched out towards the mainland, as though in token of his mighty grasp upon the soil. Viewed, however, from the neutral ground, this Protean cliff takes on a new shape altogether, and no one would suppose that the lines of that sheer precipice, towering up into a jagged pinnacle, could appear from any quarter to melt into the blunt and massive curves which mark the head and shoulders of the King of Beasts.

At last, however, we are in the harbor, and are about to land. To land! How little does that phrase convey to the inexperienced in sea travel, or to those whose voyages have begun and ended in stepping from a landing-stage on to a gangway, and from a gangway on to a deck, and vice-versâ! And how much does it mean for him to whom it comes fraught with recollections of steep descents, of heaving seas, of tossing cock-boats, perhaps of dripping garments, certainly of swindling boatmen! There are disembarkations in which you come in for them all; but not at Gibraltar, at least under normal circumstances. The waters of the port are placid, 9] and from most of the many fine vessels that touch there you descend by a ladder, of as agreeable an inclination as an ordinary flight of stairs. All you have to fear is the insidious bilingual boatman, who, unless you strictly covenant with him before entering his boat, will have you at his mercy. It is true that he has a tariff, and that you might imagine that the offense of exceeding it would be punished in a place like Gibraltar by immediate court-martial and execution; but the traveller should not rely upon this. There is a deplorable relaxation of the bonds of discipline all over the world. Moreover, it is wise to agree with the boatmen for a certain fixed sum, as a salutary check upon undue liberality. Most steamers anchor at a considerable distance from the shore, and on a hot day one might be tempted by false sentiment to give the boatman an excessive fee.

Your hosts at Gibraltar—"spoiling" as they always are for the sight of new civilian faces—show themselves determined from the first to make you at home. Private Thomas Atkins on sentry duty grins broad welcome to you from the Mole. The official to whom you have to give account of yourself and your belongings greets you with a pleasant smile, and, while your French or Spanish fellow-traveller is strictly interrogated as to his identity, profession, purpose of visit, &c., your English party is passed easily and promptly in, as men "at home" upon the soil which they are treading. Fortunate is it, if a little bewildering, for the visitor to arrive at midday, for before he has made his way from the landing-place to his hotel he will have seen a sight which has few if any parallels in the world. Gibraltar has its narrow, quiet, sleepy alleys as have all Southern towns; and any one who confined himself to strolling through and 10] along these, and avoiding the main thoroughfare, might never discover the strangely cosmopolitan character of the place. He must walk up Waterport Street at midday in order to see what Gibraltar really is—a conflux of nations, a mart of races, an Exchange for all the multitudinous varieties of the human product. Europe, Asia, and Africa meet and jostle in this singular highway. Tall,

4

stately, slow-pacing Moors from the north-west coast; white-turbaned Turks from the eastern gate of the Mediterranean; thick-lipped, and woolly-headed negroids from the African interior; quick-eyed, gesticulating Levantine Greeks; gabardined Jews, and black-wimpled Jewesses; Spanish smugglers, and Spanish sailors; "rock-scorpions," and red-coated English soldiers—all these compose, without completing, the motley moving crowd that throngs the main street of Gibraltar in the forenoon, and gathers densest of all in the market near Commercial Square.

It is hardly then as a fortress, but rather as a great entrepôt of traffic, that Gibraltar first presents itself to the newly-landed visitor. He is now too close beneath its frowning batteries and dominating walls of rock to feel their strength and menace so impressive as at a distance; and the flowing tide of many-colored life around him overpowers the senses and the imagination alike. He has to seek the outskirts of the town on either side in order to get the great Rock again, either physically or morally, into proper focus. And even before he sets out to try its height and steepness by the ancient, if unscientific, process of climbing it—nay, before he even proceeds to explore under proper guidance its mighty elements of military strength—he will discover perhaps that sternness is not its only feature. Let him stroll 11] round in the direction of the race-course to the north of the Rock, and across the parade-ground, which lies between the town and the larger area on which the reviews and field-day evolutions take place, and he will not complain of Gibraltar as wanting in the picturesque. The bold cliff, beneath which stands a Spanish café, descends in broken and irregular, but striking, lines to the plain, and it is fringed luxuriantly from stair to stair with the vegetation of the South. Marching and counter-marching under the shadow of this lofty wall, the soldiers show from a little distance like the tin toys of the nursery, and one knows not whether to think most of the physical insignificance of man beside the brute bulk of Nature, or of the moral—or immoral—power which has enabled him to press into his service even the vast Rock which stands there beetling and lowering over him, and to turn the blind giant into a sort of Titanic man-at-arms.

Such reflections as these, however, would probably whet a visitor's desire to explore the fortifications without delay; and the time for that is not yet. The town and its buildings have first to be inspected; the life of the place, both in its military and—such as there is of it—its civil aspect, must be studied; though this, truth to tell, will not engage even the minutest observer very long. Gibraltar is not famous for its shops, or remarkable, indeed, as a place to buy anything, except tobacco, which, as the Spanish Exchequer knows to its cost (and the Spanish Customs' officials on the frontier too, it is to be feared, their advantage), is both cheap and good. Business, however, of all descriptions is fairly active, as might be expected, when we recollect that the town is pretty populous for its size, and numbers some 20,000 inhabitants, in addition to its garrison of from 5,000 to 6,000 12] men. With all its civil activity, however, the visitor is scarcely likely to forget—for any length of time—that he is in a "place of arms." Not to speak of the shocks communicated to his unaccustomed nerves by morning and evening gun-fire; not to speak of the thrilling fanfare of the bugles, executed as only the bugler of a crack English regiment can execute it, and echoed and re-echoed to and fro, from face to face of the Rock, there is an indefinable air of stern order, of rigid discipline, of authority whose word is law, pervading everything. As the day wears on toward the evening this aspect of things becomes more and more unmistakable; and in the neighborhood of the gates, towards the hour of gun-fire, you may see residents hastening

5

in, and non-residents quickening the steps of their departure, lest the boom of the fatal cannon-clock should confine or exclude them for the night. After the closing of the gates it is still permitted for a few hours to perambulate the streets; but at midnight this privilege also ceases, and no one is allowed out of doors without a night-pass. On the 31st of December a little extra indulgence is allowed. One of the military bands will perhaps parade the main thoroughfare discoursing the sweet strains of "Auld Lang Syne," and the civil population are allowed to "see the old year out and the new year in." But a timid and respectful cheer is their sole contribution to the ceremony, and at about 12.15 they are marched off again to bed: such and so vigilant are the precautions against treachery within the walls, or surprise from without. In Gibraltar, undoubtedly, you experience something of the sensations of men who are living in a state of siege, or of those Knights of Branksome who ate and drank in 13] armor, and lay down to rest with corslet laced, and with the buckler for a pillow.

The lions of the town itself, as distinguished from the wonders of its fortifications, are few in number. The Cathedral, the Garrison Library, Government House, the Alameda Gardens, the drive to Europa Point exhaust the list; and there is but one of these which is likely to invite—unless for some special purpose or other—a repetition of the visit. In the Alameda, however, a visitor may spend many a pleasant hour, and—if the peace and beauty of a hillside garden, with the charms of subtropical vegetation in abundance near at hand, and noble views of coast and sea in the distance allure him—he assuredly will. Gibraltar is immensely proud of its promenade, and it has good reason to be so. From the point of view of Nature and of Art the Alameda is an equal success. General Don, who planned and laid it out some three-quarters of a century ago, unquestionably earned a title to the same sort of tribute as was bestowed upon a famous military predecessor, Marshal Wade. Anyone who had "seen" the Alameda "before it was made," might well have "lifted up his hands and blessed" the gallant officer who had converted "the Red Sands," as the arid desert once occupying this spot was called, into the paradise of geranium-trees which has taken its place. Its monuments to Elliot and Wellington are not ideal: the mysterious curse pronounced upon English statuary appears to follow it even beyond seas; but the execution of the effigies of these national heroes may, perhaps, be forgotten in the interest attaching to their subjects. The residents at any rate, whether civil or military, are inured to these efforts of the sculptor's art, and have long since ceased 14] to repine. And the afternoon promenade in these gardens—with the English officers and their wives and daughters, English nursemaids and their charges, tourists of both sexes and all ages, and the whole surrounded by a polyglot and polychromatic crowd of Oriental listeners to the military band—is a sight well worth seeing and not readily to be forgotten.

But we must pursue our tour round the peninsula of the Rock; and leaving the new Mole on our right, and farther on the little land-locked basin of Rosia Bay, we pass the height of Buena Vista, crowned with its barracks, and so on to the apex of the promontory, Europa Point. Here are more barracks and, here on Europa Flats, another open and level space for recreation and military exercises beneath the cliff wall. Doubling the point, and returning for a short distance along the eastern side of the promontory, we come to the Governor's Cottage, a cool summer retreat nestling close to the Rock, and virtually marking the limits of our exploration. For a little way beyond this the cliff rises inaccessible, the road ends, and we must retrace our steps. So far as walking or driving along the flat is concerned, the visitor who has reached the point may allege, with a

6

certain kind of superficial accuracy, that he has "done Gibraltar." No wonder that the seasoned globe-trotter from across the Atlantic thinks nothing of taking Calpe in his stride.

To those, however, who visit Gibraltar in a historic spirit, it is not to be "done" by any means so speedily as this. Indeed, it would be more correct to say that the work of a visitor of this order is hardly yet begun. For he will have come to Gibraltar not mainly to stroll on a sunny promenade, or to enjoy a shady drive round the seaward slopes of a Spanish headland, or even to feast 15]his eyes on the glow of Southern color and the picturesque varieties of Southern life; but to inspect a great world-fortress, reared almost impregnable by the hand of Nature, and raised into absolute impregnability by the art of man; a spot made memorable from the very dawn of the modern period by the rivalries of nations, and famous for all time by one of the most heroic exploits recorded in the annals of the human race. To such an one, we say, the name of Gibraltar stands before and beyond everything for the Rock of the Great Siege; and he can no more think of it in the light of a Mediterranean watering-place, with, a romantic, if somewhat limited, sea-front, than he can think of the farmhouse of La Haye as an "interesting Flemish homestead," or the Chateau of Hougoumont as a Belgian gentleman's "eligible country house."

For him the tour of the renowned fortifications will be the great event of his visit. Having furnished himself with the necessary authorization from the proper military authorities (for he will be reminded at every turn of the strict martial discipline under which he lives), he will proceed to ascend the Rock, making his first halt at a building which in all probability he will often before this have gazed upon and wondered at from below. This is the Moorish Castle, the first object to catch the eye of the newcomer as he steps ashore at the Mole, and looks up at the houses that clamber up the western slope of the Rock. Their ascending tiers are dominated by this battlemented pile, and it is from the level on which it stands that one enters the famous galleries of Gibraltar. The castle is one of the oldest Moorish buildings in Spain, the Arabic legend over the south gate recording it to have been built in 725 by Abu-Abul-Hajez. Its 16]principal tower, the Torre del Homenaje, is riddled with shot marks, the scars left behind it by the ever-memorable siege. The galleries, which are tunneled in tiers along the north front of the Rock, are from two to three miles in extent. At one extremity they widen out into the spacious crypt known as the Hall of St. George, in which Nelson was feasted. No arches support these galleries; they are simply hewn from the solid rock, and pierced every dozen yards or so by port-holes, through each of which the black muzzle of a gun looks forth upon the Spanish mainland. They front the north, these grim watchdogs, and seeing that the plain lies hundreds of feet beneath them, and with that altitude of sheer rock face between them and it, they may perhaps be admitted to represent what a witty Frenchman has called le luxe et la coquetterie d' imprenable, or as we might put it, a "refinement on the impregnable." Artillery in position implies the possibility of regular siege operations, followed perhaps by an assault from the quarter which the guns command; but though the Spanish threw up elaborate works on the neutral ground in the second year of the great siege, neither then nor at any other time has an assault on the Rock from its

7

northern side been contemplated. Yet it has once been "surprised" from its eastern side, which looks almost equally inaccessible; and farther on in his tour of exploration, the visitor will come upon traces of that unprecedented and unimitated exploit. After having duly inspected the galleries, he will ascend to the Signal Tower, known in Spanish days as El Hacho, or the Torch, the spot at which beacon fires were wont on occasion to be kindled. It is not quite the highest point of the Rock, but the view from it is one of the most imposing in the world. 17] To the north lie the mountains of Ronda, and to the far east the Sierra of the Snows that looks down on Granada, gleams pale and spectral on the horizon. Far beneath you lie town and bay, the batteries with their tiny ordnance, and the harbor with its plaything ships; while farther onward, in the same line of vision, the African "Pillar of Hercules," Ceuta, looks down upon the sunlit waters of the Strait.

A little farther on is the true highest point of the Rock, 1,430 feet; and yet a little farther, after a descent of a few feet, we come upon the tower known as O'Hara's Folly, from which also the view is magnificent, and which marks the southernmost point of the ridge. It was built by an officer of that name as a watch tower, from which to observe the movements of the Spanish fleet at Cadiz, which, even across the cape as the crow flies, is distant some fifty or sixty miles. The extent, however, of the outlook which it actually commanded has probably never been tested, certainly not with modern optical appliances, as it was struck by lightning soon after its completion. Retracing his steps to the northern end of the height, the visitor historically interested in Gibraltar will do well to survey the scene from here once more before descending to inspect the fortifications of the coast line. Far beneath him, looking landward, lies the flat sandy part of the isthmus, cut just where its neck begins to widen by the British lines. Beyond these, again, extends the zone some half mile in breadth of the neutral ground; while yet farther inland, the eye lights upon a broken and irregular line of earthworks, marking the limit, politically speaking, of Spanish soil. These are the most notable, perhaps the only surviving, relic of the great siege. In the third year of that desperate leaguer—it 18] was in 1781—the Spaniards having tried in vain, since June, 1779, to starve out the garrison, resorted to the idea of bombarding the town into surrender, and threw up across the neutral ground the great earthworks, of which only these ruins remain. They had reason, indeed, to resort to extraordinary efforts. Twice within these twenty-four months had they reduced the town to the most dreadful straits of hunger, and twice had it been relieved by English fleets. In January, 1780, when Rodney appeared in the Straits with his priceless freight of food, the inhabitants were feeding on thistles and wild onions; the hind quarter of an Algerian sheep was selling for seven pounds ten, and an English milch cow for fifty guineas. In the spring of 1781, when Admiral Darby relieved them for the second time, the price of "bad ship's biscuits full of vermin"—says Captain John Drinkwater of the 72nd, an actor in the scenes which he has recorded—was a shilling a pound; "old dried peas, a shilling and fourpence; salt, half dirt, the sweepings of ships' bottoms, and storehouses, eightpence; and English farthing candles, sixpence apiece." These terrible privations having failed to break the indomitable spirit of the besieged, bombardment had, before the construction of these lines, been resorted to. Enormous batteries, mounting 170 guns and 80 mortars, had been planted along the shore, and had played upon the town, without interruption, for six weeks. Houses were shattered and set on fire, homeless and half-starved families were driven for shelter to the southern end of the promontory, where again they were harried by Spanish ships sailing round Europa Point and firing indiscriminately on shore. The troops, shelled out of their quarters, were living in tents on the hillside, save when these also were swept 19] away by the furious rainstorms of that region. And it was to put, as was hoped, the finishing stroke to this process of torture, that the great fortifications which have been spoken of were in course of construction all through the spring and summer of 1781 on the neutral ground. General Elliot—that tough old Spartan warrior, whose food was vegetables and water, and four hours his maximum of continuous sleep, and the contagion of whose noble example could alone perhaps have given heart enough even to this sturdy garrison—watched the progress of the works with anxiety, and had made up his mind before the winter came that they must be assaulted. Accordingly, at three a. m. on the morning of November 27, 1781, he sallied forth with a picked band of two thousand men—a pair of regiments who had fought by his side at Minden two-and-twenty years before—and having traversed the three-quarters of a mile of intervening country in swift silence, fell upon the Spanish works. The alarm had been given, but only just before the assailants reached the object of their attack; and the affair was practically a surprise. The gunners, demoralized and panic-stricken, were bayoneted at their posts, the guns were spiked, and the batteries themselves set on fire with blazing faggots prepared for the purpose. In an hour the flames had gained such strength as to be inextinguishable, and General Elliot drew off his forces and retreated to the town, the last sound to greet their ears as they re-entered the gates being the roar of the explosion of the enemy's magazines. For four days the camp continued to burn, and when the fire had exhausted itself for want of materials, the work of laborious months lay in ruins, and the results of a vast military outlay were scattered to the winds. It was the last serious attempt made against the 20] garrison by the Spaniards from the landward side. The fiercest and most furious struggle of the long siege was to take place on the shore and waters to the west.

And so after all it is to the "line-wall"—to that formidable bulwark of masonry and gun-metal which fringes the town of Gibraltar from the Old Mole to Rosia Bay—that one returns as to the chief attraction from the historical point of view, of the mighty fortress. For two full miles it runs, zigzagging along the indented coast, and broken here and there by water-gate or bastion, famous in military story. Here, as we move southward from the Old Mole, is the King's Bastion, the most renowned of all. Next comes Ragged Staff Stairs, so named from the heraldic insignia of Charles V.; and farther on is Jumper's Battery, situated at what is held to be the weakest part of the Rock, and which has certainly proved itself to be so on one ever memorable occasion. For it was at the point where Jumper's Battery now stands that the first English landing-party set foot on shore; it was at this point, it may be said, that Gibraltar was carried. The fortunes of nomenclature are very capricious, and the name of Jumper—unless, indeed, it were specially selected for its appropriateness—has hardly a better right to perpetuation in this fashion than the name of Hicks. For these were the names of the two gallant officers who were foremost in their pinnaces in the race for the South Mole, which at that time occupied the spot where the landing was effected; and we are not aware that history records which was the actual winner. It was on the 23rd of July, 1704, as all the world knows, that these two gallant seamen and their boats' crews made their historic leap on shore; and after all, the accident which had preserved the name of one of them is not more of 21] what is familiarly called a "fluke" than the project of the capture itself, and the retention of the great fortress when captured. It is almost comic to think that when Sir George Rooke sailed from England, on the voyage from which he returned, figuratively speaking, with the key of the Mediterranean in his pocket, he had no more notion of attacking Gibraltar than of discovering the North-West Passage. He simply went to land England's candidate for the Spanish throne, "King Charles III.," at Lisbon; which service performed, he received orders from the English Government to sail to the relief of Nice

9

and Villa Franca, which were supposed to be in danger from the French, while at the same time he was pressed by Charles to "look round" at Barcelona, where the people, their aspirant-sovereign thought, were ready to rise in his favor. Rooke executed both commissions. That is to say, he ascertained that there was nothing for him to do in either place—that Barcelona would not rise, and that Nice was in no danger of falling; and the admiral accordingly dropped down the Mediterranean towards the Straits—where he was joined by Sir Cloudesley Shovel with another squadron—with the view of intercepting the Brest Fleet of France, which he had heard was about to attempt a junction with that of Toulon. The Brest Fleet, however, he found had already given him the slip, and thus it came about that on the 17th of July these two energetic naval officers found themselves about seven leagues to the east of Tetuan with nothing to do. It is hardly an exaggeration to say that the attack on Gibraltar was decreed as the distraction of an intolerable ennui. The stronghold was known to be weakly garrisoned, though, for that time, strongly armed; it turned out afterwards that it had only a hundred 22] and fifty gunners to a hundred guns, and it was thought possible to carry the place by a coup-de-main. On the 21st the whole fleet came to anchor in Gibraltar Bay. Two thousand men under the Prince of Hesse were landed on what is now the neutral ground, and cut off all communication with the mainland of Spain. On the 23rd Rear-Admirals Vanderdussen and Byng (the father of a less fortunate seaman) opened fire upon the batteries, and after five or six hours' bombardment silenced them, and Captain Whittaker was thereupon ordered to take all the boats, filled with seamen and marines, and possess himself of the South Mole Head. Captains Jumper and Hicks were, as has been said, in the foremost pinnaces, and were the first to land. A mine exploded under their feet, killing two officers and a hundred men, but Jumper and Hicks pressed on with their stout followers, and assaulted and carried a redoubt which lay between the Mole and the town. Whereupon the Spanish Governor capitulated, the gates on the side of the isthmus were thrown open to the Prince of Hesse and his troops, and Gibraltar was theirs. Or rather it was not theirs, except by the title of the "man in possession." It was the property of his Highness the Archduke Charles, styled his Majesty King Charles III. of Spain, and had he succeeded in making good that title in arms, England should, of course, have had to hand over to him the strongest place in his dominions, at the end of the war. But she profited by the failure of her protégé. The war of the Spanish Succession ended in the recognition of Philip V.; and almost against the will of the nation—for George I. was ready enough to give it up, and the popular English view of the matter was that it 23] was "a barren rock, an insignificant fort, and a useless charge"—Gibraltar remained on her hands.

Undoubtedly, the King's Bastion is the center of historic military interest in Gibraltar, but the line-wall should be followed along its impregnable front to complete one's conception of the sea defenses of the great fortress. A little farther on is Government House, the quondam convent, which now forms the official residence of the Governor; and farther still the landing-place, known as Ragged Staff Stairs. Then Jumper's Bastion, already mentioned; and then the line of fortification, running outwards with the coast line towards the New Mole and landing-place, returns upon itself, and rounding Rosia Bay trends again southward towards Buena Vista Point. A ring of steel indeed—a coat of mail on the giant's frame, impenetrable to the projectiles of the most terrible of the modern Titans of the seas. The casemates for the artillery are absolutely bomb-proof, the walls of such thickness as to resist the impact of shots weighing hundreds of pounds, while the mighty arches overhead are constructed to defy the explosion of the heaviest shells. As to its offensive armament, the line-wall bristles with guns of the largest caliber, some mounted on the parapet above, others on the casemates nearer the sea-level, whence their shot could be discharged with the deadliest effect at an attacking ship.

He who visits Gibraltar is pretty sure, at least if time permits, to visit Algeciras and San Roque, while from farther afield still he will be tempted by Estepona. The first of these places he will be in a hurry, indeed, if he misses; not that the place itself is very remarkable, as that it stands so prominently in evidence on the other 24] side of the bay as almost to challenge a visit. Add to this the natural curiosity of a visitor to pass over into Spanish territory and to survey Gibraltar from the landward side, and it will not be surprising that the four-mile trip across the bay is pretty generally made. On the whole it repays; for though Algeciras is modern and uninteresting enough, its environs are picturesque, and the artist will be able to sketch the great rock-fortress from an entirely new point, and in not the least striking of its aspects.

And now, before passing once for all through the storied portal of the Mediterranean, it remains to bestow at least a passing glance upon the other column which guards the entrance. Over against us, as we stand on Europa Point and look seaward, looms, some ten or a dozen miles away, the Punta de Africa, the African Pillar of Hercules, the headland behind which lies Ceuta, the principal Spanish stronghold on the Moorish coast. Of a truth, one's first thought is that the great doorway of the inland sea has monstrously unequal jambs. Except that the Punta de Africa is exactly opposite the Rock of Gibraltar, and that it is the last eminence on the southern side of the Straits—the point at which the African coast turns suddenly due southward, and all is open sea—it would have been little likely to have caught the eye of an explorer, or to have forced itself upon the notice of the geographer. Such as it is, however, it must stand for the African Pillar of Hercules, unless that demi-god is to content himself with only one. It is not imposing to approach as we make our way directly across the Straits from Gibraltar, or down and along them from Algeciras towards it: a smooth, rounded hill, surmounted by a fort with the Spanish flag floating above it, and 25] walled on the sea side, so little can its defenders trust to the very slight natural difficulties offered even by its most difficult approach. Such is Ceuta in the distance, and it is little, if at all, more impressive on a closer inspection. Its name is said to come from Sebta, a corruption of Septem, and to have been given it because of the seven hills on which it is built. Probably the seven hills would be difficult to find and count, or with a more liberal interpretation of the word, it might very likely be as easy to find fourteen.

Ceuta, like almost every other town or citadel on this battle-ground of Europe and Africa, has played its part in the secular struggle between Christendom and Islam. It is more than four centuries and a half since it was first wrested from the Moors by King John of Portugal, and in the hands of that State it remained for another two hundred years, when in 1640, it was annexed to the Crown of Castille. King John's acquisition of the place, however, was unfortunate for his family. He returned home, leaving the princes of Portugal in command of his new possession; which, after the repulse of an attempt on the part of the Moors to recapture it, he proceeded to strengthen with new fortifications and an increased garrison. Dying in 1428, he was succeeded by his eldest son, Edward, who undertook an expedition against Tangier, which turned out so unluckily that the Portuguese had to buy their retreat from Africa by a promise to restore Ceuta, the king's son, Don Ferdinand, being left in the hands of the Moors as a hostage for its delivery. In spite of this, however, the King and Council refused on their return home to carry out their undertaking; and though preparations were made for recovering the unfortunate hostage, the death of Edward prevented the 26] project from being carried out, and Prince Ferdinand remained a prisoner for several years. Ceuta was never surrendered, and passing, as has been said, in the seventeenth century from the possession of Portugal into that of Spain, it now forms one of the four or five vantage-points held by Spain on the coast of Africa and in its vicinity. Surveyed from the neighboring heights, the citadel, with the town stretching away along the neck of land at its foot, looks like anything but a powerful stronghold, and against any less effete and decaying race than the Moors who surround it, it might not possibly prove very easy to defend. Its garrison, however, is strong, whatever its forts may be, and as a basis of military operations, it proved to be of some value to Spain in her expedition against Morocco thirty years ago. In times of peace it is used by the Spaniards as a convict station.

The internal attractions of Ceuta to a visitor are not considerable. There are Roman remains in the neighborhood of the citadel, and the walls of the town, with the massive archways of its gates, are well worthy of remark. Its main feature of interest, however, is, and always will be, that rock of many names which it thrusts forth into the Straits, to form, with its brother column across the water, the gateway between the Eastern and the Western World. We have already looked upon it in the distance from El Hacho, the signal tower on the summit of the Rock of Gibraltar. Abyla, "the mountain of God," it was styled by the Phœnicians; Gibel Mo-osa, the hill of Musa, was its name among the Moors; it is the Cabo de Bullones of the Spaniard, and the Apes' Hill of the Englishman. It may be well seen, though dwarfed a little by proximity, from its neighboring 27] waters; a curious sight, if only for its strange contrast with the European Pillar that we have left behind. It is shaped like a miniature Peak of Teneriffe, with a pointed apex sloping away on either side down high-shouldered ridges towards its companion hills, and presenting a lined and furrowed face to the sea. It is its situation, as has been noted already, and not its conformation, which procured it its ancient name. But however earned, its mythical title, with all the halo of poetry and romance that the immortal myths of Hellas have shed around every spot which they have reached, remains to it for ever. And here we take our farewell look of the Pillars of Hercules to right and left, and borne onwards amidstream by the rushing current of the Straits, we pass from the modern into the ancient world.

28]

II

ALGIERS

"A Pearl set in Emeralds"—Two distinct towns, one ancient, one modern—The Great Mosque—A Mohammedan religious festival—Oriental life in perfection—The road to Mustapha Supérieur—A true Moorish villa described—Women praying to a sacred tree—Excessive rainfall.

12

"ALGIERS," says the Arab poet, with genuine Oriental love of precious stones in literature, "is a pearl set in emeralds." And even in these degenerate days of Frank supremacy in Islam, the old Moorish town still gleams white in the sun against a deep background of green hillside, a true pearl among emeralds. For it is a great mistake to imagine North Africa, as untravelled folk suppose, a dry and desert country of arid rocky mountains. The whole strip of laughing coast which has the Atlas for its backbone may rank, on the contrary, as about the dampest, greenest, and most luxuriant region of the Mediterranean system. The home of the Barbary corsairs is a land of high mountains, deep glens, great gorges; a land of vast pine forests and thick, verdant undergrowth. A thousand rills tumble headlong down its rich ravines; a thousand rivers flow fast through its fertile valleys. For wild flowers Algeria is probably unequaled in the whole world; its general aspect in many ways recalls on a 29]smaller scale the less snow-clad parts of eastern Switzerland.

When you approach the old pirate-nest from the sea, the first glimpse of the African coast that greets your expectant eye is a long, serrated chain of great sun-smitten mountains away inland and southward. As the steamer nears the land, you begin, after a while, to distinguish the snowy ridge of the glorious Djurjura, which is the Bernese Oberland of Algeria, a huge block of rearing peaks, their summits thick-covered by the virgin snow that feeds in spring a score of leaping torrents. By-and-by, with still nearer approach, a wide bay discloses itself, and a little range of green hills in the foreground detaches itself by degrees from the darker mass of the Atlas looming large in the distance behind. This little range is the Sahel, an outlier just separated from the main chain in the rear by the once marshy plain of the Metidja, now converted by drainage and scientific agriculture into the most fertile lowland region of all North Africa.

Presently, on the seaward slopes of the Sahel, a white town bursts upon the eye, a white town so very white, so close, so thick-set, that at first sight you would think it carved entire, in tier after tier, from a solid block of marble. No street or lane or house or public building of any sort stands visible from the rest at a little distance; just a group of white steps, you would say, cut out by giant hands from the solid hillside. The city of the Deys looks almost like a chalk-pit on the slope of an English down; only a chalk-pit in relief, built out, not hewn inwards.

As you enter the harbor the strange picture resolves itself bit by bit with charming effect into its component 30] elements. White houses rise up steep, one above the other, in endless tiers and rows, upon a very abrupt acclivity. Most of them are Moorish in style, square, flat-roofed boxes; all are whitewashed without, and smiling like pretty girls that show their pearly teeth in the full southern sunshine. From without they have the aspect of a single solid block of stone; you would fancy it was impossible to insert a pin's head between them. From within, to him that enters, sundry narrow and tortuous alleys

13

discover themselves here and there on close inspection; but they are too involved to produce much effect as of streets or rows on the general coup d'œil from the water.

Land at the quay, and you find at once Algiers consists of two distinct towns: one ancient, one modern; one Oriental, one Western. Now and again these intersect, but for the most part they keep themselves severely separate.

The lower town has been completely transformed within half a century by its French masters. What it has gained in civilization it has lost in picturesqueness. A spacious port has been constructed, with massive mole and huge arcaded breakwater. Inside, vast archways support a magnificent line of very modern quays, bordered by warehouses on a scale that would do honor to Marseilles or to Liverpool. Broad streets run through the length and breadth of this transformed Algiers, streets of stately shops where ladies can buy all the fripperies and fineries of Parisian dressmakers. Yet even here the traveller finds himself already in many ways en plein Orient. The general look of the new town itself is far more Eastern than that of modernized Alexandria since the days of the bombardment. Arabs, Moors and 31] Kabyles crowd the streets and market-places; muffled women in loose white robes, covered up to the eyes, flit noiselessly with slippered feet over the new-flagged pavement; turbaned Jews, who might have stepped straight out of the "Arabian Nights," chaffer for centimes at the shop-doors with hooded mountain Berbers. All is strange and incongruous; all is Paris and Bagdad shaking hands as if on the Devonshire hillsides.

Nor are even Oriental buildings of great architectural pretensions wanting to this newer French city. The conquerors, in reconstructing Algiers on the Parisian model, have at least forborne to Haussmannise in every instance the old mosques and palaces. The principal square, a broad place lined with palm-trees, is enlivened and made picturesque by the white round dome and striking minarets of the Mosquée de la Pêcherie. Hard by stands the Cathedral, a religious building of Mussulman origin, half Christianized externally by a tower at each end, but enclosing within doors its old Mohammedan mimbar and many curious remains of quaint Moorish decoration. The Archbishopric at its side is a Moorish palace of severe beauty and grandeur; the museum of Græco-Roman antiques is oddly installed in the exquisite home raised for himself by Mustapha Pasha. The Great Mosque, in the Rue Bab-el-Oued, remains to us unspoiled as the finest architectural monument of the early Mohammedan world. That glorious pile was built by the very first Arab conquerors of North Africa, the companions of the Prophet, and its exquisite horse-shoe arches of pure white marble are unsurpassed in the Moslem world for their quaintness, their oddity, and their originality.

The interior of this mosque is, to my mind, far more impressive than anything to be seen even in Cairo itself, 32] so vast it is, so imposing, so grand, so gloomy. The entire body of the building is occupied throughout by successive arcades, supported in long rows by plain, square pillars. Decoration there is none; the mosque depends for effect entirely on its architectural features and its noble proportions. But the long perspective of these endless aisles, opening out to right and left perpetually as you proceed, strikes the imagination of the beholder with a solemn sense of vastness and mystery. As you pick your way, shoeless, among the loose mats on the floor, through those empty long corridors, between those buttress-like pillars, the soul shrinks within you, awe-struck. The very absence of images or shrines, the simplicity and severity, gives one the true Semitic

14

religious thrill. No gauds or gewgaws here. You feel at once you are in the unseen presence of the Infinite and the Incomprehensible.

The very first time I went into the Great Mosque happened, by good luck, to be the day of a Mohammedan religious festival. Rows and rows of Arabs in white robes filled up the interspaces of the columns, and rose and fell with one accord at certain points of the service. From the dim depths by the niche that looks towards Mecca a voice of some unseen ministrant droned slowly forth loud Arabic prayers or long verses from the Koran. At some invisible signal, now and again, the vast throng of worshippers, all ranged in straight lines at even distances between the endless pillars, prostrated themselves automatically on their faces before Allah, and wailed aloud as if in conscious confession of their own utter unworthiness. The effect was extraordinary, electrical, contagious. No religious service I have ever seen elsewhere seemed to me to possess such a profundity of 33]earnest humiliation, as of man before the actual presence of his Maker. It appeared to one like a chapter of Nehemiah come true again in our epoch. We few intrusive Westerns, standing awe-struck by the door, slunk away, all abashed, from this scene of deep abasement. We had no right to thrust ourselves upon the devotions of these intense Orientals. We felt ourselves out of place. We had put off our shoes, for the place we stood upon was holy ground. But we slunk back to the porch, and put them on again in silence. Outside, we emerged upon the nineteenth century and the world. Yet even so, we had walked some way down the Place de la Régence, among the chattering negro pedlers, before one of us dared to exchange a single word with the other.

If the new town of Algiers is interesting, however, the old town is unique, indescribable, incomprehensible. No map could reproduce it; no clue could unravel it. It climbs and clambers by tortuous lanes and steep staircases up the sheer side of a high hill to the old fortress of the Deys that crowns the summit. Not one gleam of sunshine ever penetrates down those narrow slits between the houses, where two people can just pass abreast, brushing their elbows against the walls, and treading with their feet in the poached filth of the gutter. The dirt that chokes the sides is to the dirt of Italy as the dirt of Italy is to the dirt of Whitechapel. And yet so quaint, so picturesque, so interesting is it all, that even delicate ladies, with the fear of typhoid fever for ever before their eyes, cannot refuse themselves the tremulous joy of visiting it and exploring it over and over again; nay, more, of standing to bargain for old brass-work or Algerian embroidery with keen Arab shopkeepers in its sunless labyrinths. Except the Mooskee at Cairo, indeed, 34] I know no place yet left where you can see Oriental life in perfection as well as the old town of Algiers. For are there not tramways nowadays even in the streets of Damascus? Has not a railway station penetrated the charmed heart of Stamboul? The Frank has done his worst for the lower town of his own building, but the upper town still remains as picturesque, as mysterious, and as insanitary as ever. No Pasteur could clean out those Augean stables.

In those malodorous little alleys, where every prospect pleases and every scent is vile, nobody really walks; veiled figures glide softly as if to inaudible music; ladies, muffled up to their eyes, use those solitary features with great effect upon the casual passer-by; old Moors, in stately robes, emerge with stealthy tread from half-unseen doorways; boys clad in a single shirt sit and play pitch-and-toss for pence on dark steps. Everything reeks impartially of dirt and of mystery. All is gloom and shade. You could believe anything on

15

earth of that darkling old town. There all Oriental fancies might easily come true, all fables might revive, all dead history might repeat itself.

These two incongruous worlds, the ancient and the modern town, form the two great divisions of Algiers as the latter-day tourist from our cold North knows it. The one is antique, lazy, sleepy, unprogressive; the other is bustling, new-world, busy, noisy, commercial. But there is yet a third Algiers that lies well without the wall, the Algiers of the stranger and of the winter resident. Hither Mr. Cook conducts his eager neophytes; hither the Swiss innkeeper summons his cosmopolitan guests. It reaches its culminating point about three miles from 35] the town, on the heights of Mustapha Supérieur, where charming villas spread thick over the sunlit hills, and where the Western visitor can enjoy the North African air without any unpleasant addition of fine old crusted Moorish perfumes.

The road to Mustapha Supérieur lies through the Bab-Azzoun gate, and passes first along a wide street thronged with Arabs and Kabyles from the country and the mountains. This is the great market road of Algiers, the main artery of supplies, a broad thoroughfare lined with fondouks or caravanserais, where the weary camel from the desert deposits his bales of dates, and where black faces of Saharan negroes smile out upon the curious stranger from dense draping folds of some dirty burnouse. The cafés are filled with every variety of Moslem, Jew, Turk, and infidel. Nowhere else will you see to better advantage the wonderful variety of races and costumes that distinguishes Algiers above most other cosmopolitan Mediterranean cities. The dark M'zabite from the oases, arrayed like Joseph in a coat of many colors, stands chatting at his own door with the pale-faced melancholy Berber of the Aurès mountains. The fat and dusky Moor, over-fed on kous-kous, jostles cheek by jowl with the fair Jewess in her Paisley shawl and quaint native head-gear. Mahonnais Spaniards from the Balearic Isles, girt round their waists with red scarves, talk gaily to French missionary priests in violet bands and black cassocks. Old Arabs on white donkeys amble with grave dignity down the center of the broad street, where chasseurs in uniform and spahis in crimson cloaks keep them company on fiery steeds from the Government stud at Blidah. All is noise and bustle, hurry, scurry, 36] and worry, the ant-hill life of an English bazaar grotesquely superimposed on the movement and stir of a great European city.

You pass through the gates of the old Moorish town and find yourself at once in a modern but still busy suburb. Then on a sudden the road begins to mount the steep Mustapha slope by sharp zigzags and bold gradients. In native Algerian days, before Allah in his wisdom mysteriously permitted the abhorred infidel to bear sway in the Emerald City over the Faithful of Islam, a single narrow mule-path ascended from the town wall to the breezy heights of Mustapha. It still exists, though deserted, that old breakneck Mussulman road a deep cutting through soft stone, not unlike a Devonshire lane, all moss-grown and leafy, a favorite haunt of the naturalist and the trap-door spider. But the French engineers, most famous of road-makers, knew a more excellent way. Shortly after the conquest they carved a zigzag carriage-drive of splendid dimensions up that steep hill-front, and paved it well with macadam of most orthodox solidity. At the top, in proof of their triumph over nature and the Moslem, they raised a tiny commemorative monument, the Colonne Voirol, after their commander's name, now the Clapham Junction of all short excursions among the green dells of the Sahel.

16

The Mustapha road, on its journey uphill, passes many exquisite villas of the old Moorish corsairs. The most conspicuous is that which now forms the Governor-General's Summer Palace, a gleaming white marble pile of rather meretricious and over-ornate exterior, but all glorious within, to those who know the secret of decorative art, with its magnificent heirloom of antique tiled dados. Many of the other ancient villas, however, and 37]notably the one occupied by Lady Mary Smith-Barry, are much more really beautiful, even if less externally pretentious, than the Summer Palace. One in particular, near the last great bend of the road, draped from the ground to the flat roof with a perfect cataract of bloom by a crimson bougainvillea, may rank among the most picturesque and charming homes in the French dominions.

It is at Mustapha, or along the El Biar road, that the English colony of residents or winter visitors almost entirely congregates. Nothing can be more charming than this delicious quarter, a wilderness of villas, with its gleaming white Moorish houses half lost in rich gardens of orange, palm, and cypress trees. How infinitely lovelier these Eastern homes than the fantastic extravagances of the Californie at Cannes, or the sham antiques on the Mont Boron! The native North African style of architecture answers exactly to the country in whose midst it was developed. In our cold northern climes those open airy arcades would look chilly and out of place, just as our castles and cottages would look dingy and incongruous among the sunny nooks of the Atlas. But here, on the basking red African soil, the milk-white Moorish palace with its sweeping Saracenic arches, its tiny round domes, its flat, terraced roofs, and its deep perspective of shady windows, seems to fit in with land and climate as if each were made for the other. Life becomes absolutely fairy-like in these charming old homes. Each seems for the moment while you are in it just a dream in pure marble.

I am aware that to describe a true Moorish villa is like describing the flavor of a strawberry; the one must be tasted, the other seen. But still, as the difficulty of a 38] task gives zest to the attempt at surmounting it, I will try my hand at a dangerous word-picture. Most of the Mustapha houses have an outer entrance-court, to which you obtain admission from the road by a plain, and often rather heavy, archway. But, once you have reached the first atrium, or uncovered central court, you have no reason to complain of heaviness or want of decoration. The court-yard is generally paved with parti-colored marble, and contains in its center a Pompeian-looking fountain, whose cool water bubbles over into a shallow tank beneath it. Here reeds and tall arums lift their stately green foliage, and bright pond-blossoms rear on high their crimson heads of bloom. Round the quadrangle runs a covered arcade (one might almost say a cloister) of horse-shoe arches, supported by marble columns, sometimes Græco-Roman antiques, sometimes a little later in date, but admirably imitated from the originals. This outer court is often the most charming feature of the whole house. Here, on sultry days, the ladies of the family sit with their books or their fancy-work; here the lord of the estate smokes his afternoon cigar; here the children play in the shade during the hottest African noon-day. It is the place for the siesta, for the afternoon tea, for the lounge in the cool of the evening, for the joyous sense of the delight of mere living.

17

From the court-yard a second corridor leads into the house itself, whose center is always occupied by a large square court, like the first in ground-plan, but two-storied and glass-covered. This is the hall, or first reception room, often the principal apartment of the whole house, from which the other rooms open out in every direction. Usually the ground-floor of the hall has an open arcade, supporting a sort of balcony or gallery 39] above, which runs right round the first floor on top of it. This balcony is itself arcaded; but instead of the arches being left open the whole way up, they are filled in for the first few feet from the floor with a charming balustrade of carved Cairene woodwork. Imagine such a court, ringed round with string-courses of old Oriental tiles, and decorated with a profusion of fine pottery and native brasswork, and you may form to yourself some faint mental picture of the common remodeled Algerian villa. It makes one envious again to remember how many happy days one has spent in some such charming retreats, homes where all the culture and artistic taste of the West have been added to all the exquisite decorative instinct and insight of the Oriental architect.

Nor are fair outlooks wanting. From many points of view on the Mustapha Hill the prospect is among the most charming in the western Mediterranean. Sir Lambert Playfair, indeed, the learned and genial British Consul-General whose admirable works on Algeria have been the delight of every tourist who visits that beautiful country, is fond of saying that the two finest views on the Inland Sea are, first, that from the Greek Theater at Taormina, and, second, that from his own dining-room windows on the hill-top at El Biar. This is very strong praise, and it comes from the author of a handbook to the Mediterranean who has seen that sea in all aspects, from Gibralta to Syria; yet I fancy it is too high, especially when one considers that among the excluded scenes must be put Naples, Sorrento, Amalfi, Palermo, and the long stretch of Venice as seen from the Lido. I would myself even rank the outlook on Monaco from the slopes of Cap Martin, and the glorious panorama of Nice and the Maritime Alps from the Lighthouse Hill at 40] Antibes, above any picture to be seen from the northern spurs of the Sahel. Let us be just to Piræus before we are generous to El Biar. But all this is, after all, a mere matter of taste, and no lover of the picturesque would at any rate deny that the Bay of Algiers, as viewed from the Mustapha Hill, ranks deservedly high among the most beautiful sights of the Mediterranean. And when the sunset lights up in rosy tints the white mole and the marble town, the resulting scene is sometimes one of almost fairy-like splendor.

Indeed, the country round Mustapha is a district of singular charm and manifold beauty. The walks and drives are delicious. Great masses of pale white clematis hang in sheets from the trees, cactus and aloe run riot among the glens, sweet scents of oleander float around the deep ravines, delicious perfumes of violets are wafted on every breeze from unseen and unsuspected gardens. Nowhere do I know a landscape so dotted with houses, and nowhere are the houses themselves so individually interesting. The outlook over the bay, the green dells of the foreground, the town on its steep acclivity, the points and headlands, and away above all, in the opposite direction, the snow-clad peaks of the Djurjura, make up a picture that, after all, has few equals or superiors on our latter-day planet.

One of the sights of Mustapha is the Arab cemetery, where once a week the women go to pray and wail, with true Eastern hyperbole, over the graves of their dead relations. By the custom of Islam they are excluded from the mosques and from all overt participation in the public exercises of religion; but these open-air temples not made with hands, even the Prophet himself has never dared to close to them. Ancestor-worship and the 41]veneration of the kindred dead have always borne a large part in the domestic creed of the less civilized Semites, and, like many other traces of heathenism, this antique cult still peeps sturdily through the thin veil of Mohammedan monotheism. Every hillock in the Atlas outliers is crowned by the tiny domed tomb, or koubba, of some local saint; every sacred grove overshadows the relics of some reverend Marabout. Nay, the very oldest forms of Semitic idolatry, the cult of standing stones, of holy trees, and of special high places on the mountain-tops, survive to this day even in the midst of Islam. It is the women in particular who keep alive these last relics of pre-Moslem faith; it is the women that one may see weeping over the narrow graves of their loved ones, praying for the great desire of the Semitic heart, a man-child from Allah, before the sacred tree of their pagan ancestors, or hanging rags and dolls as offerings about the holy grove which encloses the divine spring of pure and hallowed water.

Algiers is thus in many ways a most picturesque winter resort. But it has one great drawback: the climate is moist and the rainfall excessive. Those who go there must not expect the dry desert breeze that renders Luxor and Assiout so wholesome and so unpleasant. Beautiful vegetation means rain and heat. You will get both in Algiers, and a fine Mediterranean tossing on your journey to impress it on your memory.

42]

III

MALAGA

A nearly perfect climate—Continuous existence of thirty centuries—Granada and the world-renowned Alhambra—Systems of irrigation—Vineyards the chief source of wealth—Esparto grass—The famous Cape de Gatt—The highest peak of the Sierra Nevada—Last view of Granada.

MALAGA has been very differently described and appreciated. The Arab chroniclers who knew it in the palmy days of the Moorish domination considered it "a most beautiful city, densely peopled, large and most excellent." Some rose to poetical rhapsody in describing it; they praised it as "the central jewel of a necklace, a land of paradise, the pole star, the diadem of the moon, the forehead of a bewitching beauty unveiled." A Spanish poet was not less eloquent, and sang of Malaga as "the enchantress, the home of eternal spring, bathed by the soft sea, nestling amidst flowers." Ford, on the other hand, that prince of guide-book makers, who knew the Spain of his day intimately from end to end, rather despised Malaga. He thought it a fine but purely commercial city, having "few attractions beyond climate, almonds and raisins, and sweet wine." Malaga has made great strides nevertheless in the fifty-odd years since Ford so wrote of it. While preserving many of the charming characteristics which evoked such 43] high-flown encomiums in the past, it has developed considerably in trade, population, and importance. It grows daily; building is constantly in progress, new streets are added year after year to the town. Its commerce flourishes; its port is filled with shipping which carry off its many manufactures: chocolate, liquorice, porous jars, and clay figures, the iron ores that are smelted on the spot; the multifarious products of its fertile soil, which grows in rich profusion the choicest fruits of the earth: grapes, melons, plantains, guava, quince, Japanese medlars, oranges, lemons, and prickly pears. All the appliances and luxurious aids to comfort known to our latter-day civilization are to be found in Malaga: several theaters, one of them an opera house, clubs, grand hotels, bankers, English doctors, cabs. It rejoices too in an indefeasible and priceless gift, a nearly perfect climate, the driest and balmiest in Southern Europe. Rain falls in Malaga but half a dozen days in the year, and its winter sun would shame that of an English summer. It has a southern aspect, and is sheltered from the north by an imposing range of mountains; its only trouble is the terral or north-west wind, the same disagreeable visitor as that known on the Italian Riviera as the Tramontana, and in the south of France as the Mistral. These climatic advantages have long recommended Malaga as a winter health resort for delicate and consumptive invalids, and an increasingly successful rival to Madeira, Malta, and Algiers. The general view of this city of sunshine, looking westward, to which point it lies open, is pleasing and varied; luxuriant southern vegetation, aloes, palmetto, and palms, fill up the foreground; in the middle distance are the dazzling white façades and towers of the town, the great amphitheater of the bull ring, the tall spire of 44] the Cathedral a very conspicuous object, the whole set off by the dark blue Mediterranean, and the reddish-purple background of the Sierra Bermeja or Vermilion Hills.

There is active enjoyment to be got in and near Malaga as well as the mere negative pleasure of a calm, lazy life amid beautiful scenes. It is an excellent point of departure for interesting excursions. Malaga lies on the fringe of a country full of great memories, and preserving many curious antiquarian remains. It is within easy reach by rail of Granada and the world-renowned Alhambra, whence the ascent of the great southern snowy range, the Sierra Nevada, may be made with pleasurable excitement and a minimum of discomfort. Other towns closely associated with great events may also be visited: Alhama, the mountain key of Granada, whose capture preluded that of the Moorish capital and is enshrined in Byron's beautiful verse; Ronda, the wildly picturesque town lying in the heart of its own savage hills; Almeria, Antequera, Archidona, all old Moorish towns. By the coast road westward, a two days' ride, through Estepona and Marbella, little seaside towns bathed by the tideless Mediterranean, Gibraltar may be reached. Inland, a day's journey, are the baths of Caratraca, delightfully situated in a narrow mountain valley, a cleft of the rugged hill, and famous throughout Spain. The waters are akin to those of Harrogate, and are largely patronized by crowds of the bluest-blooded hidalgos, the most fashionable people, Spaniards from La Corte (Madrid), and all parts of the Peninsula. Yet another series of riding excursions may be made into the wild Alpujarras, a desolate and uncultivated district gemmed with bright oases of verdure, which are best reached by the coast 45] road leading from Malaga through Velez Malaga, Motril to Adra, and which is perhaps the pleasantest route to Granada itself. On one side is the dark-blue sea; on the other, vine-clad hills: this is a land, to use Ford's words, "overflowing with oil and wine; here is the palm without the desert, the sugar-cane without the slave;" old Moorish castles perched like eagles' eyries crown the hills; below cluster the spires and towers of churches and convents, hemmed in by the richest vegetation. The whole of this long strip of coast is rich with the alluvial deposits brought down by the mountain torrents from the snowy Sierras above; in spring time, before the summer heats have parched the land, everything flourishes here, the sweet potato, indigo, sugar-cane and vine; masses of wild flowers in innumerable gay colors, the blue iris, the crimson oleander, geraniums, and luxuriant festoons of maidenhair ferns bedeck the landscape around. It is impossible to exaggerate the delights of these riding trips; the traveller relying upon his horse, which carries a modest kit, enjoys a strange sense of independence: he can go on or stop, as he chooses, lengthen or shorten his day's journey, which takes him perpetually and at the leisurely pace which permits ample observation of the varied views. The scene changes constantly: now he threads a half-dried watercourse, thick with palmetto and gum cistus; now he makes the slow circuit of a series of little rocky bays washed by the tideless calm of the blue sea; now he breasts the steep slope, the seemingly perilous ascent of bold cliffs, along which winds the track made centuries since when the most direct was deemed the shortest way to anywhere in spite of the difficulties that intervened.

Malaga as a seaport and place of settlement can claim 46] almost fabulous antiquity. It was first founded by the Phœnicians three thousand years ago, and a continuous existence of thirty centuries fully proves the wisdom of their choice. Its name is said to be Phœnician, and is differently derived from a word meaning salt, and another which would distinguish it as "the king's town." From the earliest ages Malaga did a thriving business in salt fish; its chief product and export were the same anchovies and the small boquerones, not unlike an English whitebait, which are still the most highly prized delicacies of the Malaga fish market. Southern Spain was among the richest and most valued of Phœnician possessions. It was a mine of wealth to them, the Tarshish of Biblical history from which they drew such vast supplies of the precious metals that their ships carried silver anchors. Hiram, King of Tyre, was a sort of goldsmith to Solomon, furnishing the wise man's house with such stores of gold and silver utensils that silver was "accounted nothing therein," as we read in the First Book of Kings. When the star of Tyre and Sidon waned, and Carthage became the great commercial center of the Mediterranean, it controlled the mineral wealth of Spain and traded largely with Malaga. Later, when Spain passed entirely into Roman hands, this southern province of Bœtica grew more and more valuable, and the wealth of the country passed through its ports eastward to the great marts of the world. Malaga however, was never the equal either in wealth or commercial importance of its more eastern and more happily placed neighbor Almeria. The latter was the once famous "Portus Magnus," or Great Port, which monopolized most of the maritime traffic with Italy and the more distant East. But Malaga rose in prosperity as Roman settlers crowded 47] into Bœtica, and Roman remains excavated in and around the town attest the size and importance of the place under the Romans. It was a municipium, had a fine ampitheater, the foundations of which were laid bare long afterwards in building a convent, while many bronzes, fragments of statuary, and Roman coins found from time to time prove the intimate relations between Malaga and the then Mistress of the World. The Goths, who came next, overran Bœtica, and although their stay was short, they rechristened the province, which is still known by their name, the modern Andal-, or Vandalucia. Malaga was a place of no importance in the time of the Visigoths, and it declined, only to rise with revived splendor under the Moors, when it reached the zenith of its greatness, and stood high in rank among the Hispano-Mauresque cities.

It was the same one-eyed Berber General, Tarik, who took Gibraltar who was the first Moorish master of Malaga. Legendary story still associates a gate in the old Moorish castle, the Gibralfaro, with the Moorish invasion. This Puerta de la Cava was called, it has been said, after the ill-used daughter of Count Julyan whose wrongs led to the appeal to Moorish intervention. But it is not known historically that Count Julyan had a daughter named La Cava, or any daughter at all; nor is it likely that the Moors would remember the Christian maiden's name as sponsor for the gate. After the Moorish conquest Malaga fell to the tribes that came from the river Jordan, a pastoral race who extended their rule to the open lands as far as Archidona. The richness of their new possession attracted great hordes of Arabs from their distant homes; there was a general exodus, and each as it came to the land of promise settled 48] where they found anything that recalled their distant homes. Thus the tribes from the deserts of Palmyra found a congenial resting-place on the arid coast near Almeria and the more rugged kingdom of Murcia; the Syrian mountaineers established themselves amidst the rocky fastness of the Ronda Serranía; while those from Damascus and Bagdad reveled in the luxuriant beauty of the fertile plains watered by the Xenil and Darro, the great Vega, with its orange-groves and jeweled gardens that still make Granada a smiling paradise.

These Moslem conquerors were admirable in their administration and development of the land they seized, quick to perceive its latent resources and make the most of them. Malaga itself became the court and seat of government of a powerful dynasty whose realms extended inland as far as Cordova, and the region around grew under their energetic and enlightened management into one great garden teeming with the most varied vegetation. What chiefly commended Malaga to the Moors was the beauty of its climate and the amazing fertility of the soil. The first was a God-sent gift, the latter made unstinting return for the labor freely but intelligently applied. Water was and still is the great need of those thirsty and nearly rainless southern lands, and the Moorish methods of irrigation, ample specimens of which still survive, were most elaborate and effective contrivances for distributing the fertilizing fluid. Many of these ancient systems of irrigation are still at work at Murcia, Valencia, Granada, and elsewhere. The Moors were masters of hydraulic science, which was never more widely or intelligently practiced than in the East. So the methods adopted and still seen in Spain have their Oriental prototypes and counterparts. They varied, of 49] course, with the character of the district to be irrigated and the sources of supply. Where rivers and running water gave the material, it was conveyed in canals; one main trunk-line or artery supplied the fluid to innumerable smaller watercourses or veins, the acequias, which formed a reticulated network of minute ramifications. The great difficulty in the plains, and this was especially the case about Malaga, was to provide a proper fall, which was effected either by carrying the water to a higher level by an aqueduct, or sinking it below the surface in subterranean channels. Where the water had to be raised from underground, the simple pole, on which worked an arm or lever with a bucket, was used, the identical "shadoof" of the Nile; or the more elaborate water-wheel, the Arab Anaoura, a name still preserved in the Spanish Noria, one of which is figured in the Almeria washing-place, where it serves the gossiping lavanderas at their work. In these norias the motive power is usually that of a patient ox, which works a revolving wheel, and so turns a second at right angles armed with jars or buckets. These descend in turn, coming up charged with water, which falls over into a reservoir or pipe, whence it flows to do its business below.

Under this admirable system the land gives forth perpetual increases. It knows no repose. Nothing lies fallow. "Man is never weary of sowing, nor the sun of calling into life." Crop succeeds crop with astonishing rapidity; three or four harvests of corn are

22

reaped in the year, twelve or fifteen of clover and lucerne. All kinds of fruit abound; the margins of the watercourses blossom with flowers that would be prized in a hothouse, and the most marvelous fecundity prevails. By these 50] means the Moors of Malaga, the most scientific and successful of gardeners, developed to the utmost the marvelously prolific soil. Moorish writers described the pomegranates of Malaga as red as rubies, and unequaled in the whole world. The brevas, or small green figs, were of exquisitely delicious flavor, and still merit that encomium. Grapes were a drug in the markets, cheap as dirt; while the raisins into which they were converted, by a process that dates back to the Phœnicians, found their way into the far East and were famous in Palestine, Arabia, and beyond. The vineyards of the Malaga district, a wide tract embracing all the southern slopes towards the Mediterranean, were, and still are, the chief source of its wealth. The wine of Malaga could tempt even Mohammedan Moors to forget their prophet's prohibition; it was so delicious that a dying Moor when commending his soul to God asked for only two blessings in Paradise, enough to drink of the wines of Malaga and Seville. As the "Mountains," this same wine was much drunk and appreciated by our forefathers. To this day "Malaga" is largely consumed, both dry and sweet, especially that known as the Lagrimas, or Tears, a cognate term to the famous Lachrymæ Christi of Naples, and which are the very essence of the rich ripe grapes, which are hung up in the sun till the juice flows from them in luscious drops. Orange groves and lemon groves abound in the Vega, and the fruit is largely exported. The collection and packing are done at points along the line of railway to which Malaga is the maritime terminus, as at La Pizarra, a small but important station which is the starting point for the Baths of Caratraca, and the mountain ride to Ronda through the 51]magnificent pass of El Burgo. Of late years Malaga has become a species of market garden, in which large quantities of early vegetables are raised, the primeurs of French gourmets, the young peas, potatoes, asparagus, and lettuce, which are sent north to Paris during the winter months by express trains. This is probably a more profitable business than the raising of the sugar-cane, an industry introduced (or more exactly, revived, for it was known to and cultivated by the Moors) in and around Malaga by the well-known General Concha, Marques del Duero. He spent the bulk of a large fortune in developing the cane cultivation, and almost ruined himself in this patriotic endeavor. Others benefited largely by his well-meant enterprise, and the sugar fields of southern Spain prospered until the German beet sugar drove the homegrown hard. The climate of Malaga, with its great dryness and absolute immunity from frost, is exceedingly favorable to the growth of the sugar-cane, and the sugar fields at the time of the cutting are picturesque centers of activity. The best idea, however, of the amazing fertility of this gifted country will be obtained from a visit to one of the private residential estates, or fincas, such as that of La Concepcion, where palms, bamboos, arums, cicads and other tropical plants thrive bravely in the open air. It is only a short drive, and is well worth a visit. The small Grecian temple is full of Roman remains, chiefly from Cartama, the site of a great Roman city which Livy has described. Some of these remains are of beautiful marble figures, which were found, like ordinary stones, built into a prison wall and rescued with some difficulty. The Malaga authorities annexed them, thinking they contained gold, then threw them away as 52] old rubbish. Other remains at La Concepcion are fragments of the Roman municipal law, on bronze tablets, found at Osuna, between Antequera and Seville.

Malaga possesses many mementoes of the Moors besides their methods of irrigation. The great citadel which this truly militant race erected upon the chief point of vantage and key to the possession of Malaga still remains. This, the Castle of Gibralfaro,

23

the rock of the lighthouse, was built by a prince of Granada, Mohammed, upon the site of a Phœnician fortress, and it was so strongly fortified and held that it long resisted the strenuous efforts of Ferdinand and Isabella in the memorable siege which prefaced the fall of Granada. How disgracefully the Catholic kings ill-treated the conquered Moors of Malaga, condemning them to slavery or the auto da fé, may be read in the pages of Prescott. The towers of the Gibralfaro still standing have each a story of its own: one was the atalaya, or watch-tower; on another, that of La Vela, a great silver cross was erected when the city surrendered. Below the Gibralfaro, but connected with it and forming part of the four deep city walls, is the Alcazaba, another fortification utilized by the Moors, but the fortress they raised stands upon Phœnician foundations. The quarter that lies below these Moorish strongholds is the most ancient part of Malaga, a wilderness of dark, winding alleys of Oriental aspect, and no doubt of Moorish origin. This is the home of the lower classes, of the turbulent masses who have in all ages been a trial and trouble to the authorities of the time. The Malagueños, the inhabitants of Malaga, whether Moors or Spaniards, have ever been rebellious subjects of their liege lords, and uncomfortable 53] neighbors to one another. In all their commotions they have generally espoused the cause which has ultimately failed.

Thus, in 1831, Riego and Torrijos having been in open revolt against the Government, were lured into embarking for Malaga from Gibraltar, where they had assembled, by its military commandant Moreno, and shot down to a man on the beach below the Carmen Convent. Among the victims was an Englishman, Mr. Boyd, whose unhappy fate led to sharp protests from England. Since this massacre a tardy tribute has been raised to the memory of the slain; it stands in the shape of a monument in the Plaza de Riego, the Alameda. Again, Malaga sided with Espartero in 1843, when he "pronounced" but had to fly into exile. Once more, in 1868, the Malagueños took up arms upon the losing side, fighting for the dethroned Isabella Segunda against the successful soldiers who had driven her from Madrid. Malaga was long and obstinately defended, but eventually succumbed after a sanguinary struggle. Last of all, after the abdication of Amadeus in 1873, the Republicans of Malaga rose, and carried their excesses so far as to establish a Communistic régime, which terrorized the town. The troops disbanded themselves, their weapons were seized by the worst elements of the population, who held the reins of power, the local authorities having taken to flight. The mob laid hands on the customhouse and all public moneys, levied contributions upon the more peaceable citizens, then quarreled among themselves and fought out their battles in the streets, sweeping them with artillery fire, and threatening a general bombardment. Order was not easily restored or without 54] the display of armed force, but the condign punishment of the more blameworthy has kept Malaga quiet ever since.

While the male sex among the masses of Malaga enjoy an indifferent reputation, her daughters of all classes are famed for their attractiveness, even in Spain, the home, par excellence, of a well-favored race. "Muchachas Malagueñas, muy halagueñas" (the girls of Malaga are most bewitching) is a proverbial expression, the truth of which has been attested by many appreciative observers. Théophile Gautier's description of them is perhaps the most complimentary. The Malagueña, he tells us, is remarkable for the even tone of her complexion (the cheek having no more color than the forehead), the rich crimson of her lips, the delicacy of her nostril, and above all the brilliancy of her Arab eyes, which might be tinged with henna, they are so languorous and so almond-shaped. "I cannot tell whether or not it was the red draperies of their headgear, but their faces exhibited gravity combined with passion that was quite Oriental in character." Gautier drew this picture of the Malagueñas as he saw them at a bull-fight, and he expresses a not unnatural surprise that sweet, Madonna-like faces, which might well inspire the painter of sacred subjects, should look on unmoved at the ghastly episodes of the blood-stained ring. It shocked him to see the deep interest with which these pale beauties followed the fight, to hear the feats of the arena discussed by sweet lips that might speak more suitably of softer things. Yet he found them simple, tender-hearted, good, and concluded that it was not cruelty of disposition but the custom of the country that drew them to this savage show. Since then the bull-fight, shorn, however, of its worst horrors, 55] has become acclimatized and most popular amidst M. Gautier's own country-women in Paris. That the beauty of the higher ranks rivals that of the lowest may be inferred from the fact that a lady whose charms were once celebrated throughout Europe is of Malagueñan descent. The mother of the Empress Eugénie, who shared with Napoleon III. the highest honors in France, was a Malaga girl, a Miss Fitzpatrick, the daughter of the British consul, but she had also Spanish blood in her veins.

A near neighbor and old rival, as richly endowed, may again pass Malaga in the great race for commercial expansion. This is Almeria, which lies farther eastward and which owns many natural advantages; its exposed port has been improved by the construction of piers and breakwaters, and it now offers a secure haven to the shipping that should ere long be attracted in increasing tonnage to carry away the rich products of the neighboring districts. Almeria is the capital of a province teeming with mineral wealth, and whose climate and soil favor the growth of the most varied and valuable crops. The silver mines of the mountains of Murcia and the fertile valleys of the Alpujarras would find their best outlet at Almeria, while Granada would once more serve as its farm. So ran the old proverb, "When Almería was really Almería, Granada was only its alquería," or source of supply. What this time-honored but almost forgotten city most needs is to be brought into touch with the railway systems of Spain. Meanwhile, Almeria, awaiting better fortune, thrives on the exports of its own products, chief among which are grapes and esparto. The first has a familiar sound to British ears, from the green grapes known as "Almerias," which are largely 56] consumed in British households. These are not equal to the delicately flavored Muscatels, but they are stronger and will bear the packing and rough usages of exportation under which the others perish. Esparto is a natural product of these favored lands, which, after long supplying local wants, has now become an esteemed item in their list of exports. It is known to botanists as the Spanish rush, or bass feather grass, the Genet d'Espagne, and is compared by Ford to the "spear grass which grows on the sandy sea-shores of Lancashire." It is still manufactured, as in the days of Pliny, into matting, baskets, ropes, and the soles for the celebrated Alpargatas, or rope sandal shoes, worn universally by Spanish peasants in the south and Spanish soldiers on the line of march. The ease and speed with which the Spanish infantry cover long distances are greatly attributed to their comfortable chaussures. Nowadays a much wider outlet has been found for esparto grass, and it is grown artificially. When rags became more and more scarce and unequal to the demands of the paper-makers, experiments were made with various substitutes, and none answered the purpose better than the wild spear-grass of southern Spain.

Almeria, while awaiting the return of maritime prosperity, can look with some complacency upon a memorable if not altogether glorious past. Its very names, Portus Magnus under the Romans, and Al Meriah, the "Conspicuous," under the Moors, attest its importance. All the agricultural produce of the prolific Vega, the silks that were woven on Moorish looms and highly prized through the East, were brought to Almeria for transmission abroad. The security and convenience of this famous port gave it an evil reputation in after years, 57] when it became an independent kingdom under Ibn Maymum. Almeria was the terror of the Mediterranean; its pirate galleys roved to and fro, making descents upon the French and Italian coasts, and carrying back their booty, slaves, and prizes to their impregnable home. Spaniards and Genoese presently combined against the common enemy, and Almeria was one of the earliest Christian conquests regained from the Moors. Later still the Algerian Moors took fresh revenge, and their corsairs so constantly threatened Almeria that Charles V. repaired its ancient fortifications, the old Moorish castle now called the Alcazaba, the center or keep, and hung a great tocsin bell upon its cathedral tower to give notice of the pirates' approach. This cathedral is the most imposing object in the decayed and impoverished town. Pigs and poultry roam at large in the streets, amidst dirt and refuse; but in the strong sunlight, white and blinding as in Africa, the mean houses glisten brightly, and the abundant color seen on awnings and lattice, upon the women's skirts and kerchiefs, in the ultramarine sea, is brought out in the most vivid and beautiful relief.

The scenery on the coast from Malaga eastward is fine, in some parts and under certain aspects magnificent. Beyond Almeria is the famous Cape de Gatt, as it is known to our mariners, the Cabo de Gata of local parlance, the Agate Cape, to give it its precise meaning. This remarkable promontory, composed of rocks encrusted with gems, is worthy a place in the "Arabian Nights." There are miles and miles of agates and crystal spar, and in one particular spot amethysts are found. Wild winds gather and constantly bluster about this richly constituted but often storm-tossed landmark. Old sailor saws have perpetuated its character in the form of a 58] proverb, "At the Cape de Gatt take care of your hat." Other portions of the coast nearer Malaga are still more forbidding and dangerous: under the Sierra Tejada, for example, where the rocky barriers which guard the land rise tier above tier as straight as a wall, in which there are no openings, no havens of safety for passing craft in an inshore gale. Behind all, a dim outline joining hands as it were with the clouds, towers the great snowy range of southern Spain, the Sierra Nevada, rejoicing in an elevation as high as the Swiss Alps, and in some respects far more beautiful.

There are, however, no such grim glaciers, no such vast snow-fields as in Switzerland, for here in the south the sun has more power, and even at these heights only the peaks and pinnacles wear white crests during the summer heats. This more genial temperature encourages a richer vegetation, and makes the ascents less perilous and toilsome. A member of the Alpine Club would laugh to scorn the conquest of Muley Hacen, or of the Picacho de la Veleta, the two crowning peaks of the range. The enterprise is within the compass of the most moderate effort. The ascent of the last-named and lowest, although the most picturesque, is the easiest made, because the road from Granada is most direct. In both cases the greatest part of the climbing is performed on horseback; but this must be done a day in advance, and thus a night has to be passed near the summit under the stars. The temperature is low, and the travellers can only defend themselves against the cold by the wraps they have brought and the fuel they can find (mere knotted roots) around their windy shelter. The ascent to where the snow still lingers, in very dirty and disreputable patches, is usually commenced about two in the 59] morning, so that the top may be reached before dawn. If the sky is clear, sunrise from the Picacho is a scene that can never be forgotten, fairly competing with, if not outrivaling, the most famous views of the kind. The Mediterranean lies below like a lake, bounded to the north and west by the Spanish coast, to the south by the African, the faintest outlines of which may often be seen in the far, dim distance. Eastward the horizon is made glorious by the bright pageants of the rising sun, whose majestic approach is heralded by rainbow-hued clouds. All around are the strangely jagged and contorted peaks, rolling down in diminishing grandeur to the lower peaks that seem to rise from the sea.

The highest peak of the Sierra Nevada is Muley Hacen, although it has only the advantage over the Picacho de la Veleta by about a couple of hundred feet. It is a longer and more difficult ascent, but in some ways the most interesting, as it can best be reached through the Alpujarras, those romantic and secluded valleys which are full of picturesque scenery and of historical associations. The starting point, as a general rule, is Trevelez, although the ascent may be equally made from Portugos, somewhat nearer Granada. Trevelez is the other side and the most convenient coming from Malaga by way of Motril. But no one would take the latter route who could travel by the former, which leads through Alhendin, that well-known village which is said to have seen the last of the departing Moors. This is the point at which Granada is finally lost to view, and it was here that Boabdil, the last king of Granada, took his last farewell of the city whose loss he wept over, under the scathing sarcasm of his more heroic mother, who told him he might well "weep like a woman for what he 60] could not defend as a man." Near this village is the little hill still known as the site of "El Ultimo Suspiro del Moro, the last sigh of the Moor." This same road leads through Lanjaron, an enchanting spot, posted high upon a spur of the hills, and famous as a bathing place with health-giving mineral springs. From Portugos or Trevelez the climb is easy enough: to be accomplished a great part of the way on horseback, and in its earlier levels ascending amid forests of evergreen oak; after that, long wastes of barren rock are passed, till at length the summit is reached, on a narrow strip of table-land, the highest in Southern Europe, and with an unrivaled view. The charm of the Muley Hacen peak is its isolation, while the Picacho looks better from it than Muley Hacen does from the Picacho, and there is a longer vista across the Mediterranean Sea.

61]

IV

BARCELONA

The flower market of the Rambla—Streets of the old town—The Cathedral of Barcelona—Description of the Columbus monument—All Saints' Day in Spain—Mont Tibidaho—Diverse centers of intellectual activity—Ancient history—Philanthropic and charitable institutions.

"BARCELONA, shrine of courtesy, harbor of the wayfarer, shelter of the poor, cradle of the brave, champion of the outraged, nurse of friendship, unique in position, unique in beauty!"

Such was the eulogium bestowed upon Barcelona by the great Cervantes several hundred years ago, an eulogium warranted by a stranger's experience in our own day. The matchless site of the second city of Spain, its luxuriant surroundings, awaken enthusiasm as of old, whilst even the briefest possible sojourn suffices to make us feel at home. A winning urbanity, a cosmopolitan amiableness, characterize the townsfolk, Spanish hauteur is here replaced by French cordiality. Softness of manner and graces of speech lend additional charm to a race conspicuous for personal beauty. The Barcelonese are described by a contemporary as laborious and energetic, ambitious of social advance, tenacious of personal dignity, highly imaginative, at the same time eminently practical, steadfast in friendship, vehement in hate. The stir and 62] magnificence of the city attest the progressive character of the inhabitants.

Few European capitals can boast of finer public monuments, few indeed possess such a promenade as its famous Rambla. The Rambla may be regarded as an epitome, not only of the entire city, but of all Spain, and here the curious traveller should take up his quarters. A dozen brilliant or moving spectacles meet the eye in a day, whilst the normal aspect is one of unimaginable picturesqueness and variety. The dark-eyed flower-girls with their rich floral displays; the country folks still adhering to the costume of Catalonia—the men sandaled and white-hosed, for headgear, slouch caps of crimson, scarlet, or peach-colored felt, the women with gorgeous silk kerchiefs pinned under the chin—the Asturian nursemaids in poppy-red skirts barred with black, and dainty gold and lace caps; the ladies fanning themselves as they go in November, with black lace mantillas over their pretty heads; the Guardia Civile in big, awe-inspiring cocked hats and long black cloaks reaching to the ankle; the trim soldiery in black and red tunics, knickerbockers and buskins, their officers ablaze with gold braid and lace; the spick-and-span city police, each neat as a dandy in a melodrama, not a hair out of place, collars and cuffs of spotless white, ironed to perfection, well-fitting costumes, swords at their sides; the priests and nuns; the seafaring folk of many nationalities; the shepherds of uncouth appearance from the neighboring mountains—all these at first make us feel as if we were taking part in a masquerade.

Now way is made for the funeral train of some rich citizen, the lofty car of sumptuous display of black and gold drapery, wreaths of fresh roses, violet, and 63]heliotrope, large as carriage-wheels, fastened to the sides, the coffin, encased in black and violet velvet, studded with gold nails; following slowly, a long procession of carriages bearing priests, choristers, and mourners. And now the sounds of martial music summon the newcomer a second time to his window. It is a soldier who is borne to his rest. Six comrades accompany the bier, carrying long inverted tapers; behind march commanding officers and men, the band playing strains all too spirited it seems for such an occasion. There is always something going on in this splendid avenue animated from early morning till past midnight, market-place, parade ground, promenade in one.

The daily flower-market of itself would almost repay the journey from London. When northern skies are gloomiest, and fogs are daily fare, the Rambla is at its best. The yellowing leaves of the plane-trees look golden under the dazzling blue sky, and brilliant as in a picture are the flower-sellers and their wares. These distractingly pretty girls, with their dark locks pulled over the brow, their lovely eyes, rich olive complexions, and gleaming white teeth, have nothing of the mendicant about them. As they offer their flowers—perhaps fastening roses to a half-finished garland with one hand, whilst with the other a pot of heliotrope is reached down—the passer-by is engagingly invited to purchase. The Spanish language, even the dialect of Catalonia, is music to begin with, and the flower-maidens make it more musical still by their gentle, caressing ways. Some wear little mantillas of black, blonde, or cashmere; others, silk kerchiefs of brightest hue— orange, crimson, deep purple, or fanciful patterns of many colors. Barcelona is a flower-garden all the year round, and in mid-winter we stroll 64]between piled-up masses of rose, carnation, and violet, to say nothing of dahlias and chrysanthemums.

It is especially on All Saints' and All Souls' Days that the flower-market of the Rambla is seen to advantage; enormous sums are spent upon wreaths and garlands for the cemetery, the poorest then contriving to pay his floral tribute to departed kith and kin.

In striking contrast with the wide, airy, ever brilliantly illuminated Rambla, electric light doing duty for sunshine at night, are the streets of the old town. The stranger may take any turning—either to right or left—he is sure to find himself in one of these dusky narrow thoroughfares, so small ofttimes the space between window and opposite window that neighbors might almost shake hands. With their open shops of gay woolen stuffs, they vividly recall Cairene bazaars. Narrow as is the accommodation without, it must be narrower still within, since when folks move from one house to another their goods and chattels are hoisted up and passed through the front windows. The sight of a chest of drawers or a sofa in cloudland is comical enough, although the system certainly has its advantages. Much manual labor is thereby spared, and the furniture doubtless escapes injury from knocking about.

The wise traveller will elect to live on the Rambla, but to spend his time in the old town. Wherever he goes he is sure to come upon some piece of antiquity, whilst here, in a great measure, he loses sight of the cosmopolitan element characterizing the new quarters. Novel and striking as is its aspect to the stranger, Barcelona must nevertheless be described as the least Spanish of Spanish towns. The second seaport of Spain is still—as it was in the Middle Ages—one of the most important seats of 65]international commerce on the Mediterranean. As we elbow our way along the crowded Rambla we encounter a diversity of types and hear a perplexing jargon of many tongues. A few minutes suffice to transport us into the old-world city familiar to Ford—not, however, to be described by the twentieth century tourist in Ford's own words. "A difficult language," he wrote just upon half a century ago, "rude manners, and a distrust of strangers, render Barcelona a disagreeable city." Nowhere nowadays is more courtesy shown to the inquiring stranger. He is not even obliged to ask his way in these narrow tortuous streets. The city police, to be found at every turn, uninvited come to his aid, and, bringing out a pocket-map, with an infinity of pains make clear to him the route he has to take. The handsome Calle San Fernando leads to the somber but grandiose old Cathedral with its lovely cloisters, magnificent towers and bells, deep-voiced as that of Big Ben itself. All churches in Spain, by the way, must be visited in the forenoon; even then the light is so dim that little can be seen of their treasures—pictures, reliquaries, marble tombs. The Cathedral of Barcelona forms no exception to the rule. Only lighted by windows of richly stained old glass, we are literally compelled to grope our way along the crowded aisles. Mass is going on from early morning till noon, and in the glimmering jeweled light we can just discern the moving figures of priests and acolytes before the high altar, and the scattered worshippers kneeling on the floor. Equally vague are the glimpses we obtain of the chapels, veritable little museums of rare and beautiful things unfortunately consigned to perpetual obscurity, veiled in never-fading twilight. What a change we find outside! The elegant Gothic cloisters, rather 66] to be described as a series of chapels, each differing from the other, each sumptuously adorned, enclose a sunny open space or patio, planted with palms, orange and lemon trees, the dazzlingly bright foliage and warm blue sky in striking contrast to the somber gray of the building-stone. A little farther off, on the other side, we may see the figures of the bell-ringers high up in the open belfry tower, swinging the huge bells backwards and forwards with tremendous effort, a sight never to be missed on Sundays and fête days.

This stately old Cathedral, like so many others, was never finished and works of reparation and restoration are perpetually going on. Close by stands the Palais de Justice, with its beautiful Gothic court and carved stone staircase, the balustrade supported by lovely little statuettes or gargoyles, each an artistic study in itself. Abutting this is the Palais de Diputacion, Provincial or local Parliament House, a building of truly Spanish grandeur. Its wide marble staircases, its elaborate ceilings of carved wood, its majestic proportions, will, perhaps, have less interest for some travellers than its art-treasures, two chefs d'œuvre of the gifted Fortuny. Barcelona was the patron of this true genius— Catalan by birth—so unhappily cut off in his early prime. With no little pride the stately officials show these canvases—the famous "Odalisque" and the "Battle of Tetuan"—the latter, alas! left unfinished. It is a superb piece of life and color, but must be seen on a brilliant day as the hall is somber. Nothing can exceed the courtesy of the Barcelonese to strangers, and these pictures are shown out of the regular hours. But let no one incautiously offer a fee. The proffered coin will be politely, even smilingly, rejected, without humiliating reproof, much less a look of affront. Ford's 67] remark that "a silver key at all times secures admission" does not hold good in these days.

Near the Cathedral, law courts, and Provincial Parliament House stands another picturesque old palace of comparatively modern date, yet Saracenic aspect, and containing one of the most curious historic treasures in Europe. This is the palace of the kings of Aragon, or Archivo General de la Corona de Aragon. The exterior, as is usual with Spanish buildings, is massive and gloomy. Inside is a look of Oriental lightness and gaiety. Slender columns, painted red, enclose an open court, and support a little terrace planted with shrubs and flowers. Here in perfect order and preservation, without a break, are stored the records of upwards of a thousand years, the earlier consisting of vellum scrolls and black letter, the latter showing the progress of printing from its beginning down to our own day. The first parchment bears date a. d. 875. Among the curiosities of the collection are no less than eight hundred and two Papal Bulls from the year 1017 to 1796. Besides the archives of Barcelona itself, and of the kingdom of Aragon, to which it was annexed in the twelfth century, the palace contains many deeply interesting manuscripts found in the suppressed monasteries.

The archives have been ingeniously arranged by the learned keeper of records. The bookcases, which are not more than six feet high, stand on either side of the vast library, at some distance from the wall, made staircase-wise; one set of volumes just above the other, with the result that no accumulation of dust is possible, and that each set is equally accessible. The effect on the eye of these symmetrically-placed volumes in white vellum is very novel and pleasing. We seem to be in a 68] hall, the walls of which are of fluted cream-colored marble.

The little museum of local antiquities in the ruined Church of Santa Agneda, the somber old churches of San Pablo del Campo, Santa Maria del Mar and Belen, the fragments of mediæval domestic architecture remaining here and there—all these will detain the archæologist. Of more general interest are the modern monuments of Barcelona. In no city have civic lavishness and public spirit shone forth more conspicuously.

A penny tramway—you may go anywhere here for a penny—takes you to the beautiful Park and Fountain of Neptune. The word "fountain" gives an inadequate notion of the splendid pile, with its vast triple-storied marble galleries, its sculptured Naiads and dolphins, and on the summit, towering above park and lake and cascades, its three gigantic sea-horses and charioteers richly gilt, gleaming as if indeed of massive gold. Is there any more sumptuous fountain in the world? I doubt it. In spite of the gilded sea-horses and chariot, there is no tawdriness here; all is bold, splendid, and imposing. Below the vast terraced galleries and wide staircases, all of pure marble, flows in a broad sheet the crystal-clear water, home of myriads of gold fish. The entourage is worthy of so superb a construction. The fountain stands in the midst of a scrupulously-kept, tastefully laid-out, ever-verdant park or public pleasure-ground. In November all is fresh and blooming as in an English June. Palms, magnolias, bananas, oleanders, camellias, the pepper-tree, make up a rich, many-tinted foliage. Flowers in winter-time are supplanted by beds of brilliant leaved plants that do duty for blossoms. The purple, crimson, and sea-green leaves are arranged with 69] great effect, and have a brilliant appearance. Here surrounded by gold green turf, are little lakes which may be sailed across in tiny pleasure skiffs. At the chief entrance, conspicuously placed, stands the fine equestrian monument to Prim, inaugurated with much civil and military pomp some years ago. It is a bold statue in red bronze. The general sits his horse, hat in hand, his fine, soldier-like face turned towards the city. On the sides of the pedestal are bas-reliefs recording episodes of his career, and on the front these words only, "Barcelona à Prim." The work is that of a Spanish artist, and the monument as a whole reflects great credit alike to local art and public spirit.

But a few minutes' drive brings us within sight of a monument to one of the world's heroes. I allude to the memorial column recently raised to Columbus by this same public-spirited and munificent city of Barcelona. Columbus, be it remembered, was received here by Ferdinand and Isabella after his discovery of America in 1493. Far and wide over hills and city, palm-girt harbor, and sea, as a lighthouse towers the tremendous obelisk, the figure of the great Genoese surmounting it, his feet placed on a golden sphere, his

31

outstretched arm pointing triumphantly in the direction of his newly-discovered continent as much as to say, "It is there!"

Never did undertaking reflect more credit upon a city than this stupendous work. The entire height of the monument is about two-thirds of the height of the Monument of London. The execution was entrusted to Barcelonese craftsmen and artists; the materials—bronze, stone, and marble—all being supplied in the neighborhood.

On the upper tier of the pedestal are statues of the 70] four noble Catalans who materially aided Columbus in his expedition—by name Fray Boyl, monk of Montserrat, Pedro Margarit, Jaime Ferrer, and Luis Sentangel. Below are allegorical figures representing, in the form of stately matrons, the four kingdoms of Catalonia, Castille, Aragon, and Leon. Bas-reliefs, illustrating scenes in the career of the discoverer, adorn the hexagonal sides, six magnificent winged lions of greystone keep jealous watch over the whole, and below these, softening the aspect of severity, is a belt of turf, the following inscription being perpetually written in flowers: "Barcelona à Colon." The column is surmounted by a globe burnished with gold, and above rises the colossal figure of Columbus.

No happier site could have been selected. The monument faces the sea, and is approached from the town by a palm-bordered walk and public garden. The first object to greet the mariner's eye as he sights land is the figure of Columbus poised on his glittering ball; the last to fade from view is that beacon-like column towering so proudly above city and shore. A little excursion must be made by boat or steamer, in order to realize the striking effect of this monument from the sea.

To obtain a bird's-eye view of Barcelona itself, the stranger should go some distance inland. The Fort of Montjuich, commanding the town from the south, or Mont Tibidaho to the north, will equally answer his purpose. A pretty winding path leads from the shore to a pleasure-garden just below the fort, and here we see the entire city spread as in a map at our feet. The panorama is somewhat monotonous, the vast congeries of white walls and grey roofs only broken by gloomy old church towers and tall factory chimneys, but thus is realized for the first time the enormous extent of the 71] Spanish Liverpool and Manchester in one. Thus, indeed, may Barcelona be styled. Looking seaward, the picture is animated and engaging—the wide harbor bristling with shipping, lateen-sailed fishing boats skimming the deep-blue sunny waves, noble vessels just discernible on the dim horizon.

The once celebrated promenade of the Murallo del Mar, eulogized by Ford and other writers, no longer exists, but the stranger will keep the sea-line in search of the new cemetery. A very bad road leads thither, on All Saints' and All Souls' days followed by an unbroken string of vehicles, omnibuses, covered carts, hackney carriages, and private broughams; their occupants, for the most part, dressed in black. The women, wearing black Cashmere mantillas, are hardly visible, being hidden by enormous wreaths, crosses, and bouquets of natural and also of artificial flowers. The new cemetery is well placed, being several miles from the city, on high ground between the open country and the sea. It is tastefully laid out in terraces—the trees and shrubs testifying to the care bestowed on them. Here are many costly monuments—mausoleums, we should rather say—of opulent Barcelonese, each family possessing its tiny chapel and burial-place.

It is to be hoped that so progressive a city as Barcelona will ere long adopt the system of cremation. Nothing can be less hygienic, one would think, than the present mode of burial in Spain. To die there is literally—not figuratively—to be laid on the shelf. The terrace-like sides of the cemetery ground have been hollowed out into pigeon-holes, and into these are thrust the coffins, the marble slab closing the aperture bearing a memorial inscription. Ivy and other creepers are trained around 72] the various divisions, and wreaths of fresh flowers and immortelles adorn them; the whole presenting the appearance of a huge chest of drawers divided into mathematically exact segments. To us there is something uncanny—nay, revolting—in such a form of burial; which, to say the least of it, cannot be warranted on æsthetic, much less scientific, principles. It is satisfactory to find that at last Protestants and Jews have their own burial-place here, shut off from the rest, it is true by a wall at least twenty feet high, but a resting-place for all that. It was not so very long ago that Malaga was the only Spanish town according Protestants this privilege, the concession being wrung from the authorities by the late much-esteemed British consul, Mr. Mark.

For some days preceding the festival of All Saints the cemetery presents a busy scene. Charwomen, gardeners, masons, and painters then take possession of the place. Marble is scoured, lettering is repainted, shrubs clipped, turf cut—all is made spick and span, in time for the great festival of the dead. It must be borne in mind that All Saints' Day in Spain has no analogy with the same date in our own calendar. Brilliant sunshine, air soft and balmy as of July, characterize the month of November here. These visits to the cemetery are, therefore, less depressing than they would be performed amid English fog and drizzle. We Northerners, moreover, cannot cast off gloomy thoughts and sad retrospection as easily as the more elastic, more joyous Southern temperament. Mass over, the pilgrimage to the cemetery paid, all is relaxation and gaiety. All Saints' and All Souls' days are indeed periods of unmitigated enjoyment and relaxation. Public offices, museums, schools, shops, 73] are closed. Holiday folk pour in from the country. The city is as animated as Paris on the 14th of July.

In the forenoon it is difficult to elbow one's way through the crowded thoroughfares. Every street is thronged, men flocking to mass as zealously as devotees of the other sex. In these early hours most of the ladies wear black; their mourning garb later in the day to be exchanged for fashionable toilettes of all colors. The children are decked out gaily, as for a fancy fair. Service is being held in every church, and from all parts may be heard the sonorous Cathedral bells. Its vast, somber interior, now blazing with wax-lights, is a sight to remember. Crowds in rapt devotion are kneeling on the bare stones, the ladies heedless of their silks; here and there the men kneeling on a glove or pocket-handkerchief, in order to protect their Sunday pantaloons. Rows of poor men—beggars, it would seem, tidied up for the occasion—sit in rows along the aisle, holding lighted tapers. The choir is filled with choristers, men and boys intoning the service so skilfully that they almost seem to sing. Soon the crowds fall back, and a procession passes from choir to high altar—priests and dignitaries in their gorgeous robes, some of black, embroidered with crosses in gold, others of white and purple or yellow, the bishop coming last, his long violet train borne by a priest; all the time the well-trained voices of the choristers—sweet treble of the boys, tenor, and base—making up for lack of music. At last the long ceremony comes to an end, and the vast congregation pours out to enjoy the balmy air, the warm sunshine, visits, confectionery, and other distractions.

Such religious holidays should not be missed by the 74] traveller, since they still stamp Spain as the most Catholic country in the world. Even in bustling, cosmopolitan, progressive Barcelona people seem to spend half their time in church.

In the capital of Catalonia, twentieth-century civilization and the mediæval spirit may still be called next-door neighbors. The airy boulevards and handsome villas of suburban Algiers are not more strikingly contrasted with the ancient Moorish streets than the new quarters of Barcelona with the old. The Rambla, its electric lights, its glittering shops, cafés, clubs, and theaters, recalls a Parisian boulevard. In many of the tortuous, malodorous streets of the old town there is hardly room for a wheelbarrow to be drawn along; no sunbeam has ever penetrated the gloom.

Let us take a penny tramway from the Rambla to the gloomy, grandiose old church of Santa Maria del Mar. Between the city and the sea rises the majestic monument to Columbus, conspicuous as a lighthouse alike from land and sea. We follow a broad palm-bordered alley and pleasure garden beyond which are seen the noble harbor bristling with masts and the soft blue Mediterranean. Under the palms lounge idle crowds listening to a band, shading themselves as best they can from the burning sun of November! What a change when we leave the tramway and the airy, handsome precincts of the park, and plunge into the dark, narrow street behind the Lonja Palace. The somber picture is not without relief. Round about the ancient façade of the church are cloth-shops, the gay wares hanging from each story, as if the shopmen made a display of all their wares. Here were reds, yellows, greens of brightest hue, some of these woolen blankets, shawls, and garments of every 75]description being gay to crudeness; grass green, scarlet, orange, sky-blue, dazzled the eye, but the general effect was picturesque and cheerful. The dingy little square looked ready for a festival. In reality, a funeral service was taking place in the church. If Spanish interiors are always dark and depressing, what must they be when draped with black? No sooner does the door swing behind us here than daylight is shut out completely as on entering a mine; we are obliged to grope our way by the feeble rays of light penetrating the old stained glass of the clerestory. The lovely lancets of the aisles are hidden by huge black banners, the vast building being only lighted by a blaze of wax tapers here and there. Sweet soft chanting of boys' voices, with a delicious organ accompaniment, was going on when I entered, soon to be exchanged for the unutterably monotonous and lugubrious intoning of black-robed choristers. They formed a procession and, chanting as they went, marched to a side altar before which a priest was performing mass. The Host elevated, all marched back again, the dreary intoning now beginning afresh. It is impossible to convey any adequate notion of the dreariness of the service. If the Spaniards understand how to enjoy to the uttermost what Browning calls "the wild joy of living," they also know how to clothe death with all the terrors of mediæval superstition. It takes one's breath away, too, to calculate the cost of a funeral here, what with the priests accomplished in the mystic dance—so does a Spanish writer designate the performance—the no less elaborate services of the choristers, the lighting up of the church, the display of funeral drapery. The expense, fortunately, can only be

34

incurred once. These ancient churches—all somberness and gloom, yet on fête 76] days ablaze with light and colors—symbolize the leading characteristics of Spanish character. No sooner does the devotee rise from his knees than the Southern passion for joy and animation asserts itself. Religious exercise and revel, penitence and enjoyment, alternate one with the other; the more devout the first, all the more eagerly indulged in the last.

On the Sunday morning following the Festival of All Saints—the 4th of November—the splendid old cathedral was the scene of a veritable pageant. Wax lights illuminated the vast interior from end to end, the brocades and satins of priestly robes blazed with gold embroidery, the rich adornments and treasure of altar and chapels could be seen in full splendor. Before the grand music of the organ and the elevation, a long, very long, sermon had to be listened to, the enormous congregation for the most part standing; scattered groups here and there squatted on the stone piers, not a chair to be had anywhere, no one seeming to find the discourse too long. When at last the preacher did conclude, the white-robed choristers, men and boys, passed out of the choir, and formed a double line. Then the bishop in solemn state descended from the high altar. He wore a crimson gown with long train borne by a priest, and on his head a violet cap, with pea-green tuft. The dresses of the attendant clergy were no less gorgeous and rich in texture, some of crimson with heavy gold trimmings, others of mauve, guinea-gold, peach color, or creamy white, several wearing fur caps. The procession made the round of the choir, then returned to the starting-point. As I sat behind the high altar on one of the high-backed wooden benches destined for the aged poor, two tiny chorister boys came up, both in white surplices, one with a pink, the other with sky-blue 77] collar. Here they chatted and laughed with their hands on the bell-rope, ready to signal the elevation. On a sudden the tittering ceased, the childish hands tugged at the rope, the tinkling of the bell was heard, and the multitude, as one man, fell on its knees, the organ meantime being played divinely. Service over, the crowds emerged into the dazzling sunshine: pleasure parties, steamboat trips, visits, theaters, bull-fights occupied the rest of the day, the Rambla presenting the appearance of a masquerade.

An excursion northwards of the city is necessary, in order to see its charming, fast-increasing suburbs. Many, as is the case with those of Paris, Passy, Auteuil, Belleville, and others, were formerly little towns, but are fast becoming part of Barcelona itself.

Most musically named is Gracia, approached by rail or tramway, where rich citizens have their orange and lemon gardens, their chateaux and villas, and where religious houses abound. In this delightful suburban retreat alone no less than six nunneries may be counted; somber prison-like buildings, with tiny barred windows, indicating the abode of cloistered nuns of ascetic orders. That of the Order of St. Domingo has been recently founded. The house looks precisely like a prison. Here also are several congregations of the other sex—the Missionaries of the Sacred Heart, the Fathers of San Filipe, and others.

Gracia may be called the Hampstead of Barcelona. Hardly a house but possesses its garden. Above the high walls trail gorgeous creepers and datura, whilst through the iron gates we obtain glimpses of dahlias in full splendor, roses red and white, and above these the glossy-leaved orange and lemon trees with their ripening 78] fruit. The pleasantest suburb of Barcelona is well worthy of its name. As Sarria is approached, the scenery becomes more rural, and under the brilliant November sunshine reminds the traveller of the East, the square, white, low-roofed houses rising amid olive and palm trees. The aloes and prickly pears on the waste ground again and again recall Algeria. Here are vast stretches of vegetable gardens and vineyards supplying the city markets, and standing in their own grounds on sunny hill-sides, the quintas or country houses of rich citizens and grandees.

From the little town of Sarria—hardly as yet to be called suburban—a glorious view is obtained of city, port, and sea. The narrow dusty streets, with their close-shuttered houses, have a sleepy look; yet Sarria possesses one of the largest cotton-mills in Spain, several thousand hands being employed by one firm. The branch railway ends at Sarria. Here tourists and holiday-makers alight; the hardy pedestrian to reach the summit of Mont Tibidaho on foot—a matter of two hours or so—the less enterprising, to accept one of the covered cars awaiting excursionists outside the station. Mont Tibidaho is the favorite holiday ground of the citizens. Even in November numerous pleasure parties are sure to be found here, and the large restaurants indicate the extent of summer patronage. On the breezy heights round about are the sumptuous mansions of nobles and merchant princes; whilst down below are numerous picturesque valleys, notably that of San Cugat. The stranger fortunate enough to obtain admission will find himself in the kind of fairyland described by Tennyson in his "Haroun-al-Raschid," Owen Meredith in "The Siege of Constantinople," or Gayangos in his delightful 79] translation of the "Chronicles of Al-Makkari." Marble courts, crystal fountains, magnificent baths, mosaic pavements, statuary, tapestries, aviaries, rare exotics, gold and silver plate, are now combined with all modern appliances of comfort. A sojourn in one of the well-appointed hotels will suffice to give some notion of Spanish society. During the holidays many families from the city take up their quarters here. Social gatherings, picnics, excursions, concerts, are the order of the day, and good military bands enliven the gardens on Sundays.

To the south-east of Barcelona lies the suburb of Barceloneta, frequented by the seafaring population. Penny boats ply between city and suburb, on Sundays and holidays the music of a barrel-organ being thrown into the bargain. The harbor is then black with spectators, and the boats and little steamers, making the cruise of the port for half a franc, are crowded with holiday-makers. The bright silk head-dresses of the women, the men's crimson or scarlet sombreros and plaids, the uniforms of the soldiers, the gay dresses of the ladies, make up a picturesque scene. On board the boats the music of the barrel-organ must on no account be paid for. A well-intentioned stranger who should offer the musician a penny is given to understand that the treat is gratuitous and generously supplied by the owners of the craft. Greed being almost universal in those parts of the world frequented by tourists, it is gratifying to be able to chronicle such exceptions. Seldom, indeed, has the sightseer at Barcelona to put his hand in his pocket.

If inferior to other Spanish cities in picturesqueness and interest generally, the capital of Catalonia atones for the deficit by its abundance of resources. It possesses nothing to be called a picture-gallery; the museums are 80] second-rate, the collections of antiquities inconsiderable. But what other city in Spain can boast of so many learned bodies and diverse centers of intellectual activity? Excessive devotion and scientific inquiry do not here seem at variance. Strange to say, a population that seems perpetually on its knees is the first to welcome modern ideas.

The Academy of Arts was founded in 1751, and owes its origin to the Junta, or Tribunal of Commerce of Catalonia. This art school is splendidly lodged in the Lonja

Palace, and attached to it is a museum, containing a few curious specimens of old Spanish masters, some rather poor copies of the Italian schools, and one real artistic treasure of the first water. This is a collection of studies in black and white by the gifted Fortuny, whose first training was received here. The sketches are masterly, and atone for the insignificance of the remaining collection. Students of both sexes are admitted to the classes, the course of study embracing painting in all its branches, modeling, etching, linear drawing and perspective, anatomy and æsthetics. It is gratifying to find that girls attend these classes, although as yet in small numbers.

The movement in favor of the higher education of women marches at a snail's pace in Spain. The vast number of convents and what are called "Escuelas Pias," or religious schools, attest the fact that even in the most cosmopolitan and enlightened Spanish town the education of girls still remains chiefly in the hands of the nuns. Lay schools and colleges exist, also a normal school for the training of female teachers, founded a few years ago. Here and there we find rich families entrusting their girls to English governesses, but such cases are rare.

81]We must remember, however, that besides the numerous "Escuelas pias" and secular schools, several exist opened under the auspices of the Spanish Evangelical body, and also the League for the Promotion of lay Teaching. We need not infer, then, that because they do not attend the municipal schools the children go untaught.

How reluctantly Catholic countries are won over to educate their women we have witnessed in France. Here in the twentieth century the chief occupation of an educated Spanish lady seems to be that of counting her beads in church.

Music is universally taught, the cultivation of the piano being nowhere more assiduous. Pianoforte teachers may be counted by the hundred; and a Conservatorium, besides academies due to private initiative, offers a thorough musical training to the student. Elegant pianos, characterized by great delicacy of tone and low price, are a leading feature of Barcelona manufacture, notably of the firm Bernareggi.

The University, attended by two thousand five hundred students, was founded so long ago as 1430, and rebuilt in 1873.

A technical school—the only complete school of arts and sciences existing in Spain—was opened under the same roof in 1850; and, in connection with it, night classes are held. Any workman provided with a certificate of good conduct can attend these classes free of cost. Schools of architecture and navigation are also attached to the University.

Thirst after knowledge characterizes all classes of the community. A workman's literary club, or Athenæum, founded a few years back, is now a flourishing institution, 82] aided by municipal funds. No kind of recreation is allowed within its walls. Night-schools opened here are attended by several hundred scholars. Barcelona also boasts of an Academy of Belles Lettres, the first founded in Spain; schools of natural science, chemistry, agriculture, of medicine and surgery, of jurisprudence, an academy devoted to the culture of the Catalonian language, and containing library and museum. This society has greatly contributed to the protection of ancient buildings throughout the province, besides amassing valuable treasure, legend, botanical and geological specimens and antiquities. The Archæological Society of Barcelona has also effected good work: to its initiative the city is mainly indebted for the charming little collection of antiquities known as the "Museo Provincial," before alluded to.

In places of public entertainment Barcelona is unusually rich. Its Opera House, holding four thousand spectators, equals in spaciousness the celebrated house of Moscow. The unpretentious exterior gives no idea of the splendor within. A dozen theaters may be counted besides. Bull-fights, alas! still disgrace the most advanced city of the Peninsula. The bull-ring was founded in 1834, and the brutal spectacle still attracts enormous crowds, chiefly consisting of natives. The bull-fight is almost unanimously repudiated by foreign residents of all ranks.

A few words must now be said about the history of this ancient place. The city founded here by Hamilcar Barco, father of the great Hannibal, is supposed to stand on the site of one more ancient still, existing long before the foundation of Rome. The Carthaginian city in 206 b. c. became a Roman colonia, under the title of "Faventia Julia Augusta Pia Barzino," which was eclipsed in 83]importance, however, by Tarragona, the Roman capital. In 409 a. d. it was taken by the Goths, and under their domination increased in size and influence, coining its own money stamped with the legend "Barcinona." On the destruction of Tarragona by the Moors Barcelona capitulated, was treated with clemency, and again became a metropolis. After many vicissitudes it was ruled in the ninth century by a Christian chief of its own, whose descendants till the twelfth governed it under the title of Counts of Barcelona, later assuming that of Kings of Aragon, to which kingdom the province was annexed. During the Middle Ages Barcelona played a foremost part in the history of commerce. In the words of Ford, "Like Carthage of old, it was the lord and terror of the Mediterranean. It divided with Italy the enriching commerce of the East. It was then a city of commerce, conquest, and courtiers, of taste, learning, and luxury—the Athens of the troubadour."

Its celebrated commercial code, framed in the thirteenth century, obtained acceptance throughout Europe. Here one of the first printing-presses in Spain was set up, and here Columbus was received by Ferdinand and Isabella after his discovery of a new world. A hundred years later a ship was launched from the port, made to move by means of steam. The story of Barcelona is henceforth but a catalogue of tyrannies and treacheries, against which the brave, albeit turbulent, city struggled single-handed. In 1711 it was bombarded and partly ruined by Philip V.; a few years later, after a magnanimous defense, it was stormed by Berwick, on behalf of Louis XIV., and given up to pillage, outrage, fire, and sword. Napoleon's fraudulent seizure of Barcelona is one of the most shameful pages of his shameful history. 84] The first city—the key of Spain, as he called it—only to be taken in fair war by eighty thousand men, was basely entrapped, and remained in the hands of the French till the Treaty of Paris in 1814. From that time Barcelona has only enjoyed fitful intervals of repose. In 1827 a popular rising took place in favor of Don Carlos. In 1834 Queen Christina was opposed, and in 1840 public opinion declared for Espartero. In 1856 and 1874 insurrections occurred, not without bloodshed.

Barcelona is a great gathering-place of merchants from all parts of Europe. In its handsome hotels is heard a very Babel of tongues. The principal manufactures consist of woolen stuffs—said to be inferior to English in quality—silk, lace, firearms, hats, hardware, pianos; the last, as has been already stated, of excellent quality, and low in price. Porcelain, crystal, furniture, and inlaid work, must be included in this list, also ironwork and stone blocks.

Beautifully situated on the Mediterranean between the mouths of two rivers,—the Llobregat and the Besos—and possessing one of the finest climates in the world, Barcelona is doubtless destined ere long to rival Algiers as a health resort. Three lines of railway now connect it directly with Paris, from which it is separated by twenty-eight hours' journey. The traveller may leave Barcelona at five o'clock in the morning and reach Lyons at midnight with only a change of carriages on the frontier. The route viâ Bordeaux is equally expeditious; that by way of Clermont-Ferrand less so, but more picturesque. Hotels in the capital of Catalonia leave nothing to desire on the score of management, hygiene, comfort, and prices strictly regulated by tariff. The only drawback to be complained of is the total absence of the feminine 85]element—not a woman to be seen on the premises. Good family hotels, provided with lady clerks and chambermaids, is a decided desideratum. The traveller wishing to attain a knowledge of the Spanish language, and see something of Spanish life and manners, may betake himself to one of the numerous boarding-houses.

Barcelona is very rich in philanthropic and charitable institutions. Foremost of these is its Hospital of Santa Cruz, numbering six hundred beds. It is under the conjoint management of sisters and brothers of charity and lay nurses of both sexes. An asylum for the insane forms part of the building, with annexes for the convalescent. The Hospital del Sagrado Corazon, founded by public subscription in 1870 for surgical cases, also speaks volumes for the munificence of the citizens. The only passport required of the patient is poverty. One interesting feature about this hospital is that the committee of management consists of ladies. The nursing staff is formed of French Sisters of St. Vincent de Paul. Besides these must be named the orphanage for upwards of two thousand children of both sexes—Casa de Caridad de la Provincia de Barcelona—asylums for abandoned infants, for the orphaned children of seamen, maternity hospitals, crèches, etc. There is also a school for the blind and deaf mutes, the first of the kind established in Spain. Here the blind of both sexes receive a thorough musical training, and deaf mutes are taught according to the system known as lip-speech. All teaching is gratuitous.

Barcelona possesses thirty-eight churches, without counting the chapels attached to convents, and a vast number of conventual houses. Several evangelical services are held on Sundays both in the city and in the 86] suburb of Barceloneta. The Protestant communities of Spain, England, France, Germany, Sweden, and other countries, have here their representative and organization. Sunday-schools and night-schools for adults are held in connection with these churches. The Protestant body seems active. We find here a branch depôt of the Religious Tract Society; various religious magazines, many of them translations from the English and German, are published. Among these are the "Revista Christiana," intended for the more thoughtful class of readers; "La Luz," organ of the Reformed Church of Spain; and several illustrated periodicals for children. Will Protestantism ever take deep root in the home of the Inquisition? Time will show.

That very advanced political opinions should be held here need hardly surprise us. We find the following Democratic clubs in existence: The Historic Republican Club

("Centro Republicano Historico"), the Possibilist Republican Club ("Circulo Republicano Possibilista"), the Democratic Progressist Club, the Federal Republican Club, and many others. When next a great popular movement takes place in Spain—and already the event looms in the distance—without doubt the first impulse will be given at Barcelona.

Electric lighting was early introduced here, a company being founded so long back as 1880, and having branches in the capital, Seville, Valencia, Bilbao, and other towns. The importance of Barcelona as a center of commerce is attested by the extraordinary number of banks. At every turn the stranger comes upon a bank. "Compared to the mighty hives of English industry and skill, here everything is petty," wrote Ford, fifty years ago. Very 87] different would be his verdict could he revisit the Manchester and Liverpool of Catalonia in our own day.

One curious feature of social life in Spain is the extraordinary number of religious fête days and public holidays. No Bank Holiday Act is needed, as in the neighboring country of France. Here is a list of days during which business is for the most part suspended in this recreation-loving city: Twelfth-cake Day is the great festival of the little ones—carnival is kept up, if with less of former splendor, nevertheless with much spirit; on Ash Wednesday rich and poor betake themselves to the country; Holy Thursday and Good Friday are celebrated with great pomp in the churches; on Easter Eve takes place a procession of shepherds in the park; Easter Monday is a day given up to rural festivity; the 19th of March St. José's Day—is a universal fête, hardly a family in Spain without a José among its number. The first Sunday in May is a feast of flowers and poetic competitions; the days consecrated to St. Juan and St. Pedro are public holidays, patronized by enormous numbers of country-folks; All Saints' and All Souls' Days are given up, as we have seen, to alternate devotion and festivity. On the 20th of December is celebrated the Feast of the Nativity, the fair and the displays of the shops attracting strangers from all parts. But it is especially the days sacred to the Virgin that are celebrated by all classes. Balls, banquets, processions, miracle-plays, illuminations, bull-fights, horse-races, scholastic fêtes, industrial exhibitions, civic ceremonial, besides solemn services, occupy old and young, rich and poor. Feasting is the order of the day, and the confectioners' windows are wonderful to behold.

88]Although many local customs are dying out, we may still see some of the curious street sights described by Ford fifty years ago, and the Mariolatry he deplored is still as active as ever. The goodly show of dainties in the shops, however, belie his somewhat acrimonious description of a Spanish reception. "Those who receive," he wrote, "provide very little refreshment unless they wish to be covered with glory; space, light, and a little bad music, are sufficient to amuse these merry, easily-pleased souls, and satisfy their frugal bodies. To those who, by hospitality and entertainment, can only understand eating and drinking—food for man and beast—such hungry proceedings will be more honored in the breach than in the observance; but these matters depend much on latitude and longitude." Be this as it may, either the climate of Barcelona has changed, or international communication has revolutionized Spanish digestion. Thirty years ago, when travelling in Spain, it was no unusual sight to see a spare, aristocratic hidalgo enter a restaurant, and, with much form and ceremony, breakfast off a tiny omelette. Nowadays we find plenty of Spanish guests at public ordinaries doing ample justice to a plentiful board. English visitors in a Spanish house will not only get good music, in addition to space and light, but abundant hospitality of material sort.

The Spain of which Ford wrote so humorously, and, it must be admitted, often so maliciously, is undergoing slow, but sure, transformation. Many national characteristics remain—the passion for the brutal bull-fight still disgraces a polished people, the women still spend the greater portion of their lives in church, religious intolerance at the beginning of the twentieth century must be laid to the charge of a slowly progressive nation. On the 89] other hand, and nowhere is the fact more patent than at Barcelona, the great intellectual and social revolution, described by contemporary Spanish novelists, is bringing the peninsula in closer sympathy with her neighbors. Many young Spaniards, for instance, are now educated in England, English is freely spoken at Malaga, and its literature is no longer unknown to Spanish readers. These facts indicate coming change. The exclusiveness which has hitherto barred the progress of this richly-dowed and attractive country is on the wane. Who shall say? We may ere long see dark-eyed students from Barcelona at Girton College, and a Spanish society for the protection of animals prohibiting the torture of bulls and horses for the public pleasure.

Already—all honor to her name—a Spanish woman novelist, the gifted Caballero, has made pathetic appeals to her country-folks for a gentler treatment of animals in general. For the most part, it must be sadly confessed, in vain!

In spite of its foremost position, in intellectual and commercial pre-eminence, Barcelona has produced no famous men. Her noblest monument is raised to an alien; Lopez, a munificent citizen, honored by a statue, was born at Santander. Prim, although a Catalan, did not first see the light in the capital. By some strange concatenation of events, this noble city owes her fame rather to the collective genius and spirit of her children than to any one. A magnanimous stepmother, she has adopted those identified with her splendor to whom she did not herself give birth.

Balzac wittily remarks that the dinner is the barometer of the family purse in Paris. One perceives whether Parisians are flourishing or no by a glance at the daily 90] board. Clothes afford a nice indication of temperature all the world over. We have only to notice what people wear, and we can construct a weather-chart for ourselves. Although the late autumn was, on the whole, favorable, I left fires, furs, and overcoats in Paris. At Lyons, a city afflicted with a climate the proper epithet of which is "muggy," ladies had not yet discarded their summer clothes, and were only just beginning to refurbish felt hats and fur-lined pelisses.

At Montpellier the weather was April-like—mild, blowy, showery; waterproofs, goloshes, and umbrellas were the order of the day. On reaching Barcelona I found a blazing sun, windows thrown wide open, and everybody wearing the lightest garments. Such facts do duty for a thermometer.

Boasting, as it does of one of the finest climates in the world, natural position of rare beauty, a genial, cosmopolitan, and strikingly handsome population, and lastly, accessibility, Barcelona should undoubtedly be a health resort hardly second to Algiers. Why it is not, I will undertake to explain.

In the first place, there is something that invalids and valetudinarians require more imperatively than a perfect climate. They cannot do without the ministrations of women.

To the suffering, the depressed, the nervous, feminine influence is ofttimes of more soothing—nay, healing—power than any medical prescription.

Let none take the flattering unction to their souls—as well look for a woman in a Bashaw's army, or on a man-of-war, as in the palatial, well-appointed, otherwise irreproachable hotels of Barcelona! They boast of marble floors, baths that would not have dissatisfied a Roman epicure, salons luxurious as those of a West-end club, 91] newspapers in a score of languages, a phalanx of gentlemanly waiters, a varied ordinary, delicious wines, but not a daughter of Eve, old or young, handsome or ugly—if, indeed, there exists an ugly woman in Barcelona—to be caught sight of anywhere! No charming landlady, as in French hotels, taking friendliest interest in her guests, no housemaids, willing and nimble as the Marys and Janes we have left at home, not even a rough, kindly, garrulous charwoman scrubbing the floors. The fashionable hotel here is a vast barrack conducted on strictly impersonal principles. Visitors obtain their money's worth, and pay their bills. There the transaction between innkeeper and traveller ends.

Good family hotels or "pensions," in which invalids would find a home-like element, are sadly needed in this engaging, highly-favored city. The next desideratum is a fast train from Port Bou—the first Spanish town on the frontier. An express on the Spanish line would shorten the journey to Lyons by several hours. New carriages are needed as much as new iron roads. Many an English third-class is cleaner and more comfortable than the so-called "first" here. It must be added that the officials are all politeness and attention, and that beyond slowness and shabbiness the traveller has nothing to complain of. Exquisite urbanity is still a characteristic of the Barcelonese as it was in the age of Cervantes. One exception will be mentioned farther on.

If there are no women within the hotel walls—except, of course, stray lady tourists—heaven be praised, there are enough, and to spare, of most bewitching kind without. Piquancy is, perhaps, the foremost charm of a Spanish beauty, whether a high-born señora in her brougham, or a flower-girl at her stall. One and all 92] seem born to turn the heads of the other sex, after the fashion of Carmen in Merimée's story. Nor is outward attraction confined to women. The city police, cab-drivers, tramway-conductors, all possess what Schopenhauer calls the best possible letter of introduction, namely, good looks.

The number of the police surprise us. These bustling, brilliant streets, with their cosmopolitan crowds, seem the quietest, most orderly in the world. It seems hard to believe that this tranquillity and contentment should be fallacious—on the surface only. Yet such is the case, as shown by the recent outbreak of rioting and bloodshed.

"I have seen revolution after revolution," said to me a Spanish gentleman of high position, an hidalgo of the old school; "I expect to see more if my life is sufficiently prolonged. Spain has no government; each in power seeks but self-aggrandizement. Our army is full of Boulangers, each ready to usurp power for his own ends. You suggest a change of dynasty? We could not hope to be thereby the gainers. A Republic, say you? That also has proved a failure with us. Ah, you English are happy; you do not need to change abruptly the existing order of things, you effect revolutions more calmly."

I observed that perhaps national character and temperament had something to do with the matter. He replied very sadly, "You are right; we Southerners are more impetuous, of fiercer temper. Whichever way I look, I see no hope for unhappy Spain."

Such somber reflections are difficult to realize by the passing traveller. Yet, when we consider the tremendous force of such a city as Barcelona, its progressive tendencies, its spirit of scientific inquiry, we can but admit that an Ultramontane regency and reactionary 93] government must be out of harmony with the tendencies of modern Spain.

There is only one occupation which seems to have a deteriorating effect upon the Spanish temper. The atmosphere of the post-office, at any rate, makes a Catalan rasping as an east wind, acrimonious as a sloe-berry. I had been advised to provide myself with a passport before revisiting Spain, but I refused to do so on principle.

What business have we with this relic of barbarism at the beginning of the twentieth century, in times of peace among a friendly people? The taking a passport under such circumstances seemed to me as much of an anachronism as the wearing of a scapular, or seeking the royal touch for scrofula. By pure accident, a registered letter containing bank notes was addressed to me at the Poste Restante. Never was such a storm in a teacup, such groaning of the mountain before the creeping forth of a tiny mouse! The delivery of registered letters in Spain is accompanied with as much form as a marriage contract in France. Let future travellers in expectation of such documents provide themselves, not only with a passport, but a copy of their baptismal register, of the marriage certificate of their parents, the family Bible—no matter its size—and any other proofs of identity they can lay hands upon. They will find none superfluous.

94]

V

MARSEILLES

Its Greek founders and early history—Superb view from the sea—The Cannebière—The Parado and Chemin de la Corniche—Château d'If and Monte-Cristo—Influence of the Greeks in Marseilles—Ravages by plague and pestilence—Treasures of the Palais des Arts—The chapel of Notre Dame de la Garde—The new Marseilles and its future.

ABOUT six hundred years before the birth of Christ, when the Mediterranean, ringed round with a long series of commercial colonies, was first beginning to transform itself with marvelous rapidity into "a Greek lake," a body of adventurous Hellenic mariners—young Columbuses of their day—full of life and vigor, sailed forth from Phocæa in Asia Minor, and steered their course, by devious routes, to what was then the

43

Far West, in search of a fitting and unoccupied place in which to found a new trading city. Hard pressed by the Persians on their native shore, these free young Greeks—the Pilgrim Fathers of modern Marseilles—left behind for ever the city of their birth, and struck for liberty in some distant land, where no Cyrus or Xerxes could ever molest them. Sailing away past Greece and Sicily, and round Messina into the almost unknown Tyrrhenian Sea, the adventurous voyagers arrived at last, after various false starts in Corsica and elsewhere, at some gaunt white hills of the Gaulish coast, 95] and cast anchor finally in a small but almost land-locked harbor, under the shelter of some barren limestone mountains. Whether they found a Phœnician colony already established on the spot or not, matters as little to history nowadays as whether their leaders' names were really Simos and Protis or quite otherwise. What does matter is the indubitable fact that Massalia, as its Greek founders called it, preserved through all its early history the impress of a truly Hellenic city; and that even to this moment much good Greek blood flows, without question, in the hot veins of all its genuine native-born citizens.

The city thus founded has had a long, a glorious, and an eventful history. Marseilles is to-day the capital of the Mediterranean, the true commercial metropolis of that inland sea which now once more has become a single organic whole, after its long division by the Mohammedan conquest of North Africa and the Levant into two distinct and hostile portions. Naples, it is true, has a larger population; but then, a population of Neapolitan lazzaroni, mere human drones lounging about their hive and basking in the sunlight, does not count for much, except for the macaroni trade. What Venice once was, that Marseilles is to-day; the chief gate of Mediterranean traffic, the main mart of merchants who go down in ships on the inland sea. In the Cannebière and the Old Port, she possesses, indeed, as Edmond About once graphically phrased it, "an open door upon the Mediterranean and the whole world." The steamers and sailing vessels that line her quays bind together the entire Mediterranean coast into a single organic commercial whole. Here is the packet for Barcelona and Malaga; there, the one for Naples, Malta, and Constantinople. By this huge liner, sunning herself at La Joliette, we can go 96] to Athens and Alexandria; by that, to Algiers, Cagliari, and Tunis. Nay, the Suez Canal has extended her bounds beyond the inland sea to the Indian Ocean; and the Pillars of Hercules no longer restrain her from free use of the great Atlantic water-way. You may take ship, if you will, from the Quai de la Fraternité for Bombay or Yokohama, for Rio or Buenos Ayres, for Santa Cruz, Teneriffe, Singapore, or Melbourne. And this wide extension of her commercial importance Marseilles owes, mainly no doubt, to her exceptional advantages of natural position, but largely also, I venture to think, to the Hellenic enterprise of her acute and vigorous Græco-Gaulish population.

And what a marvelous history has she not behind her! First of all, no doubt, a small fishing and trading station of prehistoric Gaulish or Ligurian villagers occupied the site where now the magnificent façade of the Bourse commemorates the names of Massalia's greatest Phocæan navigators. Then the Phœnicians supervened upon the changeful scene, and built those antique columns and forgotten shrines whose scanty remains were recently unearthed in the excavations for making the Rue de la République. Next came the early Phocæan colonists, reinforced a little later by the whole strength of their unconquerable townsmen, who sailed away in a body, according to the well-known legend preserved in Herodotus, when they could no longer hold out against the besieging Persian. The Greek town became as it were a sort of early Calcutta for the Gaulish trade, with its own outlying colonies at Nice, Antibes, and Hyères, and its inland "factories" (to use the old familiar Anglo-Indian word) at Tarascon, Avignon, and many other ancient towns of the Rhône valley. Her admirals sailed on every known 97] sea: Euthymenes explored the coasts of Africa as far as Senegal; Pytheas followed the European shore past Britain and Ireland to the north of the Shetlands. Till the Roman arrived upon the Gaulish coast with his dreaded short-sword, Massalia, in short, remained undisputed queen of all the western Mediterranean waters.

Before the wolf of the Capitol, however, all stars paled. Yet even under the Roman Empire Massilia (as the new conquerors called the name, with a mere change of vowel) retained her Greek speech and manners, which she hardly lost (if we may believe stray hints in later historians) till the very eve of the barbarian invasion. With the period of the Crusades, the city of Euthymenes became once more great and free, and hardly lost her independence completely up to the age of Louis XIV. It was only after the French Revolution, however, that she began really to supersede Venice as the true capital of the Mediterranean. The decline of the Turkish power, the growth of trade with Alexandria and the Levant, the final crushing of the Barbary pirates, the conquest of Algeria, and, last of all, the opening of the Suez Canal—a French work—all helped to increase her commerce and population by gigantic strides in half a dozen decades. At the present day Marseilles is the chief maritime town of France, and the acknowledged center of Mediterranean travel and traffic.

The right way for the stranger to enter Marseilles is, therefore, by sea, the old-established high road of her antique commerce. The Old Port and the Cannebière are her front door, while the railway from Paris leads you in at best, as it were, through shabby corridors, by a side entry. Seen from the sea, indeed, Marseilles is superb. I hardly know whether the whole Mediterranean has any 98] finer approach to a great town to display before the eyes of the artistic traveller. All round the city rises a semicircle of arid white hills, barren and bare indeed to look upon; but lighted up by the blue Provençal sky with a wonderful flood of borrowed radiance, bringing out every jutting peak and crag through the clear dry air in distinct perspective. Their sides are dotted with small square white houses, the famous bastides or country boxes of the good Marseillais bourgeois. In front, a group of sunlit rocky isles juts out from the bay, on one of which tower the picturesque bastions of the Chateau d'If, so familiar to the reader of "Monte-Cristo." The foreground is occupied by the town itself, with its forest of masts, and the new dome of its checkered and gaudy Byzantine Cathedral, which has quite supplanted the old cathedral of St. Lazare, of which only a few traces remain. In the middle distance the famous old pilgrimage chapel of Notre Dame de la Garde crowns the summit of a pyramidal hill, with its picturesque mass of confused architecture. Away to right and left, those endless white hills gleam on with almost wearying brightness in the sun for miles together; but full in front, where the eye rests longest, the bustle and commotion of a great trading town teem with varied life upon the quays and landing-places.

If you are lucky enough to enter Marseilles for the first time by the Old Port, you find yourself at once in the very thick of all that is most characteristic and vivid and local in the busy city. That little oblong basin, shut in on its outer side by projecting hills, was indeed the making of the great town. Of course the Old Port is now utterly insufficient for the modern wants of a first-class harbor; yet it still survives, not only as a historical relic but as a 99]living reality, thronged even to-day with the crowded ships of all nations. On the quay you may see the entire varied Mediterranean world in congress assembled.

45

Here Greeks from Athens and Levantines from Smyrna jostle cheek by jowl with Italians from Genoa and Arabs or Moors from Tangier or Tunis. All costumes and all manners are admissible. The crowd is always excited, and always animated. A babel of tongues greets your ears as you land, in which the true Marseillais dialect of the Provençal holds the chief place—a graceful language, wherein the predominant Latin element has not even yet wholly got rid of certain underlying traces of Hellenic origin. Bright color, din, life, movement: in a moment the traveller from a northern climate recognizes the patent fact that he has reached a new world—that vivid, impetuous, eager southern world, which has its center to-day on the Provençal seaboard.

Go a yard or two farther into the crowded Cannebière, and the difference between this and the chilly North will at each step be forced even more strikingly upon you. That famous thoroughfare is firmly believed by every good son of old Marseilles to be, in the familiar local phrase, "la plus belle rue de l'univers." My own acquaintance with the precincts of the universe being somewhat limited (I have never travelled myself, indeed, beyond the narrow bounds of our own solar system), I should be loth to endorse too literally and unreservedly this sweeping commendation of the Marseillais mind; but as regards our modest little planet at least, I certainly know no other street within my own experience (save Broadway, New York) that has quite so much life and variety in it as the Cannebière. It is not long, to be sure, but it is broad and airy, and from morning till night its 100] spacious trottoirs are continually crowded by such a surging throng of cosmopolitan humanity as you will hardly find elsewhere on this side of Alexandria. For cosmopolitanism is the true key-note of Marseilles, and the Cannebière is a road that leads in one direction straight to Paris, but opens in the other direction full upon Algiers and Italy, upon Egypt and India.

What a picture it offers, too, of human life, that noisy Cannebière! By day or by night it is equally attractive. On it centers all that is alive in Marseilles—big hotels, glittering cafés, luxurious shops, scurrying drays, high-stepping carriage-horses, and fashionably-dressed humanity; an endless crowd, many of them hatless and bonnetless in true southern fashion, parade without ceasing its ringing pavements. At the end of all, the Old Port closes the view with its serried masts, and tells you the wherefore of this mixed society. The Cannebière, in short, is the Rue de Rivoli of the Mediterranean, the main thoroughfare of all those teeming shores of oil and wine, where culture still lingers by its ancient cradle.

Close to the Quai, and at the entrance of the Cannebière, stands the central point of business in new Marseilles, the Bourse, where the filial piety of the modern Phocæans has done ample homage to the sacred memory of their ancient Hellenic ancestors. For in the place of honor on the façade of that great palace of commerce the chief post has been given, as was due, to the statues of the old Massaliote admirals, Pytheas and Euthymenes. It is this constant consciousness of historical continuity that adds so much interest to Mediterranean towns. One feels as one stands before those two stone figures in the crowded Cannebière, that after all humanity is one, 101] and that the Phocæans themselves are still, in the persons of their sons, among us.

The Cannebière runs nearly east and west, and is of no great length, under its own name at least; but under the transparent alias of the Rue de Noailles it continues on in a straight line till it widens out at last into the Allées de Meilhan, the favorite haunt of all the gossips and quidnuncs of Marseilles. The Allées de Meilhan, indeed, form the beau idéal of the formal and fashionable French promenade. Broad avenues of plane trees cast a mellow shade over its well-kept walks, and the neatest of nurses in marvelous caps and long silk streamers dandle the laciest and fluffiest of babies, in exquisite costumes, with ostentatious care, upon their bountiful laps. The stone seats on either side buzz with the latest news of the town; the Zouave flirts serenely with the bonnetless shop-girls; the sergeant-de-ville stalks proudly down the midst, and barely deigns to notice such human weaknesses. These Allées are the favorite haunt of all idle Marseilles, below the rank of "carriage company," and it is probable that Satan finds as much mischief still for its hands to do here as in any other part of that easy-going city.

At right angles to the main central artery thus constituted by the Cannebière, the Rue de Noailles, and the Allées de Meilhan runs the second chief stream of Marseillais life, down a channel which begins as the Rue d'Aix and the Cours Belzunce, and ends, after various intermediate disguises, as the Rue de Rome and the Prado. Just where it crosses the current of the Cannebière, this polyonymous street rejoices in the title of the Cours St. Louis. Close by is the place where the 102]flower-women sit perched up quaintly in their funny little pulpits, whence they hand down great bunches of fresh dewy violets or pinky-white rosebuds, with persuasive eloquence to the obdurate passer-by. This flower-market is one of the sights of Marseilles, and I know no other anywhere—not even at Nice—so picturesque or so old-world. It keeps up something of the true Provençal flavor, and reminds one that here, in this Greek colony, we are still in the midst of the land of roses and of Good King René, the land of troubadours, and gold and flowers, and that it is the land of sun and summer sunshine.

As the Rue de Rome emerges from the town and gains the suburb, it clothes itself in overhanging shade of plane-trees, and becomes known forthwith as the Prado—that famous Prado, more sacred to the loves and joys of the Marseillais than the Champs Elysées are to the born Parisian. For the Prado is the afternoon-drive of Marseilles, the Rotten Row of local equestrianism, the rallying-place and lounge of all that is fashionable in the Phocæan city as the Allées de Meilhan are of all that is bourgeois or frankly popular. Of course the Prado does not differ much from all other promenades of its sort in France: the upper-crust of the world has grown painfully tame and monotonous everywhere within the last twenty-five years: all flavor and savor of national costume or national manners has died out of it in the lump, and left us only in provincial centers the insipid graces of London and Paris, badly imitated. Still, the Prado is undoubtedly lively; a broad avenue bordered with magnificent villas of the meretricious Haussmannesque order of architecture; and it possesses a certain great advantage over every other similar promenade I know of 103] in the world—it ends at last in one of the most beautiful and picturesque sea-drives in all Europe.

This sea-drive has been christened by the Marseillais, with pardonable pride, the Chemin de la Corniche, in humble imitation of that other great Corniche road which winds its tortuous way by long, slow gradients over the ramping heights of the Turbia between Nice and Mentone. And a "ledge road" it is in good earnest, carved like a shelf out of the solid limestone. When I first knew Marseilles there was no Corniche: the Prado, a long flat drive through a marshy plain, ended then abruptly on the sea-front; and the hardy pedestrian who wished to return to town by way of the cliffs had to clamber along a doubtful and rocky path, always difficult, often dangerous, and much obstructed by the attentions of the prowling douanier, ever ready to arrest him as a suspected smuggler. Nowadays, however, all that is changed. The French engineers—always famous for their roads—have hewn a broad and handsome carriage-drive out of the rugged rock, here hanging on a shelf sheer above the sea; there supported from below by heavy buttresses of excellent masonwork; and have given the Marseillais one of the most exquisite promenades to be found anywhere on the seaboard of the Continent. It somewhat resembles the new highway from Villefranche to Monte Carlo; but the islands with which the sea is here studded recall rather Cannes or the neighborhood of Sorrento. The seaward views are everywhere delicious; and when sunset lights up the bare white rocks with pink and purple, no richer coloring against the emerald green bay, can possibly be imagined in art or nature. It is as good as Torquay; and how can cosmopolitan say better?

104]On the Corniche, too, is the proper place nowadays to eat that famous old Marseillais dish, immortalized by Thackeray, and known as bouillabaisse. The Réserve de Roubion in particular prides itself on the manufacture of this strictly national Provençal dainty, which proves, however, a little too rich and a little too mixed in its company for the fastidious taste of most English gourmets. Greater exclusiveness and a more delicate eclecticism in matters of cookery please our countrymen better than such catholic comprehensiveness. I once asked a white-capped Provençal chef what were the precise ingredients of his boasted bouillabaisse; and the good man opened his palms expansively before him as he answered with a shrug, "Que voulez-vous? Fish to start with; and then—a handful of anything that happens to be lying about loose in the kitchen."

Near the end of the Prado, at its junction with the Corniche, modern Marseilles rejoices also in its park or Public Garden. Though laid out on a flat and uninteresting plain, with none of the natural advantages of the Bois de Boulogne or of the beautiful Central Park at New York, these pretty grounds are nevertheless interesting to the northern visitor, who makes his first acquaintance with the Mediterranean here, by their curious and novel southern vegetation. The rich types of the south are everywhere apparent. Clumps of bamboo in feathery clusters overhang the ornamental waters; cypresses and araucarias shade the gravel walks; the eucalyptus showers down its fluffy flowers upon the grass below; the quaint Salisburia covers the ground in autumn with its pretty and curious maidenhair-shaped foliage. Yuccas and cactuses flourish vigorously in the open air, and even fan-palms manage to thrive the year round in cosy 105]corners. It is an introduction to the glories of Riveran vegetation, and a faint echo of the magnificent tones of the North African flora.

As we wind in and out on our way back to Marseilles by the Corniche road, with the water ever dashing white from the blue against the solid crags, whose corners we turn at every tiny headland, the most conspicuous object in the nearer view is the Château d'If, with the neighboring islets of Pomègues and Ratonneau. Who knows not the Château d'If, by name at least, has wasted his boyhood. The castle is not indeed of any great antiquity—it was built by order of François I—nor can it lay much claim to picturesqueness of outline or beauty of architecture; but in historical and romantic associations it is peculiarly rich, and its situation is bold, interesting, and striking. It was here that Mirabeau was imprisoned under a lettre de cachet obtained by his father, the friend of man; and it was here, to pass from history to romance, that Monte-Cristo went through those marvelous and somewhat incredible adventures which will keep a hundred generations of school-boys in breathless suspense long after Walter Scott is dead and forgotten.

But though the Prado and the Corniche are alive with carriages on sunny afternoons, it is on the quays themselves, and around the docks and basins, that the true vivacious Marseillais life must be seen in all its full flow and eagerness. The quick southern temperament, the bronzed faces, the open-air existence, the hurry and bustle of a great seaport town, display themselves there to the best advantage. And the ports of Marseilles are many and varied: their name is legion, and their shipping manifold. As long ago as 1850, the old square port, the Phocæan harbor, was felt to have become wholly 106]insufficient for the needs of modern commerce in Marseilles. From that day to this, the accommodation for vessels has gone on increasing with that incredible rapidity which marks the great boom of modern times. Never, surely, since the spacious days of great Elizabeth, has the world so rapidly widened its borders as in these latter days in which we are all living. The Pacific and the Indian Ocean have joined the Atlantic. In 1853 the Port de la Joliette was added, therefore, to the Old Harbor, and people thought Marseilles had met all the utmost demands of its growing commerce. But the Bassin du Lazaret and the Bassin d'Arenc were added shortly after; and then, in 1856, came the further need for yet another port, the Bassin National. In 1872 the Bassin de la Gare Maritime was finally executed; and now the Marseillais are crying out again that the ships know not where to turn in the harbor. Everywhere the world seems to cosmopolitanize itself and to extend its limits: the day of small things has passed away for ever; the day of vast ports, huge concerns, gigantic undertakings is full upon us.

Curiously enough, however, in spite of all this rapid and immense development, it is still to a great extent the Greek merchants who hold in their hands—even in our own time—the entire commerce and wealth of the old Phocæan city. A large Hellenic colony of recent importation still inhabits and exploits Marseilles. Among the richly-dressed crowd of southern ladies that throngs the Prado on a sunny afternoon in full season, no small proportion of the proudest and best equipped who loll back in their carriages were born at Athens or in the Ionic Archipelago. For even to this day, these modern Greeks hang together wonderfully with old Greek persistence. Their creed keeps them apart from the Catholic 107] French, in whose midst they live, and trade, and thrive; for, of course, they are all members of the "Orthodox" Church, and they retain their orthodoxy in spite of the ocean of Latin Christianity which girds them round with its flood on every side. The Greek community, in fact, dwells apart, marries apart, worships apart, and thinks apart. The way the marriages, in particular, are most frequently managed, differs to a very curious extent from our notions of matrimonial proprieties. The system—as duly explained to me one day under the shady plane-trees of the Allées de Meilhan, in very choice modern Greek, by a Hellenic merchant of Marseilles, who himself had been "arranged for" in this very manner—is both simple and mercantile to the highest degree yet practised in any civilized country. It is "marriage by purchase" pure and simple; only

49

here, instead of the husband buying the wife, it is the wife who practically buys the husband.

A trader or ship-owner of Marseilles, let us say, has two sons, partners in his concern, who he desires to marry. It is important, however, that the wives he selects for them should not clash with the orthodoxy of the Hellenic community. Our merchant, therefore, anxious to do the best in both worlds at once, writes to his correspondents of the great Greek houses in Smyrna, Constantinople, Beyrout, and Alexandria; nay, perhaps even in London, Manchester, New York, and Rio, stating his desire to settle his sons in life, and the amount of dot they would respectively require from the ladies upon whom they decided to bestow their name and affections. The correspondents reply by return of post, recommending to the favorable attention of the happy swains certain Greek young ladies in the town of their adoption, 108] whose dot and whose orthodoxy can be equally guaranteed as beyond suspicion. Photographs and lawyers' letters are promptly exchanged; settlements are drawn up to the mutual satisfaction of both the high contracting parties; and when all the business portion of the transaction has been thoroughly sifted, the young ladies are consigned, with the figs and dates, as per bill of lading, to the port of entry, where their lords await them, and are duly married, on the morning of their arrival, at the Greek church in the Rue de la Grande Armée, by the reverend archimandrite. The Greeks are an eminently commercial people, and they find this idyllic mode of conducting a courtship not only preserves the purity of the orthodox faith and the Hellenic blood, but also saves an immense amount of time which might otherwise be wasted on the composition of useless love-letters.

It was not so, however, in the earlier Greek days. Then, the colonists of Marseilles and its dependent towns must have intermarried freely with the native Gaulish and Ligurian population of all the tributary Provençal seaboard. The true antique Hellenic stock—the Aryan Achæans of the classical period—were undoubtedly a fair, a light-haired race, with a far more marked proportion of the blond type than now survives among their mixed and degenerate modern descendants. In Greece proper, a large intermixture of Albanian and Sclavonic blood, which the old Athenians would have stigmatized as barbarian or Scythian, has darkened the complexion and blackened the hair of a vast majority of the existing population. But in Marseilles, curiously enough, and in the surrounding country, the genuine old light Greek type has left its mark to this day upon the physique of the inhabitants. In the ethnographical map of France, 109] prepared by two distinguished French savants, the other Mediterranean departments are all, without exception, marked as "dark" or "very dark," while the department of the Bouches du Rhône is marked as "white," having, in fact, as large a proportion of fair complexions, blond hair, and light eyes as the eastern semi-German provinces, or as Normandy and Flanders. This curious survival of a very ancient type in spite of subsequent deluges, must be regarded as a notable instance of the way in which the popular stratum everywhere outlasts all changes of conquest and dynasty, of governing class and ruling family.

Just think, indeed, how many changes and revolutions in this respect that fiery Marseilles has gone through since the early days of her Hellenic independence! First came that fatal but perhaps indispensable error of inviting the Roman aid against her Ligurian enemies, which gave the Romans their earliest foothold in Southern Gaul. Then followed the foundation of Aquæ Sextiæ or Aix, the first Roman colony in what was soon to be the favorite province of the new conquerors. After that, in the great civil war, the Greeks of

Marseilles were unlucky enough to espouse the losing cause; and, in the great day of Cæsar's triumph, their town was reduced accordingly to the inferior position of a mere Roman dependency. Merged for a while in the all-absorbing empire, Marseilles fell at last before Visigoths and Burgundians in the stormy days of that vast upheaval, during which it is impossible for even the minutest historian to follow in detail the long list of endless conquests and re-conquests, while the wandering tribes ebbed and flowed on one another in wild surging waves of refluent confusion. Ostrogoth and Frank, Saracen and Christian, fought one after 110]another for possession of the mighty city. In the process her Greek and Roman civilization was wholly swept away and not a trace now remains of those glorious basilicas, temples, and arches, which must once, no doubt, have adorned the metropolis of Grecian Gaul far more abundantly than they still adorn mere provincial centers like Arles and Nîmes, Vienne, and Orange. But at the end of it all, when Marseilles emerges once more into the light of day as an integral part of the Kingdom of Provence, it still retains its essentially Greek population, fairer and handsomer than the surrounding dark Ligurian stock; it still boasts its clear-cut Greek beauty of profile, its Hellenic sharpness of wit and quickness of perception. And how interesting in this relation to note, too, that Marseilles kept up, till a comparatively late period in the Middle Ages, her active connection with the Byzantine Empire; and that her chief magistrate was long nominated—in name at least, if not in actual fact—by the shadowy representative of the Cæsars at Constantinople.

May we not attribute to this continuous persistence of the Greek element in the life of Marseilles something of that curious local and self-satisfied feeling which northern Frenchmen so often deride in the born Marseillais? With the Greeks, the sense of civic individuality and civic separateness was always strong. Their Polis was to them their whole world—the center of everything. They were Athenians, Spartans, Thebans first; Greeks or even Bœotians and Lacedæmonians in the second place only. And the Marseillais bourgeois, following the traditions of his Phocæan ancestry, is still in a certain sense the most thoroughly provincial, the most uncentralized and anti-Parisian of modern French citizens. He believes in Marseilles even more devoutly than the average boulevardier 111] believes in Paris. To him the Cannebière is the High Street of the world, and the Cours St. Louis the hub of the universe. How pleased with himself and all his surroundings he is, too! "At Marseilles, we do so-and-so," is a frequent phrase which seems to him to settle off-hand all questions of etiquette, of procedure, or of the fitness of things generally. "Massilia locuta est; causa finita est." That anything can be done better anywhere than it is done in the Cannebière or the Old Port is an idea that never even so much as occurs to his smart and quick but somewhat geographically limited intelligence. One of the best and cleverest of Mars's clever Marseillais caricatures exhibits a good bourgeois from the Cours Pierre Puget, in his Sunday best, abroad on his travels along the Genoese Riviera. On the shore at San Remo, the happy, easy-going, conceited fellow, brimming over to the eyes with the happy-go-lucky Cockney joy of the South, sees a couple of pretty Italian fisher-girls mending their nets, and addresses them gaily in his own soft dialect: "Hé bien, més pitchounettes, vous êtes tellement croussetillantes que, sans ézaggérer, bagasse! ze vous croyais de Marseille!" To take anyone elsewhere for a born fellow-citizen was the highest compliment his good Marseillais soul could possibly hit upon.

Nevertheless, the Marseillais are not proud. They generously allow the rest of the world to come and admire them. They throw their doors open to East and West; they invite Jew and Greek alike to flow in unchecked, and help them make their own fortunes.

They know very well that if Marseilles, as they all firmly believe, is the finest town in the round world, it is the trade with the Levant that made and keeps it so. And they take good care to lay themselves out for entertaining all and sundry 112] as they come, in the handsomest hotels in Southern Europe. The mere through passenger traffic with India alone would serve to make Marseilles nowadays a commercial town of the first importance.

Marseilles, however, has had to pay a heavy price, more than once, for her open intercourse with the Eastern world, the native home of cholera and all other epidemics. From a very early time, the city by the Rhône has been the favorite haunt of the Plague and like oriental visitants; and more than one of its appalling epidemics has gained for itself a memorable place in history. To say the truth, old Marseilles laid itself out almost deliberately for the righteous scourge of zymotic disease. The vieille ville, that trackless labyrinth of foul and noisome alleys, tortuous, deeply worn, ill-paved, ill-ventilated, has been partly cleared away by the works of the Rue de la République now driven through its midst; but enough still remains of its Dædalean maze to show the adventurous traveller who penetrates its dark and drainless dens how dirty the strenuous Provençal can be when he bends his mind to it. There the true-blooded Marseillais of the old rock and of the Greek profile still lingers in his native insanitary condition; there the only scavenger is that "broom of Provence," the swooping mistral—the fierce Alpine wind which, blowing fresh down with sweeping violence from the frozen mountains, alone can change the air and cleanse the gutters of that filthy and malodorous mediæval city. Everywhere else the mistral is a curse: in Marseilles it is accepted with mitigated gratitude as an excellent substitute for main drainage.

It is not to be wondered at that, under such conditions, Marseilles was periodically devastated by terrible epidemics. Communications with Constantinople, Alexandria, 113] and the Levant were always frequent; communications with Tunis, Algiers, and Morocco were far from uncommon. And if the germs of disease were imported from without, they found at Marseilles an appropriate nest provided beforehand for their due development. Time after time the city was ravaged by plague or pestilence; the most memorable occasion being the great epidemic of 1720, when, according to local statistics (too high, undoubtedly), as many as forty thousand persons died in the streets, "like lambs on the hill-tops." Never, even in the East itself, the native home of the plague, says Méry, the Marseilles poet-romancer, was so sad a picture of devastation seen as in the doomed streets of that wealthy city. The pestilence came, according to public belief, in a cargo of wool in May, 1720: it raged till, by September, the tale of dead per diem had reached the appalling number of a thousand.

So awful a public calamity was not without the usual effect in bringing forth counterbalancing examples of distinguished public service and noble self-denial. Chief among them shines forth the name of the Chevalier Rose, who, aided by a couple of hundred condemned convicts, carried forth to burial in the ditches of La Tourette no less than two thousand dead bodies which infected the streets with their deadly contagion. There, quicklime was thrown over the horrible festering mass, in a spot still remembered as the "Graves of the Plague-stricken." But posterity has chosen most especially to select for the honors of the occasion Monseigneur Belzunce—"Marseilles' good bishop," as Pope calls him, who returned in the hour of danger to his stricken flock from the salons of Versailles, and by offering the last consolations of religion to the sick and dying, aided

52

114]somewhat in checking the orgy of despair and of panic-stricken callousness which reigned everywhere throughout the doomed city. The picture is indeed a striking and romantic one. On a high altar raised in the Cours which now bears his name, the brave bishop celebrated Mass one day before the eyes of all his people, doing penance to heaven in the name of his flock, his feet bare, a rope round his neck, and a flaming torch held high in his hand, for the expiation of the sins that had brought such punishment. His fervent intercession, the faithful believed, was at last effectual. In May, 1721, the plague disappeared; but it left Marseilles almost depopulated. The bishop's statue in bronze, by Ramus, on the Cours Belzunce, now marks the site of this strange and unparalleled religious service.

From the Belzunce Monument, the Rue Tapis Vert and the Allées des Capucins lead us direct by a short cut to the Boulevard Longchamp, which terminates after the true modern Parisian fashion, with a vista of the great fountains and the Palais des Arts, a bizarre and original but not in its way unpleasing specimen of recent French architecture. It is meretricious, of course—that goes without the saying: what else can one expect from the France of the Second Empire? But it is distinctly, what the children call "grand," and if once you can put yourself upon its peculiar level, it is not without a certain queer rococo beauty of its own. As for the Château d'Eau, its warmest admirer could hardly deny that it is painfully baroque in design and execution. Tigers, panthers, and lions decorate the approach; an allegorical figure representing the Durance, accompanied by the geniuses of the Vine and of Corn, holds the seat of honor in the midst of the waterspouts. To right and left a 115] triton blows his shelly trumpet; griffins and fauns crown the summit; and triumphal arches flank the sides. A marvelous work indeed, of the Versailles type, better fitted to the ideas of the eighteenth century than to those of the age in which we live at present.

The Palais des Arts, one wing of this monument, encloses the usual French provincial picture-gallery, with the stereotyped Rubens, and the regulation Caraccio. It has its Raffael, its Giulio Romano, and its Andrea del Sarto. It even diverges, not without success, into the paths of Dutch and Flemish painting. But it is specially rich, of course, in Provençal works, and its Pugets in particular are both numerous and striking. There is a good Murillo and a square-faced Holbein, and many yards of modern French battles and nudities, alternating for the most part from the sensuous to the sanguinary. But the gem of the collection is a most characteristic and interesting Perugino, as beautiful as anything from the master's hand to be found in the galleries of Florence. Altogether, the interior makes one forgive the façade and the Château d'Eau. One good Perugino covers, like charity, a multitude of sins of the Marseillais architects.

Strange to say, old as Marseilles is, it contains to-day hardly any buildings of remote antiquity. One would be tempted to suppose beforehand that a town with so ancient and so continuous a history would teem with Græco-Roman and mediæval remains. As Phocæan colony, imperial town, mediæval republic, or Provençal city, it has so long been great, famous, and prosperous that one might not unnaturally expect in its streets to meet with endless memorials of its early grandeur. Nothing could be farther from the actual fact. While Nîmes, a mere second-rate provincial municipality, and Arles, a 116] local Roman capital, have preserved rich mementoes of the imperial days—temples, arches, aqueducts, amphitheaters—Marseilles, their mother city, so much older, so much richer, so much greater, so much more famous, has not a single Roman building; scarcely even a second-rate mediæval chapel. Its ancient cathedral has been long since pulled down; of its oldest church but a spire now remains, built into a vulgar modern pseudo-Gothic Calvary. St. Victor alone, near the Fort St. Nicolas, is the one really fine piece of mediæval architecture still left in the town after so many ages.

St. Victor itself remains to us now as the last relic of a very ancient and important monastery, founded by St. Cassian in the fifth century, and destroyed by the Saracens— those incessant scourges of the Provençal coast—during one of their frequent plundering incursions. In 1040 it was rebuilt, only to be once more razed to the ground, till, in 1350, Pope Urban V., who himself had been abbot of this very monastery restored it from the base, with those high, square towers, which now, in their worn and battered solidity, give it rather the air of a castellated fortress than of a Christian temple. Doubtless the strong-handed Pope, warned by experience, intended his church to stand a siege, if necessary, on the next visit to Marseilles of the Paynim enemy. The interior, too, is not unworthy of notice. It contains the catacombs where, according to the naïve Provençal faith, Lazarus passed the last days of his second life; and it boasts an antique black image of the Virgin, attributed by a veracious local legend to the skilful fingers of St. Luke the Evangelist. Modern criticism ruthlessly relegates the work to a nameless but considerably later Byzantine sculptor.

117]By far the most interesting ecclesiastical edifice in Marseilles, however, even in its present charred and shattered condition, is the ancient pilgrimage chapel of Notre Dame de la Garde, the antique High Place of primitive Phœnician and Ligurian worship. How long a shrine for some local cult has existed on the spot it would be hard to say, but, at least, we may put it at two dozen centuries. All along the Mediterranean coast, in fact, one feels oneself everywhere thus closely in almost continuous contact with the earliest religious beliefs of the people. The paths that lead to these very antique sacred sites, crowning the wind-swept hills that overlook the valley, are uniformly worn deep by naked footsteps into the solid rock—a living record of countless generations of fervent worshipers. Christianity itself is not nearly old enough to account for all those profoundly-cut steps in the schistose slate or hard white limestone of the Provençal hills. The sanctity of the High Places is more ancient by far than Saint or Madonna. Before ever a Christian chapel crested these heights they were crested by forgotten Pagan temples; and before the days of Aphrodite or Pallas, in turn, they were crested by the shrines of some long since dead-and-buried Gaulish or Ligurian goddess. Religions change, creeds disappear, but sacred sites remain as holy as ever; and here where priests now chant their loud hymns before the high altar, some nameless bloody rites took place, we may be sure, long ages since, before the lonely shrine of some Celtic Hesus or some hideous and deformed Phœnician Moloch.

It is a steep climb even now from the Old Port or the Anse des Catalans to the Colline Notre Dame; several different paths ascend to the summit, all alike of remote antiquity, and all ending at last in fatiguing steps. 118] Along the main road, hemmed in on either side by poor southern hovels, wondrous old witches of true Provençal ugliness drive a brisk trade in rosaries, and chaplets, and blessed medals. These wares are for the pilgrim; but to suit all tastes, the same itinerant chapwomen offer to the more worldly-minded tourist of the Cookian type appropriate gewgaws, in the shape of photographs, images, and cheap trinkets. At the summit stand the charred and blackened ruins of Notre Dame de la Garde. Of late years, indeed, that immemorial shrine has fallen on evil times and evil days in many matters. To begin with, the needs of modern defence compelled the Government some years since to erect on the height a fort, which encloses in its midst the ancient chapel. Even military necessities, however, had to yield in part to the persistent religious sentiment of the community; and though fortifications girt it round on every side, the sacred site of Our Lady remained unpolluted in the center of the great defensive works of the fortress. Passing through the gates of those massive bastions a strongly-guarded path still guided the faithful sailor-folk of Marseilles to the revered shrine of their ancestral Madonna. Nay, more; the antique chapel of the thirteenth century was superseded by a gorgeous Byzantine building, from designs by Espérandieu, all glittering with gold, and precious stones, and jewels. On the topmost belfry stood a gigantic gilded statue of Our Lady. Dome and apse were of cunning workmanship—white Carrara marble and African rosso antico draped the interior with parti-colored splendor. Corsican granite and Esterel porphyry supported the massive beams of the transepts; frescoes covered every inch of the walls: the pavement was mosaic, the high altar was inlaid with costly Florentine stonework. Every 119] Marseilles fisherman rejoiced in heart that though the men of battle had usurped the sanctuary, their Madonna was now housed by the sons of the Faithful in even greater magnificence and glory than ever.

But in 1884 a fire broke out in the shrine itself, which wrecked almost irreparably the sumptuous edifice. The statue of the Virgin still crowns the façade, to be sure, and the chapel still shows up bravely from a modest distance; but within, all the glory has faded away, and the interior of the church is no longer accessible. Nevertheless, the visitor who stands upon the platform in front of the doorway and gazes down upon the splendid panoramic view that stretches before him in the vale beneath, will hardly complain of having had his stiff pull uphill for nothing. Except the view of Montreal and the St. Lawrence River from Mont Royal Mountain, I hardly know a town view in the world to equal that from Notre Dame de la Garde, for beauty and variety, on a clear spring morning.

Close at our feet lies the city itself, filling up the whole wide valley with its mass, and spreading out long arms of faubourg, or roadway, up the lateral openings. Beyond rise the great white limestone hills, dotted about like mushrooms, with their glittering bastides. In front lies the sea—the blue Mediterranean—with that treacherous smile which has so often deceived us all the day before we trusted ourselves too rashly, with ill-deserved confidence, upon its heaving bosom. Near the shore the waves chafe the islets and the Château d'If; then come the Old Port and the busy bassins; and, beyond them all, the Chain of Estaques, rising grim and gray in serrated outline against the western horizon. A beautiful prospect though barren and treeless, for nowhere in the world are mountains 120] barer than those great white guardians of the Provençal seaboard.

The fortress that overhangs the Old Port at our feet itself deserves a few passing words of polite notice; for it is the Fort St. Nicolas, the one link in his great despotic chain by which Louis Quatorze bound recalcitrant Marseilles to the throne of the Tuileries. The town—like all great commercial towns—had always clung hard to its ancient liberties. Ever rebellious when kings oppressed, it was a stronghold of the Fronde; and when Louis at last made his entry perforce into the malcontent city, it was through a breach he had effected in the heavy ramparts. The king stood upon this commanding spot, just above the harbor, and, gazing landward, asked the citizens round him how men called those little square boxes which he saw dotted about over the sunlit hillsides. "We call them bastides, sire," answered a courtly Marseillais. "Every citizen of our town has one." "Moi aussi, je veux avoir ma bastide à Marseille," cried the theatrical monarch, and straightway gave orders for building the Fort St. Nicolas: so runs the tale that passes for history. But as the fort stands in the very best possible position, commanding the port, and could only have been arranged for after consultation with the engineers of the period—it was Vauban who planned it—I fear we must set down Louis's bon mot as one of those royal epigrams which has been carefully prepared and led up to beforehand.

In every town, however, it is a favorite theory of mine that the best of all sights is the town itself: and nowhere on earth is this truism truer than here at Marseilles. After one has climbed Notre Dame, and explored the Prado and smiled at the Château d'Eau and stood beneath 121] the frowning towers of St. Victor, one returns once more with real pleasure and interest to the crowded Cannebière and sees the full tide of human life flow eagerly on down that picturesque boulevard. That, after all, is the main picture that Marseilles always leaves photographed on the visitor's memory. How eager, how keen, how vivacious is the talk; how fiery the eyes; how emphatic the gesture! With what teeming energy, with what feverish haste, the great city pours forth its hurrying thousands! With what endless spirit they move up and down in endless march upon its clattering pavements! Circulez, messieurs, circulez: and they do just circulate! From the Quai de la Fraternité to the Allées de Meilhan, what mirth and merriment, what life and movement! In every café, what warm southern faces! At every shop-door, what quick-witted, sharp-tongued, bartering humanity! I have many times stopped at Marseilles, on my way hither and thither round this terraqueous globe, farther south or east; but I never stop there without feeling once more the charm and interest of its strenuous personality. There is something of Greek quickness and Greek intelligence left even now about the old Phocæan colony. A Marseillais crowd has to this very day something of the sharp Hellenic wit; and I believe the rollicking humor of Aristophanes would be more readily seized by the public of the Alcazar than by any other popular audience in modern Europe.

"Bon chien chasse de race," and every Marseillais is a born Greek and a born littérateur. Is it not partly to this old Greek blood, then, that we may set down the long list of distinguished men who have drawn their first breath in the Phocæan city? From the days of the Troubadours, Raymond des Tours and Barral des Baux, Folquet, and 122] Rostang, and De Salles, and Bérenger, through the days of D'Urfé, and Mascaron, and Barbaroux, and De Pastoret, to the days of Méry, and Barthélemy, and Taxile Delord, and Joseph Autran, Marseilles has always been rich in talent. It is enough to say that her list of great men begins with Petronius Arbiter, and ends with Thiers, to show how long and diversely she has been represented in her foremost citizens. Surely, then, it is not mere fancy to suppose that in all this the true Hellenic blood has counted for something! Surely it is not too much to believe that with the Greek profile and the Greek complexion the inhabitants have still preserved to this day some modest measure of the quick Greek intellect, the bright Greek fancy, and the plastic and artistic Greek creative faculty! I love to think it, for Marseilles is dear to me; especially when I land there after a sound sea-tossing.

Unlike many of the old Mediterranean towns, too, Marseilles has not only a past but also a future. She lives and will live. In the middle of the past century, indeed, it might almost have seemed to a careless observer as if the Mediterranean were "played out." And so in part, no doubt, it really is; the tracks of commerce and of international intercourse have shifted to wider seas and vaster waterways. We shall never again find that inland basin ringed round by a girdle of the great merchant cities that do the carrying trade and finance of the world. Our area has widened, so that New York, Rio, San Francisco, Yokohama, Shanghai, Calcutta, Bombay, and Melbourne have taken the place of Syracuse, Alexandria, Tyre, and Carthage, of Florence, Genoa, Venice, and Constantinople. But in spite of this cramping change, this degradation of the Mediterranean from the center of the world 123] into a mere auxiliary or side-avenue of the Atlantic, a certain number of Mediterranean ports have lived on uninterruptedly by force of position from one epoch into the other. Venice has had its faint revival of recent years; Trieste has had its rise; Barcelona, Algiers, Smyrna, Odessa, have grown into great harbors for cosmopolitan traffic. Of this new and rejuvenescent Mediterranean, girt round by the fresh young nationalities of Italy and the Orient, and itself no longer an inland sea, but linked by the Suez Canal with the Indian Ocean and so turned into the main highway of the nations between East and West, Marseilles is still the key and the capital. That proud position the Phocæan city is not likely to lose. And as the world is wider now than ever, the new Marseilles is perforce a greater and a wealthier town than even the old one in its proudest days. Where tribute came once from the North African, Levantine, and Italian coasts alone, it comes now from every shore of Europe, Asia, Africa, and America, with Australia and the Pacific Isles thrown in as an afterthought. Regions Cæsar never knew enrich the good Greeks of the Quai de la Fraternité: brown, black, and yellow men whom his legions never saw send tea and silk, cotton, corn, and tobacco to the crowded warehouses of the Cannebière and the Rue de la République.

124]

VI

NICE

The Queen of the Riviera—The Port of Limpia—Castle Hill—Promenade des Anglais—The Carnival and Battle of Flowers—Place Masséna, the center of business—Beauty of the suburbs—The road to Monte Carlo—The quaintly picturesque town of Villefranche—Aspects of Nice and its environs.

WHO loves not Nice, knows it not. Who knows it, loves it. I admit it is windy, dusty, gusty. I allow it is meretricious, fashionable, vulgar. I grant its Carnival is a noisy orgy, its Promenade a meeting place for all the wealthiest idlers of Europe or America, and its clubs more desperate than Monte Carlo itself in their excessive devotion to games of hazard. And yet, with all its faults, I love it still. Yes, deliberately love it; for nothing that man has done or may ever do to mar its native beauty can possibly deface that beauty itself as God made it. Nay, more, just because it is Nice, we can readily pardon it these obvious faults and minor blemishes. The Queen of the Riviera, with all her coquettish little airs and graces, pleases none the less, like some proud and haughty girl in court

57

costume, partly by reason of that very finery of silks and feathers which we half-heartedly deprecate. If she were not herself, she would be other than she is. Nice is Nice, and that is enough for us.

125]Was ever town more graciously set, indeed, in more gracious surroundings? Was ever pearl girt round with purer emeralds? On every side a vast semicircle of mountains hems it in, among which the bald and naked summit of the Mont Cau d'Aspremont towers highest and most conspicuous above its darkling compeers. In front the blue Mediterranean, that treacherous Mediterranean all guile and loveliness, smiles with myriad dimples to the clear-cut horizon. Eastward, the rocky promontories of the Mont Boron and the Cap Ferrat jut boldly out into the sea with their fringe of white dashing breakers. Westward, the longer and lower spit of the point of Antibes bounds the distant view, with the famous pilgrimage chapel of Notre Dame de la Garoupe just dimly visible on its highest knoll against the serrated ridge of the glorious Esterel in the background. In the midst of all nestles Nice itself, the central gem in that coronet of mountains. There are warmer and more sheltered nooks on the Riviera, I will allow: there can be none more beautiful. Mentone may surpass it in the charm of its mountain paths and innumerable excursions; Cannes in the rich variety of its nearer walks and drives; but for mingled glories of land and sea, art and nature, antiquity and novelty, picturesqueness and magnificence, Nice still stands without a single rival on all that enchanted coast that stretches its long array of cities and bays between Marseilles and Genoa. There are those, I know, who run down Nice as commonplace and vulgarized. But then they can never have strayed one inch, I feel sure, from the palm-shaded trottoir of the Promenade des Anglais. If you want Italian mediævalism, go to the Old Town; if you want quaint marine life, go to the good Greek port of Limpia; if you want a grand view of sea and land and 126] snow mountains in the distance, go to the Castle Hill; if you want the most magnificent panorama in the whole of Europe, go to the summit of the Corniche Road. No, no; these brawlers disturb our pure worship. We have only one Nice, let us make the most of it.

It is so easy to acquire a character for superiority by affecting to criticize what others admire. It is so easy to pronounce a place vulgar and uninteresting by taking care to see only the most vulgar and uninteresting parts of it. But the old Riveran who knows his Nice well, and loves it dearly, is troubled rather by the opposite difficulty. Where there is so much to look at and so much to describe, where to begin? what to omit? how much to glide over? how much to insist upon? Language fails him to give a conception of this complex and polychromatic city in a few short pages to anyone who knows it by name alone as the cosmopolitan winter capital of fashionable seekers after health and pleasure. It is that, indeed, but it is so much more that one can never tell it.

For there are at least three distinct Nices, Greek, Italian, French; each of them beautiful in its own way, and each of them interesting for its own special features. To the extreme east, huddled in between the Mont Boron and the Castle Hill, lies the seafaring Greek town, the most primitive and original Nice of all; the home of the fisher-folk and the petty coasting sailors; the Nicæa of the old undaunted Phocæan colonists; the Nizza di Mare of modern Italians; the mediæval city; the birthplace of Garibaldi. Divided from this earliest Nice by the scarped rock on whose summit stood the château of the Middle Ages, the eighteenth century Italian town (the Old Town as tourists nowadays usually call it, the central 127] town of the three) occupies the space between the Castle Hill and the half dry bed of the Paillon torrent. Finally, west of the Paillon, again, the modern fashionable pleasure resort extends its long line of villas, hotels, and palaces in front of the sea to the little stream of the Magnan on the road to Cannes, and stretches back in endless boulevards and avenues and gardens to the smiling heights of Cimiez and Carabacel. Every one of these three towns, "in three different ages born," has its own special history and its own points of interest. Every one of them teems with natural beauty, with picturesque elements, and with varieties of life, hard indeed to discover elsewhere.

The usual guide-book way to attack Nice is, of course, the topsy-turvey one, to begin at the Haussmannised white façades of the Promenade des Anglais and work backwards gradually through the Old Town to the Port of Limpia and the original nucleus that surrounds its quays. I will venture, however, to disregard this time-honored but grossly unhistorical practice, and allow the reader and myself, for once in our lives, to "begin at the beginning." The Port of Limpia, then, is, of course, the natural starting point and prime original of the very oldest Nice. Hither, in the fifth century before the Christian era, the bold Phocæan settlers of Marseilles sent out a little colony, which landed in the tiny land-locked harbor and called the spot Nicæa (that is to say, the town of victory) in gratitude for their success against its rude Ligurian owners. For twenty-two centuries it has retained that name almost unchanged, now perhaps, the only memento still remaining of its Greek origin. During its flourishing days as a Hellenic city Nicæa ranked among the chief commercial entrepôts of the 128] Ligurian coast; but when "the Province" fell at last into the hands of the Romans, and the dictator Cæsar favored rather the pretensions of Cemenelum or Cimiez on the hill-top in the rear, the town that clustered round the harbor of Limpia became for a time merely the port of its more successful inland rival. Cimiez still possesses its fine ruined Roman amphitheater and baths, besides relics of temples and some other remains of the imperial period; but the "Quartier du Port," the ancient town of Nice itself, is almost destitute of any architectural signs of its antique greatness.

Nevertheless, the quaint little seafaring village that clusters round the harbor, entirely cut off as it is by the ramping crags of the Castle Hill from its later representative, the Italianized Nice of the last century, may fairly claim to be the true Nice of history, the only spot that bore that name till the days of the Bourbons. Its annals are far too long and far too eventful to be narrated here in full. Goths, Burgundians, Lombards, and Franks disputed for it in turn, as the border fortress between Gaul and Italy; and that familiar round white bastion on the eastern face of the Castle Hill, now known to visitors as the Tour Bellanda, and included (such is fate!) as a modern belvedere in the grounds of the comfortable Pension Suisse, was originally erected in the fifth century after Christ to protect the town from the attacks of these insatiable invaders. But Nice had its consolations, too, in these evil days, for when the Lombards at last reduced the hill fortress of Cimiez, the Roman town, its survivors took refuge from their conquerors in the city by the port, which thus became once more, by the fall of its rival, unquestioned mistress of the surrounding littoral.

129]The after story of Nice is confused and confusing. Now a vassal of the Frankish kings; now again a member of the Genoese league; now engaged in a desperate conflict with the piratical Saracens; and now constituted into a little independent republic on the Italian model; Nizza struggled on against an adverse fate as a fighting-ground of the races, till it fell finally into the hands of the Counts of Savoy, to whom it owes whatever little still remains of the mediæval castle. Continually changing hands between France and the kingdom of Sardinia in later days, it was ultimately made over to Napoleon III. by the Treaty of Villafranca, and is now completely and entirely Gallicized. The native dialect, however, remains even to the present day an intermediate form between Provençal and Italian, and is freely spoken (with more force than elegance) in the Old Town and around the enlarged modern basins of the Port of Limpia. Indeed, for frankness of expression and perfect absence of any false delicacy, the ladies of the real old Greek Nice surpass even their London compeers at Billingsgate.

One of the most beautiful and unique features of Nice at the present day is the Castle Hill a mass of solid rearing rock, not unlike its namesake at Edinburgh in position, intervening between the Port and the eighteenth century town, to which latter I will in future allude as the Italian city. It is a wonderful place, that Castle Hill—wonderful alike by nature, art, and history, and I fear I must also add at the same time "uglification." In earlier days it bore on its summit or slopes the château fort of the Counts of Provence with the old cathedral and archbishop's palace (now wholly destroyed), and the famous deep well, long ranked among the wonders of the world in the way of engineering. But military necessity knows 130] no law; the cathedral gave place in the fifteenth century to the bastions of the Duke of Savoy's new-fangled castle; the castle itself in turn was mainly battered down in 1706 by the Duke of Berwick; and of all its antiquities none now remain save the Tour Bellanda, in its degraded condition of belvedere, and the scanty ground-plan of the mediæval buildings.

Nevertheless, the Castle Hill is still one of the loveliest and greenest spots in Nice. A good carriage road ascends it to the top by leafy gradients, and leads to an open platform on the summit, now converted into charming gardens, rich with palms and aloes and cactuses and bright southern flowers. On one side, alas! a painfully artificial cataract, fed from the overflow of the waterworks, falls in stiff cascades among hand-built rockwork; but even that impertinent addition to the handicraft of nature can hardly offend the visitor for long among such glorious surroundings. For the view from the summit is one of the grandest in all France. The eye ranges right and left over a mingled panorama of sea and mountains, scarcely to be equaled anywhere round the lovely Mediterranean, save on the Ligurian coast and the neighborhood of Sorrento. Southward lies the blue expanse of water itself, bounded only in very clear and cloudless weather by the distant peaks of Corsica on the doubtful horizon. Westward, the coast-line includes the promontory of Antibes, basking low on the sea, the Iles Lérins near Cannes, the mouth of the Var, and the dim-jagged ridge of the purple Esterel. Eastward, the bluff headland of the Mont Boron, grim and brown, blocks the view towards Italy. Close below the spectator's feet the three distinct towns of Nice gather round the Port and the two banks of the Paillon, spreading their garden 131] suburbs, draped in roses and lemon groves, high up the spurs of the neighboring mountains. But northward a tumultuous sea of Alps rises billow-like to the sky, the nearer peaks frowning bare and rocky, while the more distant domes gleam white with virgin snow. It is a sight, once seen, never to be forgotten. One glances around entranced, and murmurs to oneself slowly, "It is good to be here." Below, the carriages are rolling like black specks along the crowded Promenade, and the band is playing gaily in the Public Garden; but up there you look across to the eternal hills, and feel yourself face to face for one moment with the Eternities behind them.

60

One may descend from the summit either by the ancient cemetery or by the Place Garibaldi, through bosky gardens of date-palm, fan-palm, and agave. Cool winding alleys now replace the demolished ramparts, and lovely views open out on every side as we proceed over the immediate foreground.

At the foot of the Castle Hill, a modern road, hewn in the solid rock round the base of the seaward escarpment, connects the Greek with the Italian town. The angle where it turns the corner, bears on native lips the quaint Provençal or rather Niçois name of Raüba Capeu or Rob-hat Point, from the common occurrence of sudden gusts of wind, which remove the unsuspecting Parisian headgear with effective rapidity, to the great joy of the observant gamins. Indeed, windiness is altogether the weak point of Nice, viewed as a health-resort; the town lies exposed in the open valley of the Paillon, down whose baking bed the mistral, that scourge of Provence, sweeps with violent force from the cold mountain-tops in the rear; and so it cannot for a moment compete in point of climate with Cannes, Monte Carlo, Mentone or San 132] Remo, backed up close behind by their guardian barrier of sheltering hills. But not even the mistral can make those who love Nice love her one atom the less. Her virtues are so many that a little wholesome bluster once in a while may surely be forgiven her. And yet the dust does certainly rise in clouds at times from the Promenade des Anglais.

The Italian city, which succeeds next in order, is picturesque and old-fashioned, but is being daily transformed and Gallicized out of all knowledge by its modern French masters. It dates back mainly to the seventeenth and eighteenth centuries, when the population became too dense for the narrow limits of the small Greek town, and began to overflow, behind the Castle Hill, on to the eastern banks of the Paillon torrent. The sea-front in this quarter, now known as the Promenade du Midi, has been modernized into a mere eastward prolongation of the Promenade des Anglais, of which "more anon;" but the remainder of the little triangular space between the Castle Hill and the river-bed still consists of funny narrow Italian lanes, dark, dense, and dingy, from whose midst rises the odd and tile-covered dome of the cathedral of St. Réparate. That was the whole of Nice as it lived and moved till the beginning of this century; the real Nice of to-day, the Nice of the tourist, the invalid, and the fashionable world, the Nice that we all visit or talk about, is a purely modern accretion of some half-dozen decades.

This wonderful modern town, with its stately sea-front, its noble quays, its dainty white villas, its magnificent hotels, and its Casino, owes its existence entirely to the vogue which the coast has acquired in our own times as a health-resort for consumptives. As long ago as Smollett's time, the author of "Roderick Random" 133]remarks complacently that an acquaintance, "understanding I intended to winter in the South of France, strongly recommended the climate of Nice in Provence, which indeed I had often heard extolled," as well he might have done. But in those days visitors had to live in the narrow and dirty streets of the Italian town, whose picturesqueness itself can hardly atone for their unwholesome air and their unsavory odors. It was not till the hard winters of 1822-23-24 that a few kind-hearted English residents, anxious to find work for the starving poor, began the construction of a sea-road beyond the Paillon, which still bears the name of the Promenade des Anglais. Nice may well commemorate their deed to this day, for to them she owes as a watering-place her very existence.

The western suburb, thus pushed beyond the bed of the boundary torrent, has gradually grown in wealth and prosperity till it now represents the actual living Nice of the tourist and the winter resident. But how to describe that gay and beautiful city; that vast agglomeration of villas, pensions, hotels, and clubs; that endless array of sun-worshipers gathered together to this temple of the sun from all the four quarters of the habitable globe? The sea-front consists of the Promenade des Anglais itself, which stretches in an unbroken line of white and glittering houses, most of them tasteless, but all splendid and all opulent, from the old bank of the Paillon to its sister torrent, the Magnan, some two miles away. On one side the villas front the shore with their fantastic façades; on the other side a walk, overshadowed with date-palms and purple-flowering judas-trees, lines the steep shingle beach of the tideless sea.

There is one marked peculiarity of the Promenade des Anglais, however, which at once distinguishes it from 134] any similar group of private houses to be found anywhere in England. There the British love of privacy, which has, of course, its good points, but has also its compensating disadvantages, leads almost every owner of beautiful grounds or gardens to enclose them with a high fence or with the hideous monstrosity known to suburban Londoners as "park paling." This plan, while it ensures complete seclusion for the fortunate few within, shuts out the deserving many outside from all participation in the beauty of the grounds or the natural scenery. On the Promenade des Anglais, on the contrary, a certain generous spirit of emulation in contributing to the public enjoyment and the general effectiveness of the scene as a whole has prompted the owners of the villas along the sea-front to enclose their gardens only with low ornamental balustrades or with a slight and unobtrusive iron fence, so that the passers-by can see freely into every one of them, and feast their eyes on the beautiful shrubs and flowers. The houses and grounds thus form a long line of delightful though undoubtedly garish and ornate decorations, in full face of the sea. The same plan has been adopted in the noble residential street known as Euclid Avenue at Cleveland, Ohio, and in many other American cities. It is to be regretted that English tastes and habits do not oftener thus permit their wealthier classes to contribute, at no expense or trouble to themselves, to the general pleasure of less fortunate humanity.

The Promenade is, of course, during the season the focus and center of fashionable life at Nice. Here carriages roll, and amazons ride and flâneurs lounge in the warm sunshine during the livelong afternoon. In front are the baths, bathing being practicable at Nice from the beginning of March; behind are the endless hotels and 135] clubs of this city of strangers. For the English are not alone on the Promenade des Anglais; the American tongue is heard there quite as often as the British dialect, while Germans, Russians, Poles, and Austrians cluster thick upon the shady seats beneath the planes and carob-trees. During the Carnival especially Nice resolves itself into one long orgy of frivolous amusement. Battles of flowers, battles of confetti, open-air masquerades, and universal tom-foolery pervade the place. Everybody vies with everybody else in making himself ridiculous; and even the staid Briton, released from the restraints of home or the City, abandons himself contentedly for a week at a time to a sort of prolonged and glorified sunny southern Derby Day. Mr. Bultitude disguises himself as a French clown;

Mr. Dombey, in domino, flings roses at his friends on the seats of the tribune. Everywhere is laughter, noise, bustle, and turmoil; everywhere the manifold forms of antique saturnalian freedom, decked out with gay flowers or travestied in quaint clothing, but imported most incongruously for a week in the year into the midst of our modern work-a-day twentieth-century Europe.

Only a comparatively few winters ago fashionable Nice consisted almost entirely of the Promenade des Anglais, with a few slight tags and appendages in either direction. At its eastern end stood (and still stands) the Jardin Public, that paradise of children and of be-ribboned French nursemaids, where the band discourses lively music every afternoon at four, and all the world sits round on two-sou chairs to let all the rest of the world see for itself it is still in evidence. These, and the stately quays along the Paillon bank, lined with shops where female human nature can buy all the tastiest and most expensive gewgaws in Europe, constituted the real Nice 136] of the early eighties. But with the rapid growth of that general taste for more sumptuous architecture which marks our age, the Phocæan city woke up a few years since with electric energy to find itself in danger of being left behind by its younger competitors. So the Niçois conscript fathers put their wise heads together, in conclave assembled, and resolved on a general transmogrification of the center of their town. By continuously bridging and vaulting across the almost dry bed of the Paillon torrent they obtained a broad and central site for a new large garden, which now forms the natural focus of the transformed city. On the upper end of this important site they erected a large and handsome casino in the gorgeous style of the Third Republic, all glorious without and within, as the modern Frenchman understands such glory, and provided with a theater, a winter garden, restaurants, cafés, ball-rooms, petits chevaux, and all the other most pressing requirements of an advanced civilization. But in doing this they sacrificed by the way the beautiful view towards the mountains behind, which can now only be obtained from the Square Masséna or the Pont Vieux farther up the river. Most visitors to Nice, however, care little for views, and a great deal for the fitful and fearsome joys embodied to their minds in the outward and visible form of a casino.

This wholesale bridging over of the lower end of the Paillon has united the French and Italian towns and abolished the well-marked boundary line which once cut them off so conspicuously from one another. The inevitable result has been that the Italian town too has undergone a considerable modernization along the sea-front, so that the Promenade des Anglais and the Promenade du Midi now practically merge into one continuous 137] parade, and are lined along all their length with the same clipped palm-trees and the same magnificent white palatial buildings. When the old theater in the Italian town was burnt down in the famous and fatal conflagration some years since the municipality erected a new one on the same site in the most approved style of Parisian luxury. A little behind lie the Préfecture and the beautiful flower market, which no visitor to Nice should ever miss; for Nice is above all things, even more than Florence, a city of flowers. The sheltered quarter of the Ponchettes, lying close under the lee of the Castle Hill, has become of late, owing to these changes, a favorite resort for invalids, who find here protection from the cutting winds which sweep with full force down the bare and open valley of the Paillon over the French town.

I am loth to quit that beloved sea-front, on the whole the most charming marine parade in Europe, with the Villefranche point and the pseudo-Gothic, pseudo-Oriental

63

monstrosity of Smith's Folly on one side and the delicious bay towards Antibes on the other. But there are yet various aspects of Nice which remain to be described: the interior is almost as lovely in its way as the coast that fringes it. For this inner Nice, the Place Masséna, called (like the Place Garibaldi) after another distinguished native, forms the starting point and center. Here the trams from all quarters run together at last; hence the principal roads radiate in all directions. The Place Masséna is the center of business, as the Jardin Public and the Casino are the centers of pleasure. Also (verbum sap.) it contains an excellent pâtisserie, where you can enjoy an ice or a little French pastry with less permanent harm to your constitution and morals than anywhere in Europe. Moreover, it forms the approach 138] to the Avenue de la Gare, which divides with the Quays the honor of being the best shopping street in the most fashionable watering-place of the Mediterranean. If these delights thy soul may move, why, the Place Masséna is the exact spot to find them in.

Other great boulevards, like the Boulevard Victor Hugo and the Boulevard Dubouchage, have been opened out of late years to let the surplus wealth that flows into Nice in one constant stream find room to build upon. Châteaux and gardens are springing up merrily on every side; the slopes of the hills gleam gay with villas; Cimiez and Carabacel, once separate villages, have now been united by continuous dwellings to the main town; and before long the city where Garibaldi was born and where Gambetta lies buried will swallow up in itself the entire space of the valley, and its border spurs from mountain to mountain. The suburbs, indeed, are almost more lovely in their way than the town itself; and as one wanders at will among the olive-clad hills to westward, looking down upon the green lemon-groves that encircle the villas, and the wealth of roses that drape their sides, one cannot wonder that Joseph de Maistre, another Niçois of distinction, in the long dark evenings he spent at St. Petersburg, should time and again have recalled with a sigh "ce doux vallon de Magnan." Nor have the Russians themselves failed to appreciate the advantages of the change, for they flock by thousands to the Orthodox Quarter on the heights of Saint Philippe, which rings round the Greek chapel erected in memory of the Czarewitch Nicholas Alexandrowitch, who died at Nice in 1865.

After all, however, to the lover of the picturesque Nice town itself is but the threshold and starting point for that 139] lovely country which spreads on all sides its endless objects of interest and scenic beauty from Antibes to Mentone. The excursions to be made from it in every direction are simply endless. Close by lie the monastery and amphitheater of Cimiez; the Italianesque cloisters and campanile of St. Pons; the conspicuous observatory on the Mont Gros, with its grand Alpine views; the hillside promenades of Le Ray and Les Fontaines. Farther afield the carriage-road up the Paillon valley leads direct to St. André through a romantic limestone gorge, which terminates at last in a grotto and natural bridge, overhung by the moldering remains of a most southern château. A little higher up, the steep mountain track takes one on to Falicon, perched "like an eagle's nest" on its panoramic hill-top, one of the most famous points of view among the Maritime Alps. The boundary hills of the Magnan, covered in spring with the purple flowers of the wild gladiolus; the vine-clad heights of Le Bellet, looking down on the abrupt and rock-girt basin of the Var; the Valley of Hepaticas, carpeted in March with innumerable spring blossoms; the longer drive to Contes in the very heart of the mountains: all alike are lovely, and all alike tempt one to linger in their precincts among the shadow of the cypress trees or under the cool grottos green and lush with spreading fronds of wild maidenhair.

64

Among so many delicious excursions it were invidious to single out any for special praise; yet there can be little doubt that the most popular, at least with the general throng of tourists, is the magnificent coast-road by Villefranche (or Villafranca) to Monte Carlo and Monaco. This particular part of the coast, between Nice and Mentone, is the one where the main range of the Maritime 140] Alps, abutting at last on the sea, tumbles over sheer with a precipitous descent from four thousand feet high to the level of the Mediterranean. Formerly, the barrier ridge could only be surmounted by the steep but glorious Corniche route; of late years, however, the French engineers, most famous of road-makers, have hewn an admirable carriage-drive out of the naked rock, often through covered galleries or tunnels in the cliff itself, the whole way from Nice to Monte Carlo and Mentone. The older portion of this road, between Nice and Villefranche, falls well within the scope of our present subject.

You leave modern Nice by the quays and the Pont Garibaldi, dash rapidly through the new broad streets that now intersect the Italian city, skirt the square basins lately added to the more shapeless ancient Greek port of Limpia, and begin to mount the first spurs of the Mont Boron among the villas and gardens of the Quartier du Lazaret. Banksia roses fall in cataracts over the walls as you go; looking back, the lovely panorama of Nice opens out before your eyes. In the foreground, the rocky islets of La Réserve foam white with the perpetual plashing of that summer sea. In the middle distance, the old Greek harbor, with its mole and lighthouse, stands out against the steep rocks of the Castle Hill. The background rises up in chain on chain of Alps, allowing just a glimpse at their base of that gay and fickle promenade and all the Parisian prettinesses of the new French town. The whole forms a wonderful picture of the varied Mediterranean world, Greek, Roman, Italian, French, with the vine-clad hills and orange-groves behind merging slowly upward into the snow-bound Alps.

Turning the corner of the Mont Boron by the grotesque vulgarisms of the Château Smith (a curious 141]semi-oriental specimen of the shell-grotto order of architecture on a gigantic scale) a totally fresh view bursts upon our eyes of the Rade de Villefranche, that exquisite land-locked bay bounded on one side by the scarped crags of the Mont Boron itself, and on the other by the long and rocky peninsula of St. Jean, which terminates in the Cap Ferrat and the Villefranche light. The long deep bay forms a favorite roadstead and rendezvous for the French Mediterranean squadron, whose huge ironclad monsters may often be seen ploughing their way in single file from seaward round the projecting headlands, or basking at ease on the calm surface of that glassy pond. The surrounding heights, of course, bristle with fortifications, which, in these suspicious days of armed European tension, the tourist and the sketcher are strictly prohibited from inspecting with too attentive an eye. The quaintly picturesque town of Villefranche itself, Italian and dirty, but amply redeemed by its slender bell-tower and its olive-clad terraces, nestles snugly at the very bottom of its pocket-like bay. The new road to Monte Carlo leaves it far below, with true modern contempt for mere old-world beauty; the artist and the lover of nature will know better than to follow the example of those ruthless engineers; they will find many subjects for a sketch among those whitewashed walls, and many a rare sea-flower tucked away unseen among those crannied crags.

And now, when all is said and done, I, who have known and loved Nice for so many bright winters, feel only too acutely how utterly I have failed to set before those of my readers who know it not the infinite charms of that gay and rose-wreathed queen of the smiling Riviera. For what words can paint the life and movement of the sparkling sea-front? the manifold humors of 142] the Jardin Public? the southern vivacity of the washer-women who pound their clothes with big stones in the dry bed of the pebbly Paillon? the luxuriant festoons of honeysuckle and mimosa that drape the trellis-work arcades of Carabacel and Cimiez? Who shall describe aright with one pen the gnarled olives of Beaulieu and the palace-like front of the Cercle de la Méditerranée? Who shall write with equal truth of the jewelers' shops on the quays, of the oriental bazaars of the Avenue, and of the dome after dome of bare mountain tops that rise ever in long perspective to the brilliant white summits of the great Alpine backbone? Who shall tell in one breath of the carmagnoles of the Carnival, or the dust-begrimed bouquets of the Battle of Flowers, and of the silent summits of the Mont Cau and the Cime de Vinaigrier, or the vast and varied sea-view that bursts on the soul unawares from the Corniche near Eza? There are aspects of Nice and its environs which recall Bartholomew Fair, or the Champs Élysées after a Sunday review; and there are aspects which recall the prospect from some solemn summit of the Bernese Oberland, mixed with some heather-clad hill overlooking the green Atlantic among the Western Highlands. Yet all is so graciously touched and lighted with Mediterranean color and Mediterranean sunshine, that even in the midst of her wildest frolics you can seldom be seriously angry with Nice. The works of God's hand are never far off. You look up from the crowd of carriages and loungers on the Promenade des Anglais, and the Cap Ferrat rises bold and bluff before your eyes above the dashing white waves of the sky-blue sea: you cross the bridge behind the Casino amid the murmur of the quays, and the great bald mountains soar aloft to heaven above the brawling 143] valley of the snow-fed Paillon. It is a desecration, perhaps, but a desecration that leaves you still face to face with all that is purest and most beautiful in nature.

And then, the flowers, the waves, the soft air, the sunshine! On the beach, between the bathing places, men are drying scented orange peel to manufacture perfumes: in the dusty high roads you catch whiffs as you pass of lemon blossom and gardenia: the very trade of the town is an expert trade in golden acacia and crimson anemones: the very gamins pelt you in the rough horse-play of the Carnival with sweet-smelling bunches of syringa and lilac. Luxury that elsewhere would move one to righteous wrath is here so democratic in its display that one almost condones it. The gleaming white villas, with carved caryatides or sculptured porches of freestone nymphs, let the wayfarer revel as he goes in the riches of their shrubberies or their sunlit fountains and in the breezes that blow over their perfumed parterres. Nice vulgar! Pah, my friend, if you say so, I know well why. You have a vulgar soul that sees only the gewgaws and the painted ladies. You have never strolled up by yourself from the noise and dust of the crowded town to the free heights of the Mont Alban or the flowery olive-grounds of the Magnan valley. You have never hunted for purple hellebore among the gorges of the Paillon or picked orchids and irises in big handfuls upon the slopes of Saint André. I doubt even whether you have once turned aside for a moment from the gay crowd of the Casino and the Place Masséna into the narrow streets of the Italian town; communed in their own delicious dialect with the free fisherfolk of the Limpia quarter; or looked out with joy upon the tumbled plain of mountain heights from 144] the breezy level of the Castle platform. Probably you have only sat for days in the balcony of your hotel, rolled at your ease down the afternoon Promenade, worn a false nose at the evening parade of the Carnival, or returned late at night by the last train from Monte Carlo with your pocket much lighter and your heart much heavier than when you left by the morning express in search of fortune. And then you say Nice is vulgar! You have no eyes, it seems, for sea, or shore, or sky, or mountain; but you look down curiously at the dust in the street, and you mutter to yourself that you find it uninteresting. When you go to Nice again, walk alone up the hills to Falicon, returning by Le Ray, and then say, if you dare, Nice is anything on earth but gloriously beautiful.

145]

VII

THE RIVIERA

In the days of the Doges—Origin of the name—The blue bay of Cannes—Ste. Marguerite and St. Honorat—Historical associations—The Rue L'Antibes—The rock of Monaco—"Notre Dame de la Roulette"—From Monte Carlo to Mentone—San Remo— A romantic railway.

"OH, Land of Roses, what bulbul shall sing of thee?" In plain prose, how describe the garden of Europe? The Riviera! Who knows, save he who has been there, the vague sense of delight which the very name recalls to the poor winter exile, banished by frost and cold from the fogs and bronchitis of more northern climes? What visions of gray olives, shimmering silvery in the breeze on terraced mountain slopes! What cataracts of Marshal Niels, falling in rich profusion over gray limestone walls! What aloes and cactuses on what sun-smitten rocks! What picnics in December beneath what cloudless blue skies! But to those who know and appreciate it best, the Riviera is something more than mere scenery and sunshine. It is life, it is health, it is strength, it is rejuvenescence. The return to it in autumn is as the renewal of youth. Its very faults are dear to us, for they are the defects of its virtues. We can put up with its dust when we remember that dust means sun and dry air; we can forgive its 146] staring white roads when we reflect to ourselves that they depend upon almost unfailing fine weather and bright, clear skies, when northern Europe is wrapped in fog and cold and wretchedness.

And what is this Riviera that we feeble folk who "winter in the south" know and adore so well? Has everybody been there, or may one venture even now to paint it in words once more for the twentieth time? Well, after all, how narrow is our conception of "everybody!" I suppose one out of every thousand at a moderate estimate, has visited that smiling coast that spreads its entrancing bays between Marseilles and Genoa; my description is, therefore, primarily for the nine hundred and ninety-nine who have not been there. And even the thousandth himself, if he knows his Cannes and his Mentone well, will not grudge me a reminiscence of those delicious gulfs and those charming headlands that must be indelibly photographed on his memory.

The name Riviera is now practically English. But in origin it is Genoese. To those seafaring folk, in the days of the Doges, the coasts to east and west of their own princely city were known, naturally enough, as the Riviera di Levante and the Riviera di Ponente respectively, the shores of the rising and the setting sun. But on English lips the qualifying clause "di Ponente" has gradually in usage dropped out altogether, and we speak nowadays of this favored winter resort, by a somewhat illogical clipping, simply as "the Riviera." In our modern and specially English sense, then, the Riviera means the long and fertile strip of coast between the arid mountains and the Ligurian Sea, beginning at St. Raphael and ending at Genoa. Hyères, it is true, is commonly reckoned of late among Riviera towns, but by 147] courtesy only. It lies, strictly speaking, outside the charmed circle. One may say that the Riviera, properly so called, has its origin where the Estérel abuts upon the Gulf of Fréjus, and extends as far as the outliers of the Alps skirt the Italian shore of the Mediterranean.

Now, the Riviera is just the point where the greatest central mountain system of all Europe topples over most directly into the warmest sea. And its best-known resorts, Nice, Monte Carlo, Mentone, occupy the precise place where the very axis of the ridge abuts at last on the shallow and basking Mediterranean. They are therefore as favorably situated with regard to the mountain wall as Pallanza or Riva, with the further advantage of a more southern position and of a neighboring extent of sunny sea to warm them. The Maritime Alps cut off all northerly winds; while the hot air of the desert, tempered by passing over a wide expanse of Mediterranean waves, arrives on the coast as a delicious breeze, no longer dry and relaxing, but at once genial and refreshing. Add to these varied advantages the dryness of climate due to an essentially continental position (for the Mediterranean is after all a mere inland salt lake), and it is no wonder we all swear by the Riviera as the fairest and most pleasant of winter resorts. My own opinion remains always unshaken, that Antibes, for climate, may fairly claim to rank as the best spot in Europe or round the shores of the Mediterranean.

Not that I am by any means a bigoted Antipolitan. I have tried every other nook and cranny along that delightful coast, from Carqueyranne to Cornigliano, and I will allow that every one of them has for certain purposes its own special advantages. All, all are charming. Indeed, the Riviera is to my mind one long feast of 148]delights. From the moment the railway strikes the sea near Fréjus the traveller feels he can only do justice to the scenery on either side by looking both ways at once, and so "contracting a squint," like a sausage-seller in Aristophanes. Those glorious peaks of the Estérel alone would encourage the most prosaic to "drop into poetry," as readily as Mr. Silas Wegg himself in the mansion of the Boffins. How am I to describe them, those rearing masses of rock, huge tors of red porphyry, rising sheer into the air with their roseate crags from a deep green base of Mediterranean pinewood? When the sun strikes their sides, they glow like fire. There they lie in their beauty, like a huge rock pushed out into the sea, the advance-guard of the Alps, unbroken save by the one high-road that runs boldly through their unpeopled midst, and by the timider railway that, fearing to tunnel their solid porphyry depths, winds cautiously round their base by the craggy sea-shore, and so gives us as we pass endless lovely glimpses into sapphire bays with red cliffs and rocky lighthouse-crowned islets. On the whole, I consider the Estérel, as scenery alone, the loveliest "bit" on the whole Riviera; though wanting in human additions, as nature it is the best, the most varied in outline, the most vivid in coloring.

Turning the corner by Agay, you come suddenly, all unawares, on the blue bay of Cannes, or rather on the Golfe de la Napoule, whose very name betrays unintentionally the intense newness and unexpectedness of all this populous coast, this "little England beyond France" that has grown up apace round Lord Brougham's villa on the shore by the mouth of the Siagne. For when the bay beside the Estérel received its present name, La Napoule, not Cannes, was still the principal village on its 149] bank. Nowadays, people drive over on a spare afternoon from the crowded fashionable town to the slumbrous little hamlet; but in older days La Napoule was a busy local market when Cannes was nothing more than a petty hamlet of Provençal fishermen.

The Golfe de la Napoule ends at the Croisette of Cannes, a long, low promontory carried out into the sea by a submarine bank, whose farthest points re-emerge as the two Iles Lérins, Ste. Marguerite and St. Honorat. Their names are famous in history. A little steamer plies from Cannes to "the Islands," as everybody calls them locally; and the trip, in calm weather, if the Alps are pleased to shine out, is a pleasant and instructive one. Ste. Marguerite lies somewhat the nearer of the two, a pretty little islet, covered with a thick growth of maritime pines, and celebrated as the prison of that mysterious being, the Man with the Iron Mask, who has given rise to so much foolish and fruitless speculation. Near the landing-place stands the Fort, perched on a high cliff and looking across to the Croisette. Uninteresting in itself, this old fortification is much visited by wonder-loving tourists for the sake of its famous prisoner, whose memory still haunts the narrow terrace corridor, where he paced up and down for seventeen years of unrelieved captivity.

St. Honorat stands farther out to sea than its sister island, and, though lower and flatter, is in some ways more picturesque, in virtue of its massive mediæval monastery and its historical associations. In the early middle ages, when communications were still largely carried on by water, the convent of the Iles Lérins enjoyed much reputation as a favorite stopping-place, one might almost say hotel, for pilgrims to or from Rome; 150] and most of the early British Christians in their continental wanderings found shelter at one time or another under its hospitable roof. St. Augustine stopped here on his way to Canterbury; St. Patrick took the convent on his road from Ireland; Salvian wrote within its walls his dismal jeremiad; Vincent de Lérins composed in it his "Pilgrim's Guide." The somber vaults of the ancient cloister still bear witness by their astonishingly thick and solid masonry to their double use as monastery and as place of refuge from the "Saracens," the Barbary corsairs of the ninth, tenth, and eleventh centuries. Indeed, Paynim fleets plundered the place more than once, and massacred the monks in cold blood.

Of Cannes itself, marvelous product of this gad-about and commercial age, how shall the truthful chronicler speak with becoming respect and becoming dignity? For Cannes has its faults. Truly a wonderful place is that cosmopolitan winter resort. Rococo châteaux, glorious gardens of palm-trees, imitation Moorish villas, wooden châlets from the scene-painter's ideal Switzerland, Elizabethan mansions stuck in Italian grounds, lovely groves of mimosa, eucalyptus, and judas-trees, all mingle together in so strange and incongruous a picture that one knows not when to laugh, when to weep, when to admire, when to cry "Out on it!" Imagine a conglomeration of two or three white-faced Parisian streets, interspersed with little bits of England, of Brussels, of Algiers, of Constantinople, of Pekin, of Bern, of Nuremberg and of Venice, jumbled side by side on a green Provençal hillside before a beautiful bay, and you get modern Cannes; a Babel set in Paradise; a sort of boulevardier Bond Street, with a view across blue waves to the serrated peaks of the ever lovely Estérel. Nay; try as it 151] will, Cannes cannot help being beautiful. Nature has done so much for it that art itself, the debased French art of the Empire and the Republic, can never for one moment succeed in making it ugly; though I am bound to admit it has striven as hard as it knew for that laudable object. But Cannes is Cannes still, in spite of Grand Dukes and landscape gardeners and architects. And the Old Town, at least, is yet wholly unspoilt by the speculative builder. Almost every Riviera watering-place has such an old-world nucleus or kernel of its own, the quaint fisher village of ancient days, round which the meretricious modern villas have clustered, one by one, in irregular succession. At Cannes the Old Town is even more conspicuous than elsewhere; for it clambers up the steep sides of a little seaward hillock, crowned by the tower of an eleventh century church, and is as picturesque, as gray, as dirty, as most other haunts of the hardy Provençal fisherman. Strange, too, to see how the two streams of life flow on ever, side by side, yet ever unmingled. The Cannes of the fishermen is to this day as unvaried as if the new cosmopolitan winter resort had never grown up, with its Anglo-Russian airs and graces, its German-American frivolities, round that unpromising center.

The Rue d'Antibes is the principal shopping street of the newer and richer Cannes. If we follow it out into the country by its straight French boulevard it leads us at last to the funny old border city from which it still takes its unpretending name. Antibes itself belongs to that very first crop of civilized Provençal towns which owe their origin to the sturdy old Phocæan colonists. It is a Greek city by descent, the Antipolis which faced and defended the harbor of Nicæa; and for picturesqueness 152] and beauty it has not its equal on the whole picturesque and beautiful Riviera. Everybody who has travelled by the "Paris, Lyon, Méditerranée" knows well the exquisite view of the mole and harbor as seen in passing from the railway. But that charming glimpse, quaint and varied as it is, gives by no means a full idea of the ancient Phocæan city. The town stands still surrounded by its bristling fortification, the work of Vauban, pierced by narrow gates in their thickness, and topped with noble ramparts. The Fort Carré that crowns the seaward promontory, the rocky islets, and the two stone breakwaters of the port (a small-scale Genoa), all add to the striking effect of the situation and prospect. Within, the place is as quaint and curious as without: a labyrinth of narrow streets, poor in memorials of Antipolis, but rich in Roman remains, including that famous and pathetic inscription to the boy Septentrio, qvi antipoli in theatro bidvo saltavit et placvit. The last three words borrowed from this provincial tombstone, have become proverbial of the short-lived glory of the actor's art.

The general aspect of Antibes town, however, is at present mediæval, or even seventeenth century. A flavor as of Louis Quatorz pervades the whole city, with its obtrusive military air of a border fortress; for, of course, while the Var still formed the frontier between France and Italy, Antibes ranked necessarily as a strategic post of immense importance; and at the present day, in our new recrudescence of military barbarism, great barracks surround the fortifications with fresh white-washed walls, and the "Hun! Deusse!" of the noisy French drill-sergeant resounds all day long from the exercise-ground by the railway station. Antibes itself is therefore by no means a place to stop at; it is the Cap 153] d'Antibes close by that attracts now every year an increasing influx of peaceful and cultivated visitors. The walks and drives are charming; the pine-woods, carpeted with wild anemones, are a dream of delight; and the view from the Lighthouse Hill behind the town is one of the loveliest and most varied on the whole round Mediterranean.

70

But I must not linger here over the beauties of the Cap d'Antibes, but must be pushing onwards towards Monaco and Monte Carlo.

It is a wonderful spot, this little principality of Monaco, hemmed in between the high mountains and the assailing sea, and long hermetically cut off from all its more powerful and commercial neighbors. Between the palm-lined boulevards of Nice and the grand amphitheater of mountains that shuts in Mentone as with a perfect semicircle of rearing peaks, one rugged buttress, the last long subsiding spur of the great Alpine axis, runs boldly out to seaward, and ends in the bluff rocky headland of the Tête de Chien that overhangs Monte Carlo. Till very lately no road ever succeeded in turning the foot of that precipitous promontory: the famous Corniche route runs along a ledge high up its beetling side, past the massive Roman ruin of Turbia, and looks down from a height of fifteen hundred feet upon the palace of Monaco. This mountain bulwark of the Turbia long formed the real boundary line between ancient Gaul and Liguria; and on its very summit, where the narrow Roman road wound along the steep pass now widened into the magnificent highway of the Corniche, Augustus built a solid square monument to mark the limit between the Province and the Italian soil, as well as to overawe the mountaineers of this turbulent region. A round 154]mediæval tower, at present likewise in ruins, crowns the Roman work. Here the Alps end abruptly. The rock of Monaco at the base is their last ineffectual seaward protest.

And what a rock it is, that quaint ridge of land, crowned by the strange capital of that miniature principality! Figure to yourself a huge whale petrified, as he basks there on the shoals his back rising some two hundred feet from the water's edge, his head to the sea, and his tail just touching the mainland, and you have a rough mental picture of the Rock of Monaco. It is, in fact, an isolated hillock, jutting into the Mediterranean at the foot of the Maritime Alps (a final reminder, as it were, of their dying dignity), and united to the Undercliff only by a narrow isthmus at the foot of the crag which bears the mediæval bastions of the Prince's palace. As you look down on it from above from the heights of the Corniche, I have no hesitation in saying it forms the most picturesque town site in all Europe. On every side, save seaward, huge mountains gird it round; while towards the smiling blue Mediterranean itself the great rock runs outward, bathed by tiny white breakers in every part, except where the low isthmus links it to the shore; and with a good field-glass you can see down in a bird's eye view into every street and courtyard of the clean little capital. The red-tiled houses, the white palace with its orderly gardens and quadrangles, the round lunettes of the old wall, the steep cobbled mule-path which mounts the rock from the modern railway-station, all lie spread out before one like a pictorial map, painted in the bright blue of Mediterranean seas, the dazzling gray of Mediterranean sunshine, and the brilliant russet of Mediterranean roofs.

155]There can be no question at all that Monte Carlo even now, with all its gew-gaw additions, is very beautiful: no Haussmann could spoil so much loveliness of position; and even the new town itself, which grows apace each time I revisit it, has a picturesqueness of hardy arch, bold rock, well-perched villa, which redeems it to a great extent from any rash charge of common vulgarity. All looks like a scene in a theater, not like a prosaic bit of this work-a-day world of ours. Around us is the blue Mediterranean, broken into a hundred petty sapphire bays. Back of us rise tier after tier of Maritime Alps, their huge summits clouded in a fleecy mist. To the left stands the white rock of Monaco; to the right, the green Italian shore, fading away into the purple mountains that guard the

Gulf of Genoa. Lovely by nature, the immediate neighborhood of the Casino has been made in some ways still more lovely by art. From the water's edge, terraces of tropical vegetation succeed one another in gradual steps towards the grand façade of the gambling-house; clusters of palms and aloes, their base girt by exotic flowers, are thrust cunningly into the foreground of every point in the view, so that you see the bay and the mountains through the artistic vistas thus deftly arranged in the very spots where a painter's fancy would have set them. You look across to Monaco past a clump of drooping date-branches; you catch a glimpse of Bordighera through a framework of spreading dracænas and quaintly symmetrical fan-palms.

Once more under way, and this time on foot. For the road from Monte Carlo to Mentone is almost as lovely in its way as that from Nice to Monte Carlo. It runs at first among the ever-increasing villas and hotels of the capital of Chance, and past that sumptuous 156] church, built from the gains of the table, which native wit has not inaptly christened "Nôtre Dame de la Roulette." There is one point of view of Monaco and its bay, on the slopes of the Cap Martin, not far from Roquebrune, so beautiful that though I have seen it, I suppose, a hundred times or more, I can never come upon it to this day without giving vent to an involuntary cry of surprise and admiration.

Roquebrune itself, which was an Italian Roccabruna when I first knew it, has a quaint situation of its own, and a quaint story connected with it. Brown as its own rocks, the tumbled little village stands oddly jumbled in and out among huge masses of pudding-stone, which must have fallen at some time or other in headlong confusion from the scarred face of the neighboring hillside. From the Corniche road it is still quite easy to recognize the bare patch on the mountain slope whence the landslip detached itself, and to trace its path down the hill to its existing position. But local legend goes a little farther than that: it asks us to believe that the rock fell as we see it with the houses on top; in other words, that the village was built before the catastrophe took place, and that it glided down piecemeal into the tossed-about form it at present presents to us. Be this as it may, and the story makes some demand on the hearer's credulity, it is certain that the houses now occupy most picturesque positions: here perched by twos and threes on broken masses of conglomerate, there wedged in between two great walls of beetling cliff, and yonder again hanging for dear life to some slender foothold on the precipitous hillside.

We reach the summit of the pass. The Bay of Monaco is separated from the Bay of Mentone by the long, 157]low-headland of Cap Martin, covered with olive groves and scrubby maritime pines. As one turns the corner from Roquebrune by the col round the cliff, there bursts suddenly upon the view one of the loveliest prospects to be beheld from the Corniche. At our feet, embowered among green lemons and orange trees, Mentone half hides itself behind its villas and its gardens. In the middle distance the old church with its tall Italian campanile stands out against the blue peaks of that magnificent amphitheater. Beyond, again, a narrow gorge marks the site of the Pont St. Louis and the Italian frontier. Farther eastward the red rocks merge half indistinctly into the point of La Mortola, with Mr. Hanbury's famous garden; then come the cliffs and fortifications of Ventimiglia, gleaming white in the sun; and last of all, the purple hills that hem in San Remo. It is an appropriate approach to a most lovely spot; for Mentone ranks high for beauty, even among her bevy of fair sisters on the Ligurian sea-board.

Yes, Mentone is beautiful, most undeniably beautiful; and for walks and drives perhaps it may bear away the palm from all rivals on that enchanted and enchanting Riviera. Five separate valleys, each carved out by its own torrent, with dry winter bed, converge upon the sea within the town precincts. Four principal rocky ridges divide these valleys with their chine-like backbone, besides numberless minor spurs branching laterally inland. Each valley is threaded by a well-made carriage-road, and each dividing ridge is climbed by a bridle-path and footway. The consequence is that the walks and drives at Mentone are never exhausted, and excursions among the hills might occupy the industrious pedestrian for many successive winters. What hills they are, too, those 158] great bare needles and pinnacles of rock, worn into jagged peaks and points by the ceaseless rain of ages, and looking down from their inaccessible tops with glittering scorn upon the green lemon groves beneath them!

The next town on the line, Bordighera, is better known to the world at large as a Rivieran winter resort, though of a milder and quieter type, I do not say than Nice or Cannes, but than Mentone or San Remo. Bordighera, indeed, has just reached that pleasant intermediate stage in the evolution of a Rivieran watering-place when all positive needs of the northern stranger are amply supplied, while crowds and fashionable amusements have not yet begun to invade its primitive simplicity. The walks and drives on every side are charming; the hotels are comfortable, and the prices are still by no means prohibitive.

San Remo comes next in order of the cosmopolitan winter resorts: San Remo, thickly strewn with spectacled Germans, like leaves in Vallombrosa, since the Emperor Frederick chose the place for his last despairing rally. The Teuton finds himself more at home, indeed, across the friendly Italian border than in hostile France; and the St. Gotthard gives him easy access by a pleasant route to these nearer Ligurian towns, so that the Fatherland has now almost annexed San Remo, as England has annexed Cannes, and America Nice and Cimiez. Built in the evil days of the Middle Ages, when every house was a fortress and every breeze bore a Saracen, San Remo presents to-day a picturesque labyrinth of streets, lanes, vaults, and alleys, only to be surpassed in the quaint neighboring village of Taggia. This is the heart of the earthquake region, too; and to protect themselves against that frequent and unwelcome visitor, whose mark 159]may be seen on half the walls in the outskirts, the inhabitants of San Remo have strengthened their houses by a system of arches thrown at varying heights across the tangled paths, which recalls Algiers or Tunis. From certain points of view, and especially from the east side, San Remo thus resembles a huge pyramid of solid masonry, or a monstrous pagoda hewn out by giant hands from a block of white free-stone. As Dickens well worded it, one seems to pass through the town by going perpetually from cellar to cellar. A romantic railway skirts the coast from San Remo to Alassio and Savona. It forms one long succession of tunnels, interspersed with frequent breathing spaces beside lovely bays, "the peacock's neck in hue," as the Laureate sings of them. One town after another sweeps gradually into view round the corner of a promontory, a white mass of houses crowning some steep point of rock, of which Alassio alone has as yet any pretensions to be considered a home for northern visitors.

160]

VIII

GENOA

Early history—Old fortifications—The rival of Venice—Changes of twenty-five years—From the parapet of the Corso—The lower town—The Genoese palazzi—Monument to Christopher Columbus—The old Dogana—Memorials in the Campo Santo—The Bay of Spezzia—The Isola Palmeria—Harbor scenes.

GENOVA la Superba—Genoa the Proud—an epithet not inappropriate for this city of merchant princes of olden days, which was once the emporium of the Tyrrhenian, as was Venice of the Adriatic sea, and the rival of the latter for the commerce of the Eastern Mediterranean. No two cities, adapted to play a similar part in history, could be more unlike in their natural environments: Venice clustered on a series of mud banks, parted by an expanse of water from a low coast-line, beyond which the far-away mountains rise dimly in the distance, a fleet, as it were, of houses anchored in the shallows of the Adriatic; Genoa stretching along the shore by the deepening water, at the very feet of the Apennines, climbing up their slopes, and crowning their lower summits with its watch-towers. No seaport in Italy possesses a site so rich in natural beauty, not even Spezzia in its bay, for though the scenery in the neighborhood certainly surpasses that around Genoa, the town itself is built upon an almost level plain; not 161] even Naples itself, notwithstanding the magnificent sweep of its bay, dominated by the volcanic cone of Vesuvius, and bounded by the limestone crags of the range of Monte S. Angelo. Genoa, however, like all places and persons, has had its detractors. Perhaps of no town has a more bitter sarcasm been uttered, than the well known one, which no doubt originated in the mouth of some envious Tuscan, when the two peoples were contending for the mastery of the western sea, and the maker of the epigram was on the losing side. Familiar as it is to many, we will venture to quote it again, as it may be rendered in our own tongue: "Treeless hills, a fishless sea, faithless men, shameless women." As to the reproach in the first clause, one must admit there is still some truth; and in olden days, when gardens were fewer and more land was left in its natural condition, there may have been even more point. The hills around Genoa undoubtedly seem a little barren, when compared with those on the Riviera some miles farther to the south, with their extraordinary luxuriance of vegetation, their endless slopes of olives, which only cease to give place to oak and pine and myrtle. There is also, I believe, some truth in the second clause; but as to the rest it is not for a comparative stranger to express an opinion. So far however as the men are concerned the reproach is not novel. Centuries since, Liguria, of which Genoa is the principal town, was noted for the cunning and treacherous disposition of its people, who ethnologically differ considerably from their neighbors. In Virgil's "Æneid" a Ligurian chief shows more cunning than courage in a fight with an Amazon, and is thus apostrophized before receiving his death-blow from a woman's hand: "In vain, O shifty one, hast thou tried thy hereditary craft." The people of this part of 162] Italy form one of a series of ethnological islands; where a remnant, by no means inconsiderable, of an earlier race has survived the invading flood of a stronger people. This old-world race—commonly called the Iberian—is characteristically short in stature, dark in hair, eyes, and complexion. Representatives of it survive in Brittany, Wales, Ireland, the Basque Provinces, and other out-of-the-way corners of Europe; insulated or pressed back, till they could no farther go, by the advance of the Aryan race, by some or other representative of which Europe is now peopled. On the Ligurian coast, however, as might be expected, in the track of two thousand years of commerce and civilization, the races, however different in origin and formerly naturally hostile, have been almost fused together by intermarriage; and this, at any rate in Genoa, seems to have had a fortuitous result in the production of an exceptionally good-looking people, especially in the case of the younger women. I well remember some years since, when driving out on a summer evening on the western side of Genoa, to have passed crowds of women, most of them young, returning from work in the factories, and certainly I never saw so large a proportion of beautiful faces as there were among them.

Genoa for at least two thousand years has been an important center of commerce; though, of course, like most other places, it has not been uniformly prosperous. It fell under the Roman power about two centuries before the Christian era, the possession of it for a time being disputed with the Carthaginians; then it became noted as a seaport town for the commerce of the western part of the Mediterranean, it declined and suffered during the decadence and fall of the Empire, and then gradually rose into eminence during the Middle Ages. Even 163] in the tenth century Genoa was an important community; its citizens, as beseemed men who were hardy sailors, found a natural pleasure in any kind of disturbance; they joined in the Crusades, and turned religious enthusiasm to commercial profit by the acquisition of various towns and islands in the East. The rather unusual combination of warrior and merchant, which the Genoese of the Middle Ages present, is no doubt due not only to social character, but also to exceptional circumstances. "The constant invasions of the Saracens united the professions of trade and war, and its greatest merchants became also its greatest generals, while its naval captains were also merchants."

Genoa, as may be supposed, had from the first to contend with two formidable rivals: the one being Pisa in its own waters; the other Venice, whose citizens were equally anxious for supremacy in the Levant and the commerce of the East. With both these places the struggle was long and fierce, but the fortune of war on the whole was distinctly favorable to Genoa nearer home, and unfavorable in regard to the more distant foe. Pisa was finally defeated in the neighborhood of Leghorn, and in the year 1300 had to cede to her enemy a considerable amount of territory, including the island of Corsica; while Venice, after more than a century of conflict with very varying fortune, at last succeeded in obtaining the supremacy in the Eastern Mediterranean.

The internal history of the city during all this period was not more peaceful than its external. Genoa presents the picture of a house divided against itself; and, strange to say, falsifies the proverb by prospering instead of perishing. If there were commonly wars without, there were yet more persistent factions within. Guelphs, headed 164] by the families of Grimaldi and Fieschi, and Ghibellines, by those of Spinola and Doria, indulged in faction-fights and sometimes in civil warfare, until at last some approach to peace was procured by the influence of Andrea Doria, who, in obtaining the freedom of the state from French control, brought about the adoption of most important constitutional changes, which tended to obliterate the old and sharply divided party lines. Yet even he narrowly escaped overthrow from a conspiracy, headed by one of the Fieschi; his great-nephew and heir was assassinated, and his ultimate triumph was due rather to a fortunate accident, which removed from the scene the leader of his opponents, than to his personal power. Then the tide of prosperity began to turn against the Genoese. The Turk made himself master of their lands and cities in the East. Venice ousted them from the commerce of the Levant. War arose with France, and the city itself was captured by that power in the year 1684. The following century was far from being a prosperous time for Genoa, and near the close it opened its gates to the Republican troops, a subjugation which ultimately resulted in no little suffering to the inhabitants.

Genoa at that time was encircled on the land side by a double line of fortifications, a considerable portion of which still remains. The outer one, with its associated detached forts, mounted up the inland slopes to an elevation of some hundreds of feet above the sea, and within this is an inner line of much greater antiquity. As it was for those days a place of exceptional strength, its capture became of the first importance, in the great struggle between France and Austria, as a preliminary to driving the Republican troops out of Italy. The city was defended by the French under the command of 165] Massena; it was attacked on the land side by the Imperialist force, while it was blockaded from the sea by the British fleet. After fifteen days of hard fighting among the neighboring Apennines, Massena was finally shut up in the city. No less desperate fighting followed around the walls, until at last the defending force was so weakened by its losses that further aggressive operations became impossible on its part, and the siege was converted into a blockade. The results were famine and pestilence. A hundred thousand persons were cooped up within the walls. "From the commencement of the siege the price of provisions had been extravagantly high, and in its latter days grain of any sort could not be had at any cost.... The neighboring rocks within the walls were covered with a famished crowd, seeking, in the vilest animals and the smallest traces of vegetation, the means of assuaging their intolerable pangs.... In the general agony, not only leather and skins of every kind were consumed, but the horror at human flesh was so much abated that numbers were supported on the dead bodies of their fellow citizens. Pestilence, as usual, came in the rear of famine, and contagious fevers swept off multitudes, whom the strength of the survivors was unable to inter." Before the obstinate defense was ended, and Massena, at the end of all his resources, was compelled to capitulate on honorable terms, twenty thousand of the inhabitants had perished from hunger or disease. The end of this terrible struggle brought little profit to the conquerors, for before long the battle of Marengo, and the subsequent successes of Napoleon in Northern Italy, led to the city being again surrendered to the French. It had to endure another siege at the end of Napoleon's career, for in 1814 it was attacked by 166]English troops under Lord William Bentinck. Fortunately for the inhabitants, the French commander decided to surrender after a few days' severe struggle around the outer defenses. On the settlement of European affairs which succeeded the final fall of Napoleon, Genoa was annexed to the kingdom of Sardinia, and now forms part of united Italy; though, it is said, the old instincts of the people give them a theoretic preference for a republican form of government.

Genoa, like so many of the chief Italian towns, has been greatly altered during the last twenty-five years. Its harbors have been much enlarged; its defenses have been extended far beyond their ancient limits. Down by the water-side, among the narrow streets on the shelving ground that fringes the sea, we are still in old Genoa—the city of the merchant princes of the fifteenth and sixteenth centuries; but higher up the slopes a new town has sprung up, with broad streets and fine modern houses, and a "corso," bordered by trees and mansions, still retains in its zigzag outline the trace of the old fortifications which enclosed the arm of Massena. More than one spot, on or near this elevated road, commands a splendid outlook over the city and neighborhood.

From such a position the natural advantages of the site of Genoa, the geographical conditions which have almost inevitably determined its history, can be apprehended at a glance. Behind us rise steeply, as has been already said, the hills forming the southernmost zone of the Apennines. This, no doubt, is a defect in a military point of view, because the city is commanded by so many positions of greater elevation; but this defect was less serious in ancient days, when the range of ordnance was comparatively short; while the difficulty of access which 167] these positions presented, and the obstacles which the mountain barrier of the Apennines offered to the advance of an enemy from the comparatively distant plains of Piedmont, rendered the city far more secure than it may at first sight have appeared. Beneath us lies a deeply recessed bay, in outline like the half of an egg, guarded on the east by a projecting shoulder; while on the western side hills descend, at first rapidly, then more gently, to a point which projects yet farther to the south. This eastern shoulder is converted into a kind of peninsula, rudely triangular in shape, by the valley of the Bisagno, a stream of considerable size which thus forms a natural moat for the fortifications on the eastern side of the town. In a bay thus sheltered on three sides by land, vessels were perfectly safe from most of the prevalent winds; and it was only necessary to carry out moles from the western headland and from some point on the eastern shore, to protect them also from storms which might blow from the south. The first defense was run out from the latter side, and still bears the name of the Molo Vecchio; then the port was enlarged, by carrying out another mole from the end of the western headland; this has been greatly extended, so that the town may now be said to possess an inner and an outer harbor. From the parapet of the Corso these topographical facts are seen at a glance, as we look over the tall and densely-massed houses to the busy quays, and the ships which are moored alongside. Such a scene cannot fail to be attractive, and the lighthouse, rising high above the western headland, is less monotonous in outline than is usual with such buildings, and greatly enhances the effect of the picture. The city, however, when regarded from this elevated position is rather wanting 168] in variety. We look down over a crowded mass of lofty houses, from which, indeed, two or three domes or towers rise up; but there is not enough diversity in the design of the one, or a sufficiently marked pre-eminence in the others, to afford a prospect which is comparable with that of many other ancient cities. Still some variety is given by the trees, which here and there, especially towards the eastern promontory, are interspersed among the houses; while the Ligurian coast on the one hand, and the distant summits of the Maritime Alps on the other, add to the scene a never-failing charm.

Of the newer part of the town little more need be said. It is like the most modern part of any Continental city, and only differs from the majority of these by the natural steepness and irregularity of the site. In Genoa, except for a narrow space along the shore, one can hardly find a plot of level ground. Now that the old limits of the enceinte have been passed, it is still growing upwards; but beyond and above the farthest houses the hills are still crowned by fortresses, keeping watch and ward over the merchant city. These, of course, are of modern date; but some of them have been reconstructed on the ancient sites, and still encrust, as can be seen at a glance, towers and walls which did their duty in the olden times. For a season, indeed, there was more to be protected than merchandise, for, till lately, Genoa was the principal arsenal of the Italian kingdom; but this has now been removed to Spezzia. Italy, however, does not seem to feel much confidence in that immunity from plunder which has been sometimes accorded to "open towns," or in the platitudes of peace-mongers; and appears to take ample precautions that an enemy in command of the sea shall not thrust his hand into a full purse without a 169] good chance of getting nothing better than crushed fingers.

But in the lower town we are still in the Genoa of the olden time. There is not, indeed, very much to recall the city of the more strictly mediæval epoch; though two churches date from days before the so-called "Renaissance," and are good examples of its work. Most of what we now see belongs to the Genoa of the sixteenth century; or, at any rate, is but little anterior in age to this. The lower town, however, even where its buildings are comparatively modern, still retains in plan—in its narrow, sometimes irregular, streets; in its yet narrower alleys, leading by flights of steps up the steep hill side; in its crowded, lofty houses; in its "huddled up" aspect, for perhaps no single term can better express our meaning—the characteristics of an ancient Italian town. In its streets even the summer sun—let the proverb concerning the absence of the sun and the presence of the doctor say what it may—can seldom scorch, and the bitter north wind loses its force among the maze of buildings. Open spaces of any kind are rare; the streets, in consequence of their narrowness, are unusually thronged, and thus produce the idea of a teeming population; which, indeed, owing to the general loftiness of the houses, is large in proportion to the area. They are accordingly ill-adapted for the requirements of modern traffic.

Genoa, like Venice, is noted for its palazzi—for the sumptuous dwellings inhabited by the burgher aristocracy of earlier days, which are still, in not a few cases, in possession of their descendants. But in style and in position nothing can be more different. We do not refer to the obvious distinction that in the one city the highway 170] is water, in the other it is dry land; or to the fact that buildings in the so-called Gothic style are common in Venice, but are not to be found among the mansions of Genoa. It is rather to this, that the Via Nuova, which in this respect holds the same place in Genoa as the Grand Canal does in Venice, is such a complete contrast to it, that they must be compared by their opposites. The latter is a broad and magnificent highway, affording a full view and a comprehensive survey of the stately buildings which rise from its margin. The former is a narrow street, corresponding in dimensions with one of the less important among the side canals in the other city. It is thus almost impossible to obtain any good idea of the façade of the Genoese palazzi. The passing traveller has about as much chance of doing this as he would have of studying the architecture of Mincing Lane; and even if he could discover a quiet time, like Sunday morning in the City, he would still have to strain his neck by staring upwards at the overhanging mass of masonry, and find a complete view of any one building almost impossible. But so far as these palazzi can be seen, how far do they repay examination? It is a common-place with travellers to expatiate on the magnificence of the Via Nuova, and one or two other streets in Genoa. There is an imposing magniloquence in the word palazzo, and a "street of palaces" is a formula which impels many minds to render instant homage.

But, speaking for myself, I must own to being no great admirer of this part of Genoa; to me the design of these palazzi appears often heavy and oppressive. They are sumptuous rather than dignified, and impress one more with the length of the purse at the architect's command than with the quality of his genius or the 171] fecundity of his conceptions. No doubt there are some fine buildings—the Palazzo Spinola, the Palazzo Doria Tursi, the Palazzo del' Universita, and the Palazzo Balbi, are among those most generally praised. But if I must tell the plain, unvarnished truth, I never felt and never shall feel much enthusiasm for the "city of palaces." It has been some relief to me to find that I am not alone in this heresy, as it will appear to some. For on turning to the pages of Fergusson,[1] immediately after penning the above confession, I read for the first time the following passage (and it must be admitted that, though not free from occasional "cranks" as to archæological questions, he was a critic of extensive knowledge and no mean authority):—"When Venice adopted the Renaissance style, she used it with an aristocratic elegance that relieves even its most fantastic forms in the worst age. In Genoa there is a pretentious parvenu vulgarity, which offends in spite of considerable architectural merit. Their size, their grandeur, and their grouping may force us to admire the palaces of Genoa; but for real beauty or architectural propriety of design they will not stand a moment's comparison with the contemporary or earlier palaces of Florence, Rome, or Venice." Farther on he adds very truly, after glancing at the rather illegitimate device by which the façades have been rendered more effective by the use of paint, instead of natural color in the materials employed, as in the older buildings of Venice, he adds:—"By far the most beautiful feature of the greater palaces of Genoa is their courtyards" (a feature obviously which can only make its full appeal to a comparatively limited number of visitors), "though these, architecturally, consist of nothing but ranges of arcades, resting on 172]attenuated Doric pillars. These are generally of marble, sometimes grouped in pairs, and too frequently with a block of an entablature over each, under the springing of the arch; but notwithstanding these defects, a cloistered court is always and inevitably pleasing, and if combined with gardens and scenery beyond, which is generally the case in this city, the effect, as seen from the streets, is so poetic as to disarm criticism. All that dare be said is that, beautiful as they are, with a little more taste and judgment they might have been ten times more so than they are now."

Several of these palazzi contain pictures and art-collections of considerable value, and the interest of those has perhaps enhanced the admiration which they have excited in visitors. One of the most noteworthy is the Palazzo Brignole Sale, commonly called the Palazzo Rosso, because its exterior is painted red. This has now become a memorial of the munificence of its former owner, the Duchess of Galliera, a member of the Brignole Sale family, who, with the consent of her husband and relations, in the year 1874 presented this palace and its contents to the city of Genoa, with a revenue sufficient for its maintenance. The Palazzo Reale, in the Via Balbi, is one of those where the garden adds a charm to an otherwise not very striking, though large, edifice. This, formerly the property of the Durazzo family, was purchased by Charles Albert, King of Sardinia, and has thus become a royal residence. The Palazzo Ducale, once inhabited by the Doges of Genoa, has now been converted into public offices, and the palazzo opposite to the Church of St. Matteo bears an inscription which of itself gives the building an exceptional interest: "Senat. Cons. Andreæ de Oria, patriæ liberatori, munus 173] publicum." It is this, the earlier home of the great citizen of Genoa, of which Rogers has written in the often-quoted lines:—

"He left it for a better; and 'tis now
A house of trade, the meanest merchandise
Cumbering its floors. Yet, fallen as it is,
'Tis still the noblest dwelling—even in Genoa!
And hadst thou, Andrea, lived there to the last,
Thou hadst done well: for there is that without,
That in the wall, which monarchs could not give
Nor thou take with thee—that which says aloud,
It was thy country's gift to her deliverer!"

The great statesman lies in the neighboring church, with other members of his family, and over the high altar hangs the sword which was given to him by the Pope. The church was greatly altered—embellished it was doubtless supposed—by Doria himself; but the old cloisters, dating from the earliest part of the fourteenth century, still remain intact. The grander palazzo which he erected, as an inscription outside still informs us, was in a more open, and doubtless then more attractive, part of the city. In the days of Doria it stood in ample gardens, which extended on one side down to a terrace overlooking the harbor, on the other some distance up the hillside. From the back of the palace an elaborate structure of ascending flight of steps in stone led up to a white marble colossal statue of Hercules, which from this elevated position seemed to keep watch over the home of the Dorias and the port of Genoa. All this is sadly changed; the admiral would now find little pleasure in his once stately home. It occupies a kind of peninsula between two streams of twentieth-century civilization. Between the terrace wall and the sea the railway connecting the harbor 174] with the main line has intervened, with its iron tracks, its sheds, and its shunting-places—a dreary unsightly outlook, for the adjuncts of a terminus are usually among the most ugly appendages of civilization. The terraced staircase on the opposite side of the palace has been swept away by the main line of the railway, which passes within a few yards of its façade, thus severing the gardens and isolating the shrine of Hercules, who looks down forlornly on the result of labors which even he might have deemed arduous, while snorting, squealing engines pass and repass— beasts which to him would have seemed more formidable than Lernæan hydra or Nemaean lion.

The palace follows the usual Genoese rule of turning the better side inwards, and offering the less attractive to the world at large. The landward side, which borders a narrow street, and thus, one would conjecture, must from the first have been connected with the upper gardens by a bridge, or underground passage, is plain, almost heavy, in its design, but it does not rise to so great an elevation as is customary with the palazzi in the heart of the city. The side which is turned towards the sea is a much more attractive composition, for it is associated with the usual cloister of loggia which occupies three sides of an oblong. This, as the ground slopes seaward, though on the level of the street outside, stands upon a basement story, and communicates by flights of steps with the lower gardens. The latter are comparatively small, and in no way remarkable; but in the days—not so very distant—when their terraces looked down upon the Mediterranean, when the city and its trade were on a smaller scale, when the picturesque side of labor had not yet been extruded by the dust and 175] grime of over-much toil, no place in Genoa could have been more pleasant for the evening stroll, or for dreamy repose in some shaded nook during the heat of the day. The palazzo itself shows signs of neglect—the family, I believe, have for some time past ceased to use it for a residence; two or three rooms are still retained in their original condition, but the greater part of the building is let off. In the corridor, near the entrance, members of the Doria family, dressed in classic garb, in conformity with the taste which prevailed in the sixteenth century, are depicted in fresco upon the walls. On the roof of the grand saloon Jupiter is engaged in overthrowing the Titans. These frescoes are the work of Perini del Vaga, a pupil of Raphael. The great admiral, the builder of the palace, is represented among the figures in the corridor, and by an oil painting in the saloon, which contains some remains of sumptuous furniture and a few ornaments of interest. He was a burly man, with a grave, square, powerful face, such a one as often looks out at us from the canvas of Titian or of Tintoret—a man of kindly nature, but masterful withal; cautious and thoughtful, but a man of action more than of the schools or of the library; one little likely to be swayed by passing impulse or transient emotion, but clear and firm of purpose, who meant to attain his end were it in mortal to command success, and could watch and wait for the time. Such men, if one may trust portraits and trust history, were not uncommon in the great epoch when Europe was shaking itself free from the fetters of mediæval influences, and was enlarging its mental no less than its physical horizon. Such men are the makers of nations, and not only of their own fortunes; they become rarer in the days of frothy stump oratory and 176] hysteric sentiment, when a people babbles as it sinks into senile decrepitude.

Andrea Doria himself—"Il principe" as he was styled—had a long and in some respects a checkered career. In his earlier life he obtained distinction as a successful naval commander, and in the curious complications which prevailed in those days among the Italian States and their neighbors ultimately became Admiral of the French fleet. But he found that Genoa would obtain little good from the French King, who was then practically its master; so he transferred his allegiance to the Emperor Charles, and by his aid expelled from his native city the troops with which he had formerly served. So great was his influence in Genoa that he might easily have obtained supreme power; but at this, like a true patriot, he did not grasp, and the Constitution, which was adopted under his influence, gradually put an end to the bitter party strife which had for so long been the plague of Genoa, and it remained in force until the French Revolution. Still, notwithstanding the gratitude generally felt for his great services to the State, he experienced in his long life—for he died at the age of ninety-two—the changefulness of human affairs. He had no son, and his heir and grand-nephew—a young man—was unpopular, and, as is often the case, the sapling was altogether inferior in character to the withering tree. The members of another great family—the Fieschi—entered into a conspiracy, and collected a body of armed men on the pretext of an expedition against the corsairs who for so long were the pests of the Mediterranean. The outbreak was well planned; on New Year's night, in the year 1547, the chief posts in the city were seized. Doria himself was just warned in time, and escaped capture; but 177] his heir was

81

assassinated, and his enemies seemed to have triumphed. But their success was changed to failure by an accident. Count Fiescho in passing along a plank to a galley in the harbor made a false step, and fell into the sea. In those days the wearing of armor added to the perils of the deep; the count sank like a stone, and so left the conspirators without a leader exactly at the most critical moment. They were thus before long defeated and dispersed, and had to experience the truth of the proverb, "Who breaks pays," for in those days men felt little sentimental tenderness for leaders of sedition and disturbers of the established order. The Fieschi were exiled, and their palace was razed to the ground. So the old admiral returned to his home and his terrace-walk overlooking the sea, until at last his long life ended, and they buried him with his fathers in the Church of S. Matteo.

Not far from the Doria Palace is the memorial to another admiral, of fame more world-wide than that of Doria. In the open space before the railway station—a building, a façade of which is not without architectural merit—rises a handsome monument in honor of Christopher Columbus. He was not strictly a native of the city, but he was certainly born on Genoese soil, and, as it seems to be now agreed, at Cogoleto, a small village a few miles west of the city. He was not, however, able to convince the leaders of his own State that there were wide parts of the world yet to be discovered; and it is a well-known story how for a long time he preached to deaf ears, and found, like most heralds of startling physical facts, his most obstinate opponents among the ecclesiastics of his day. Spain at last, after Genoa and Portugal and England had all refused, placed Columbus 178] in command of a voyage of discovery; and on Spanish ground also—in neglect and comparative poverty, worn out by toil and anxieties—the great explorer ended his checkered career. Genoa, however, though inattentive to the comparatively obscure enthusiast, has not failed to pay honor to the successful discoverer; and is glad to catch some reflected light from the splendor of successes to the aid of which she did not contribute. In this respect, however, the rest of the world cannot take up their parable at her; men generally find that on the whole it is less expensive, and certainly less troublesome, to build the tombs of the prophets, instead of honoring them while alive; then, indeed, whether bread be asked or no, a stone is often given. So now the effigy of Columbus stands on high among exotic plants, where all the world can see, for it is the first thing encountered by the traveller as he quits the railway station.

One of the most characteristic—if not one of the sweetest—places in Genoa is the long street, which, under more than one name, intervenes between the last row of houses in the town and the harbor. From the latter it is, indeed, divided by a line of offices and arched halls; these are covered by a terrace-roof and serve various purposes more or less directly connected with the shipping. The front walls of houses which rise high on the landward side are supported by rude arches. Thus, as is so common in Italian towns, there is a broad foot-walk, protected alike from sun and rain, replacing the "ground-floor front," with dark shops at the back, and stalls, for the sale of all sorts of odds and ends, pitched in the spaces between the arches. In many towns these arcades are often among the most ornamental features; but in Genoa, though not without a certain quaintness, they are 179] so rude in design and construction that they hardly deserve this title. The old Dogana, one of the buildings in the street, gives a good idea of the commercial part of Genoa before the days of steam, and has a considerable interest of its own. In the first place, it is a standing memorial of the bitter feud between Genoa and Venice, for it is built with the stones of a castle which, being captured by the one from the other, was pulled down and shipped to Genoa in the year 1262. Again, within its walls was the Banca di San Georgio, which had its origin in a municipal debt incurred in order to equip an expedition to stop the forays of a family named Grimaldi, who had formed a sort of Cave of Adullam at Monaco. The institution afterwards prospered, and held in trust most of the funds for charitable purposes, till "the French passed their sponge over the accounts, and ruined all the individuals in the community." It has also an indirect connection with English history, for on the defeat of the Grimaldi many of their retainers entered the service of France, and were the Genoese bowmen who fought at Cressy. Lastly, against its walls the captured chains of the harbor of Pisa were suspended for nearly six centuries, for they were only restored to their former owners a comparatively few years since.

Turning up from this part of the city we thread narrow streets, in which many of the principal shops are still located. We pass, in a busy piazza, the Loggia dei Banchi Borsa—the old exchange—a quaint structure of the end of the sixteenth century, standing on a raised platform; and proceed from it into the Via degli Orefici—a street just like one of the lanes which lead from Cheapside to Cannon Street, if, indeed, it be not still narrower, but full of tempting shops. Genoa is noted for its work 180] in coral and precious metals, but the most characteristic, as all visitors know, is a kind of filigree work in gold or silver, which is often of great delicacy and beauty, and is by no means so costly as might be anticipated from the elaborate workmanship.

The most notable building in Genoa, anterior to the days when the architecture of the Renaissance was in favor, is the cathedral, which is dedicated to S. Lorenzo. The western façade, which is approached by a broad flight of steps, is the best exposed to view, the rest of the building being shut in rather closely after the usual Genoese fashion. It is built of alternating courses of black and white marble, the only materials employed for mural decoration, so far as I remember, in the city. The western façade in its lower part is a fine example of "pointed" work, consisting of a triple portal which, for elegance of design and richness of ornamentation, could not readily be excelled. It dates from about the year 1307, when the cathedral was almost rebuilt. The latter, as a whole, is a very composite structure, for parts of an earlier Romanesque cathedral still remain, as in the fine "marble" columns of the nave; and important alterations were made at a much later date. These, to which belongs the mean clerestory, painted in stripes of black and white, to resemble the banded courses of stone below, are generally most unsatisfactory; and here, as in so many other buildings, one is compelled, however reluctantly, "to bless the old and ban the new." The most richly decorated portion of the interior is the side chapel, constructed at the end of the fifteenth century, and dedicated to St. John the Baptist; here his relics are enshrined for the reverence of the faithful and, as the guide-books inform us, are placed in a magnificent silver-gilt 181] shrine, which is carried in solemn procession on the day of his nativity. We are also informed that women, as a stigma for the part which the sex played in the Baptist's murder, are only permitted to enter the chapel once in a year. This is not by any means the only case where the Church of Rome gives practical expression to its decided view as to which is the superior sex. The cathedral possesses another great, though now unhappily mutilated, treasure in the sacro catino. This, in the first place, was long supposed to have been carved from a single emerald; in the next, it was a relic of great antiquity and much sanctity; though as to its precise claims to honor in this respect authorities differed. According to one, it had been a gift from the Queen of Sheba to Solomon; according to another, it had contained the paschal lamb at the Last Supper; while a third asserted that in this dish Joseph of Arimathea had caught the blood which flowed from the pierced side of the crucified

Saviour. Of its great antiquity there can at least be no doubt, for it was taken by the Genoese when they plundered Cæsarea so long since as the year 1101, and was then esteemed the most precious thing in the spoil. The material is a green glass—a conclusion once deemed so heretical that any experiment on the catino was forbidden on pain of death. As regards its former use, no more can be said than that it might possibly be as old as the Christian era. It is almost needless to say that Napoleon carried it away to Paris; but the worst result of this robbery was that when restitution was made after the second occupation of that city, the catino, through some gross carelessness, was so badly packed that it was broken on the journey back, and has been pieced together by a gold-setting of filigree, according to the 182] guide-books. An inscription in the nave supplies us with an interesting fact in the early history of Genoa which perhaps ought not to be omitted. It is that the city was founded by one Janus, a great grandson of Noah; and that another Janus, after the fall of Troy, also settled in it. Colonists from that ill-fated town really seem to have distributed themselves pretty well over the known world.

More than one of the smaller churches of Genoa is of archæological interest, and the more modern fabric, called L'Annunziata, is extremely rich in its internal decorations, though these are more remarkable for their sumptuousness than for their good taste. But one structure calls for some notice in any account of the city. This is the Campo Santo, or burial-place of Genoa, situated at some distance without the walls in the Valley of the Bisagno. A large tract of land on the slope which forms the right bank of that stream has been converted into a cemetery, and was laid out on its present plan rather more than twenty-five years since. Extensive open spaces are enclosed within and divided by corridors with cloisters; terraces also, connected by flights of steps, lead up to a long range of buildings situated some distance above the river, in the center of which is a chapel crowned with a dome, supported internally by large columns of polished black Como marble. The bodies of the poorer people are buried in the usual way in the open ground of the cemetery, and the floor of the corridors appears to cover a continuous series of vaults, closed, as formerly in our churches, with great slabs of stone; but a very large number of the dead rest above the ground in vaults constructed on a plan which has evidently been borrowed from catacombs like those of Rome. There is, 183] however, this difference, that in the latter the "loculi," or separate compartments to contain the corpses, were excavated in the rock, while here they are constructed entirely of masonry. In both cases the "loculus" is placed with its longer axis parallel to the outer side, as was occasionally the method in the rock-hewn tombs of Palestine, instead of having an opening at the narrower end, so that the corpse, whether coffined or not, lies in the position of a sleeper in the berth of a ship. After a burial, the loculus, as in the catacombs, is closed, and an inscription placed on a slab outside. Thus in the Campo Santo at Genoa we walk through a gallery of tombs. On either hand are ranges of low elongated niches, rising tier above tier, each bearing a long white marble tablet, surrounded by a broad border of dark serpentine breccia. The interior generally is faced with white marble, which is toned down by the interspaces of the darker material, and the effect produced by these simple monumental corridors, these silent records of those who have rested from their labors, is impressive, if somewhat melancholy. In the cloisters, as a rule, the more sumptuous memorials are to be found. Here commonly sections of the wall are given up to the monuments of a family, the vaults, as I infer, being underneath the pavement. These memorials are often elaborate in design, and costly in their materials. They will be, and are, greatly admired by those to whose minds sumptuousness is the chief element in beauty, and rather second-rate execution of conceptions distinctly third-rate gives no offense. Others, however, will be chiefly impressed with the inferiority of modern statuary to the better work of classic ages, and will doubt whether the more ambitious compositions which met our eyes in these 184]galleries are preferable to the simple dignity of the mediæval altar tomb, and the calm repose of its recumbent figure.

The drive to the Campo Santo, in addition to affording a view of one of the more perfect parts of the old defensive enclosure of Genoa, of which the Porta Chiappia, one of the smaller gates, may serve as an example, passes within sight, though at some distance below, one of the few relics of classic time which the city has retained. This is the aqueduct which was constructed by the Romans. Some portions of it, so far as can be seen from below, appear to belong to the original structure; but, as it is still in use, it has been in many parts more or less reconstructed and modernized.

The environs of Genoa are pleasant. On both sides, particularly on the eastern, are country houses with gardens. The western for a time is less attractive. The suburb of Sanpierdarena is neither pretty nor interesting; but at Conigliano, and still more at Sestre Ponente, the grimy finger-marks of commerce become less conspicuous, and Nature is not wholly expelled by the two-pronged fork of mechanism. Pegli, still farther west, is a very attractive spot, much frequented in the summer time for sea-bathing. On this part of the coast the hills in places draw near to the sea, and crags rise from the water; the rocks are of interest in more than one respect to the geologist. One knoll of rock rising from the sand in the Bay of Pra is crowned by an old fortress, and at Pegli itself are one or two villas of note. Of these the gardens of the Villa Pallavicini commonly attract visitors. They reward some by stalactite grottoes and "sheets of water with boats, under artificial caverns, a Chinese pagoda, and an Egyptian obelisk;" others will be more attracted by the beauty of the vegetation, for palms 185] and oleanders, myrtles, and camellias, with many semi-tropical plants, flourish in the open air.

We may regard Genoa as the meeting-place of the two Rivieras. The coast to the west—the Riviera di Ponente—what has now, by the cession of Nice, become in part French soil, is the better known; but that to the east, the Riviera di Levante, though less accessible on the whole, and without such an attractive feature as the Corniche road, in the judgment of some is distinctly the more beautiful. There is indeed a road which, for a part of the way, runs near the sea; but the much more indented character of the coast frequently forces it some distance inland, and ultimately it has to cross a rather considerable line of hills in order to reach Spezzia. The outline of the coast, indeed, is perhaps the most marked feature of difference between the two Rivieras. The hills on the eastern side descend far more steeply to the water than they do upon the western. They are much more sharply furrowed with gullies and more deeply indented by inlets of the sea; thus the construction of a railway from Genoa to Spezzia has been a work involving no slight labor. There are, it is stated, nearly fifty tunnels between the two towns, and it is strictly true that for a large part of the distance north of the latter place the train is more frequently under than above ground. Here it is actually an advantage to travel by the slowest train that can be found, for this may serve as an epitome of the journey by an express: "Out of a tunnel; one glance, between rocks and olive-groves, up a ravine, into which a picturesque old village is wedged; another glance down the same to the sea, sparkling in the sunlight below; a shriek from the engine, and another plunge into darkness." So narrow are some of these gullies, up which, 186] however, a village climbs, that, if I may trust my memory, I have seen a train halted at a station with the engine in the opening of one tunnel and the last car not yet clear of another.

But the coast, when explored, is full of exquisite nooks, and here and there, where by chance the hills slightly recede, or a larger valley than usual comes down to the sea, towns of some size are situated, from which, as halting-places, the district might be easily explored, for trains are fairly frequent, and the distances are not great. For a few miles from Genoa the coast is less hilly than it afterwards becomes; nevertheless, the traveller is prepared for what lies before him by being conducted from the main station, on the west side of Genoa, completely beneath the city to near its eastern wall. Then Nervi is passed, which, like Pegli, attracts not a few summer visitors, and is a bright and sunny town, with pleasant gardens and villas. Recco follows, also bright and cheerful, backed by the finely-outlined hills, which form the long promontory enclosing the western side of the Bay of Rapallo. Tunnels and villages, as the railway now plunges into the rock, now skirts the margin of some little bay, lead first to Rapallo and then to Chiavari, one with its slender campanile, the other with its old castle. The luxuriance of the vegetation in all this district cannot fail to attract notice. The slopes of the hills are grey with olives; oranges replace apples in the orchards, and in the more sheltered nooks we espy the paler gold of the lemon. Here are great spiky aloes, there graceful feathering palms; here pines of southern type, with spreading holm-oaks, and a dozen other evergreen shrubs.

Glimpse after glimpse of exquisite scenery flashes upon us as we proceed to Spezzia, but, as already said, its full 187] beauty can only be appreciated by rambling among the hills or boating along the coast. There is endless variety, but the leading features are similar: steep hills furrowed by ravines, craggy headlands and sheltered coves; villages sometimes perched high on a shoulder, sometimes nestling in a gully; sometimes a campanile, sometimes a watch-tower; slopes, here clothed with olive groves, here with their natural covering of pine and oak scrub, of heath, myrtle, and strawberry-trees. A change also in the nature of the rock diversifies the scenery, for between Framura and Bonasola occurs a huge mass of serpentine, which recalls, in its peculiar structure and tints, the crags near the Lizard in England. This rock is extensively quarried in the neighborhood of Levanto, and from that little port many blocks are shipped.

Spezzia itself has a remarkable situation. A large inlet of the sea runs deep into the land, parallel with the general trend of the hills, and almost with that of the coast-line. The range which shelters it on the west narrows as it falls to the headland of Porto Venere, and is extended yet farther by rocky islands; while on the opposite coast, hills no less, perhaps yet more, lofty, protect the harbor from the eastern blasts. In one direction only is it open to the wind, and against this the comparative narrowness of the inlet renders the construction of artificial defenses possible. At the very head of this deeply embayed sheet of water is a small tract of level ground—the head, as it were, of a valley—encircled by steep hills. On this little plain, and by the waterside, stands Spezzia. Formerly it was a quiet country town, a small seaport with some little commerce; but when Italy ceased to be a geographical expression, and became practically one nation, Spezzia was chosen, wisely it must be 188] admitted, as the site of the chief naval arsenal. A single glance shows its natural advantages for such a purpose. Access from the land must always present difficulties, and every road can be commanded by forts, perched on yet more elevated positions; while a hostile fleet, as it advances up the inlet, must run the gauntlet of as many batteries as the defenders can build. Further, the construction of a breakwater across the middle of the channel at once has been a protection from the storms, and has compelled all who approach to pass through straits commanded by cannon. The distance of the town from its outer defenses and from the open sea seems enough to secure it even from modern ordnance; so that, until the former are crushed, it cannot be reached by projectiles. But it must be confessed that the change has not been without its drawbacks. The Spezzia of to-day may be a more prosperous town than the Spezzia of a quarter of a century since, but it has lost some of its beauty. A twentieth-century fortress adds no charm to the scenery, and does not crown a hill so picturesquely as did a mediæval castle. Houses are being built, roads are being made, land is being reclaimed from the sea for the construction of quays. Thus the place has a generally untidy aspect; there is a kind of ragged selvage to town and sea, which, at present, on a near view, is very unsightly. Moreover, the buildings of an arsenal can hardly be picturesque or magnificent; and great factories, more or less connected with them, have sprung up in the neighborhood, from which rise tall red brick chimneys, the campaniles of the twentieth century. The town itself was never a place of any particular interest; it has neither fine churches nor old gateways nor picturesque streets—a ruinous fort among the olive groves overlooking the 189] streets is all that can claim to be ancient—so that its growth has not caused the loss of any distinctive feature—unless it be a grove of old oleanders, which were once a sight to see in summer time. Many of these have now disappeared, perhaps from natural decay; and the survivors are mixed with orange trees. These, during late years, have been largely planted about the town. In one of the chief streets they are growing by the side of the road, like planes or chestnuts in other towns. The golden fruit and the glossy leaves, always a delight to see, appear to possess a double charm by contrast with the arid flags and dusty streets. Ripe oranges in dozens, in hundreds, all along by the pathway, and within two or three yards of the pavement! Are the boys of Spezzia exceptionally virtuous? or are these golden apples of the Hesperides a special pride of the populace, and does "Father Stick" still rule in home and school, and is this immunity the result of physical coercion rather than of moral suasion? Be this as it may, I have with mine own eyes seen golden oranges by hundreds hanging on the trees in the streets of Spezzia, and would be glad to know how long they would remain in a like position in those of an English town, among "the most law-abiding people in the universe!"

But if the vicinity of the town has lost some of its ancient charm, if modern Spezzia reminds us too much, now of Woolwich, now of a "new neighborhood" on the outskirts of London, we have but to pass into the uplands, escaping from the neighborhood of forts, to find the same beauties as the mountains of this coast ever afford. There the sugar-cane and the vine, the fig and the olive cease, though the last so abounds that one might suppose it an indigenous growth; there the broken slopes 190] are covered with scrub oak and dwarf pine; there the myrtle blossoms, hardly ceasing in the winter months; there the strawberry-tree shows its waxen flowers, and is bright in season with its rich crimson berries. Even the villages add a beauty to the landscape—at any rate, when regarded from a distance; some are perched high up on the shoulders of hills, with distant outlooks over land and sea; others lie down by the water's edge in sheltered coves, beneath some ruined fort, which in olden time protected the fisher-folk from the raids of corsairs. Such are Terenza and Lerici, looking at each other across the waters of the little "Porto;" and many another village, in which grey and white and pink tinted houses blend into one pleasant harmony of color. For all this part of the coast is a series of rocky headlands and tiny bays, one succession of quiet nooks, to which the sea alone forms a natural highway. Not less irregular, not less sequestered, is the western coast of the Bay of Spezzia, which has been already mentioned. Here, at Porto Venere, a little village still carries us back in its name to classic times; and the old church on the rugged headland stands upon a site which was once not unfitly occupied by a temple of the seaborn goddess. The beauty of the scene is enhanced by a rocky wooded island, the Isola Palmeria, which rises steeply across a narrow strait; though the purpose to which it has been devoted—a prison for convicts—neither adds to its charm nor awakens pleasant reflections.

To some minds also the harbor itself, busy and bright as the scene often is, will suggest more painful thoughts than it did in olden days. For it is no preacher of "peace at any price," and is a daily witness that millennial days are still far away from the present epoch. 191] Here may be seen at anchor the modern devices for naval war: great turret-ships and ironclads, gunboats and torpedo launches—evils, necessary undoubtedly, but evils still; outward and visible signs of the burden of taxation, which is cramping the development of Italy, and is indirectly the heavy price which it has to pay for entering the ranks of the great Powers of Europe. These are less picturesque than the old line-of-battle ships, with their high decks, their tall masts, and their clouds of canvas; still, nothing can entirely spoil the harbor of Spezzia, and even these floating castles group pleasantly in the distance with the varied outline of hills and headlands, which is backed at last, if we look southward, by the grand outline of a group of veritable mountains—the Apuan Alps.

192]

IX

THE TUSCAN COAST

Shelley's last months at Lerici—Story of his death—Carrara and its marble quarries—Pisa—Its grand group of ecclesiastical buildings—The cloisters of the Campo Santo—Napoleon's life on Elba—Origin of the Etruscans—The ruins of Tarquinii—Civita Vecchia, the old port of Rome—Ostia.

THE Bay of Spezzia is defined sharply enough on its western side by the long, hilly peninsula which parts it from the Mediterranean, but as this makes only a small angle with the general trend of the coast-line, its termination is less strongly marked on the opposite side. Of its beauties we have spoken in an earlier article, but there is a little town at the southern extremity which, in connection with the coast below, has a melancholy interest to every lover of English literature. Here, at Lerici, Shelley spent what proved to be the last months of his life. The town itself, once strongly fortified by its Pisan owners against their foes of Genoa on the one side and Lucca on the other, is a picturesque spot. The old castle crowns a headland, guarding the little harbor and overlooking the small but busy town. At a short distance to the southeast is the Casa Magni, once a Jesuit seminary, which was occupied by Shelley. Looking across the beautiful gulf to the hills on its opposite shore and the island of Porto Venere, but a few miles 193] from the grand group of the Carrara mountains, in the middle of the luxuriant scenery of the Eastern Riviera, the house, though in itself not very attractive, was a fit home for a lover of nature. But Shelley's residence within its walls was too soon cut short. There are strange tales (like those told with bated breath by old nurses by the fireside) that as the closing hour approached the spirits of the unseen world took bodily form and became visible to the poet's eye; tales of a dark-robed figure standing by his bedside beckoning him to follow; of a laughing child rising from the sea as he walked by moonlight on the terrace, clapping its hands in glee; and of other warnings that the veil which parted him from the spirit world was vanishing away. Shelley delighted in the sea. On the 1st of July he left Lerici for Leghorn in a small sailing vessel. On the 8th he set out to return, accompanied only by his friend, Mr. Williams, and an English lad. The afternoon was hot and sultry, and as the sun became low a fearful squall burst upon the neighboring sea. What happened no one exactly knows, but they never came back to the shore. Day followed day, and the great sea kept its secret; but at last, on the 22d, the corpse of Shelley was washed up near Viareggio and that of Williams near Bocca Lerici, three miles away. It was not till three weeks afterwards that the body of the sailor lad came ashore. Probably the felucca had either capsized or had been swamped at the first break of the storm; but when it was found, some three months afterwards, men said that it looked as if it had been run down, and even more ugly rumors got abroad that this was no accident, but the work of some Italians, done in the hope of plunder, as it was expected that the party had in charge a considerable sum of money. 194] The bodies were at first buried in the sand with quicklime; but at that time the Tuscan law required "any object then cast ashore to be burned, as a precaution against plague," so, by the help of friends, the body of Shelley was committed to the flames "with fuel and frankincense, wine, salt, and oil, the accompaniments of a Greek cremation," in the presence of Byron Leigh Hunt, and Trelawny. The corpse of Williams had been consumed in like fashion on the previous day. "It was a glorious day and a splendid prospect; the cruel and calm sea before, the Appennines behind. A curlew wheeled close to the pyre, screaming, and would not be driven away; the flames arose golden and towering." The inurned ashes were entombed, as everyone knows, in the Protestant burial ground at Rome by the side of Keats' grave, near the pyramid of Cestius. Much as there was to regret in Shelley's life, there was more in his death, for such genius as his is rare, and if the work of springtide was so glorious, what might have been the summer fruitage?

As the Gulf of Spezzia is left behind, the Magra broadens out into an estuary as it enters the sea, the river which formed in olden days the boundary between Liguria and Etruria. Five miles from the coast, and less than half the distance from the river, is Sarzana, the chief city of the province, once fortified, and still containing a cathedral of some interest. It once gave birth to a Pope, Nicholas V., the founder of the Vatican Library, and in the neighborhood the family of the Buonapartes had their origin, a branch of it having emigrated to Corsica. Sarzana bore formerly the name of Luna Nova, as it had replaced another Luna which stood near to the mouth of the river. This was in ruins 195] even in the days of Lucan, and now the traveller from Saranza to Pisa sees only "a strip of low, grassy land intervening between him and the sea. Here stood the ancient city. There is little enough to see. Beyond a few crumbling tombs and a fragment or two of Roman ruins, nothing remains of Luna. The fairy scene described by Rutilus, so appropriate to the spot which bore the name of the virgin-queen of heaven, the 'fair white walls' shaming with their brightness the untrodden snow, the smooth, many-tinted rocks overrun with laughing lilies, if not the pure creation of the poet, have now vanished from the sight. Vestiges of an amphitheater, of a semicircular building which may be a theater, of a circus, a piscina, and fragments of columns, pedestals for statues, blocks of pavement and inscriptions, are all that Luna has now to show."

But all the while the grand group of the Carrara hills is in view, towering above a lowland region which rolls down towards the coast. A branch line now leads from Avenza, a small seaport town from which the marble is shipped, to the town of Carrara, through scenery of singular beauty. The shelving banks and winding slopes of the foreground hills are clothed with olives and oaks and other trees; here and there groups of houses, white and grey and pink, cluster around a campanile tower on some coign of vantage, while at the back rises the great mountain wall of the Apuan Alps, with its gleaming crags, scarred, it must be admitted, rather rudely and crudely by its marble quarries, though the long slopes of screes beneath these gashes in the more distant views almost resemble the Alpine snows. The situation of the town is delightful, for it stands at the entrance of a rapidly narrowing valley, in a sufficiently elevated 196]position to command a view of this exquisitely rich lowland as it shelves and rolls down to the gleaming sea. Nor is the place itself devoid of interest. One of its churches at least, S. Andrea, is a really handsome specimen of the architecture of this part of Italy in the thirteenth century, but the quarries dominate, and their products are everywhere. Here are the studios of sculptors and the ateliers of workmen. The fair white marble here, like silver in the days of Solomon, is of little account; it paves the street, builds the houses, serves even for the basest uses, and is to be seen strewn or piled up everywhere to await dispersal by the trains to more distant regions. Beyond the streets of Carrara, in the direction of the mountains, carriage roads no longer exist. Lanes wind up the hills here and there in rather bewildering intricacy, among vines and olive groves, to hamlets and quarries; one, indeed, of rather larger size and more fixity of direction, keeps for a time near the river, if indeed the stream which flows by Carrara be worthy of that name, except when the storms are breaking or the snows are melting upon the mountains. But all these lanes alike terminate in a quarry, are riven with deep ruts, ploughed up like a field by the wheels of the heavy wagons that bring down the great blocks of marble. One meets these grinding and groaning on their way, drawn by yokes of dove-colored oxen (longer than that with which Elisha was ploughing when the older prophet cast his mantle upon his shoulders), big, meek-looking beasts, mild-eyed and melancholy as the lotus-eaters. To meet them is not always an unmixed pleasure, for the lanes are narrow, and there is often no room to spare; how the traffic is regulated in some parts is a problem which I have not yet solved.

197]Carrara would come near to being an earthly paradise were it not for the mosquitos, which are said to be such that they would have made even the Garden of Eden untenable, especially to its first inhabitants. Of them, however, I cannot speak, for I have never slept in the town, or even visited it at the season when this curse of the earth is at its worst; but I have no hesitation in asserting that the mountains of Carrara are not less beautiful in outline than those of any part of the main chain of the Alps of like elevation, while they are unequalled in color and variety of verdure.

To Avenza succeeds Massa, a considerable town, beautifully situated among olive-clad heights, which are spotted with villas and densely covered with foliage. Like Carrara, it is close to the mountains, and disputes with Carrara for the reputation of its quarries. This town was once the capital of a duchy, Massa-Carrara, and the title was borne by a sister of Napoleon I. Her large palace still remains; her memory should endure, though not precisely in honor, for according to Mr. Hare, she pulled down the old cathedral to improve the view from her windows. But if Massa is beautiful, so is Pietra Santa, a much smaller town enclosed by old walls and singularly picturesque in outline. It has a fine old church, with a picturesque campanile, which, though slightly more modern than the church itself, has seen more than four centuries. The piazza, with the Town Hall, this church and another one, is a very characteristic feature. In the baptistry of one of the churches are some bronzes by Donatello. About half a dozen miles away, reached by a road which passes through beautiful scenery, are the marble quarries of Seravezza, which were first opened by Michael Angelo, and are still in full work. 198] There is only one drawback to travelling by railway in this region; the train goes too fast. Let it be as slow as it will, and it can be very slow, we can never succeed in coming to a decision as to which is the most picturesquely situated place or the most lovely view. Comparisons notoriously are odious, but delightful, as undoubtedly is the Riviera di Ponenta to me, the Riviera di Levante seems even more lovely.

After Pietra Santa, however, the scenery becomes less attractive, the Apuan Alps begin to be left behind, and a wider strip of plain parts the Apennines from the sea. This, which is traversed by the railway, is in itself flat, stale, though perhaps not unprofitable to the husbandman. Viareggio, mentioned on a previous page, nestles among its woods of oaks and pines, a place of some little note as a health resort; and then the railway after emerging from the forest strikes away from the sea, and crosses the marshy plains of the Serchio, towards the banks of the Arno.

It now approaches the grand group of ecclesiastical buildings which rise above the walls of Pisa. As this town lies well inland, being six miles from the sea, we must content ourselves with a brief mention. But a long description is needless, for who does not know of its cathedral and its Campo Santo, of its baptistry and its leaning tower? There is no more marvelous or complete group of ecclesiastical buildings in Europe, all built of the white marble of Carrara, now changed by age into a delicate cream color, but still almost dazzling in the glory of the mid-day sun, yet never so beautiful as when walls, arches, and pinnacles are aglow at its rising, or flushed at its setting. In the cloisters of the Campo Santo you may see monuments which range over nearly 199] five centuries, and contrast ancient and modern art; the frescoes on their walls, though often ill preserved, and not seldom of little merit, possess no small interest as illustrating medieval notions of a gospel of love and peace. Beneath their roof at the present time are sheltered a few relics of Roman and Etruscan days which will repay examination. The very soil also of this God's acre is not without an interest, for when the Holy Land was lost to the Christians, fifty-and-three shiploads of earth were brought hither from Jerusalem that the dead of Pisa might rest in ground which had been sanctified by the visible presence of their Redeemer. The cathedral is a grand example of the severe but stately style which was in favor about the end of the eleventh century, for it was consecrated in the year 1118. It commemorates a great naval victory won by the Pisans, three years before the battle of Hastings, and the columns which support the arches of the interior were at once the spoils of classic buildings and the memorials of Pisan victories. The famous leaning tower, though later in date, harmonizes well in general style with the cathedral. Its position, no doubt, attracts most attention, for to the eye it seems remarkably insecure, but one cannot help wishing that the settlement had never occurred, for the slope is sufficient to interfere seriously with the harmony of the group. The baptistry also harmonizes with the cathedral, though it was not begun till some forty years after the latter was completed, and not only was more than a century in building, but also received some ornamental additions in the fourteenth century. But though this cathedral group is the glory and the crown of Pisa, the best monument of its proudest days, there are other buildings of interest in the town itself; and the 200] broad quays which flank the Arno on each side, the Lungarno by name, which form a continuous passage from one end of the town to the other, together with the four bridges which link its older and newer part, are well worthy of more than a passing notice.

The land bordering the Arno between Pisa and its junction with the Mediterranean has no charm for the traveller, however it may commend itself to the farmer. A few miles south of the river's mouth is Leghorn, and on the eleven miles' journey by rail from it to Pisa the traveller sees as much, and perhaps more, than he could wish of the delta of the Arno. It is a vast alluvial plain, always low-lying, in places marshy; sometimes meadow land, sometimes arable. Here and there are slight and inconspicuous lines of dunes, very probably the records of old sea margins as the river slowly encroached upon the Mediterranean, which are covered sometimes with a grove of pines.

Leghorn is not an old town, and has little attraction for the antiquarian or the artist. In fact, I think it, for its size, the most uninteresting town, whether on the sea or inland, that I have entered in Italy. Brindisi is a dreary hole, but it has one or two objects of interest. Bari is not very attractive, but it has two churches, the architecture of which will repay long study; but Leghorn is almost a miracle of commonplace architecture and of dullness. Of course there is a harbor, of course there are ships, of course there is the sea, and all these possess a certain charm; but really this is about as small as it can be under the circumstances. The town was a creation of the Medici, "the masterpiece of that dynasty." In the middle of the sixteenth century it was an insignificant place, with between seven and eight hundred 201]inhabitants. But it increased rapidly when the princes of that family took the town in hand and made it a cave of Adullam, whither the discontented or oppressed from other lands might resort: Jews and Moors from Spain and Portugal, escaping from persecution; Roman Catholics from England, oppressed by the retaliatory laws of Elizabeth; merchants from Marseilles, seeking refuge from civil war. Thus fostered, it was soon thronged by men of talent and energy; it rapidly grew into an important center of commerce, and now the town with its suburbs contains nearly a hundred thousand souls.

Leghorn is intersected by canals, sufficiently so to have been sometimes called a "Little Venice," and has been fortified, but as the defenses belong to the system of Vauban, they add little to either the interest or the picturesqueness of the place. Parts of the walls and the citadel remain, the latter being enclosed by a broad water-ditch. The principal street has some good shops, and there are two fairly large piazzas; in one, bearing the name of Carlo Alberto, are statues of heroic size to the last Grand Duke and to his predecessor. The inscription on the latter is highly flattering; but that on the former states that the citizens had come to the conclusion that the continuance of the Austro-Lorenese dynasty was incompatible with the good order and happiness of Tuscany, and had accordingly voted union with Italy. The other piazza now bears Victor Emmanuel's name; in it are a building which formerly was a royal palace, the town hall, and the cathedral; the last a fair-sized church, but a rather plain specimen of the Renaissance style, with some handsome columns of real marble and a large amount of imitation, painted to match. There 202] are also some remains of the old fortifications, though they are not so very old, by the side of the inner or original harbor. As this in course of time proved too shallow for vessels of modern bulk, the Porto Nuovo, or outer harbor, was begun nearly fifty years since, and is protected from the waves by a semicircular mole. Among the other lions of the place, and they are all very small, is a statue of Duke Ferdinand I., one of the founders of Leghorn, with four Turkish slaves about the pedestal. The commerce of Leghorn chiefly consists of grain, cotton, wool, and silk, and is carried on mainly with the eastern ports of the Mediterranean. There is also an important shipbuilding establishment. It has, however, one link of interest with English literature, for in the Protestant cemetery was buried Tobias Smollet. There is a pleasant public walk by the sea margin outside the town, from where distant views of Elba and other islands are obtained.

The hilly ground south of the broad valley of the Arno is of little interest, and for a considerable distance a broad strip of land, a level plain of cornfields and meadow, intervenes between the sea and the foot of the hills. Here and there long lines of pine woods seem almost to border the former; the rounded spurs of the latter are thickly wooded, but are capped here and there by grey villages, seemingly surrounded by old walls, and are backed by the bolder outlines of the more distant Apennines. For many a long mile this kind of scenery will continue, this flat, marshy, dyke-intersected plain, almost without a dwelling upon it, though village after village is seen perched like epaulettes on the low shoulders of the hills. It is easy to understand why they are 203] placed in this apparently inconvenient position, for we are at the beginning of the Tuscan Maremma, a district scourged by malaria during the summer months, and none too healthy, if one may judge by the looks of the peasants, during any time of the year. But one cannot fail to observe that towards the northern extremity houses have become fairly common on this plain, and many of them are new, so that the efforts which have been made to improve the district by draining seem to have met with success. For some time the seaward views are very fine; comparatively near to the coast a hilly island rises steeply from the water and is crowned with a low round tower. Behind this lies Elba, a long, bold, hilly ridge, and far away, on a clear day, the great mountain mass of Corsica looms blue in the distance.

Elba has its interests for the geologist, its beauties for the lover of scenery. It has quarries of granite and serpentine, but its fame rests on its iron mines, which have been noted from very early times and from which fine groups of crystals of hematite are still obtained. So famed was it in the days of the Roman Empire as to call forth from Virgil the well-known line, "Insula inexhaustis chalybum generosa metallis." When these, its masters, had long passed away, it belonged in turn to Pisa, to Genoa, to Lucca, and, after others, to the Grand Duke Cosimo of Florence. Then it became Neapolitan, and at last French. As everyone knows, it was assigned to Napoleon after his abdication, and from May, 1814, to February, 1815, he enjoyed the title of King of Elba. Then, while discontent was deepening in France, and ambassadors were disputing round the Congress-table at

Vienna, he suddenly gave the slip to the vessels which 204] were watching the coast and landed in France to march in triumph to Paris, to be defeated at Waterloo, and to die at St. Helena.

The island is for the most part hilly, indeed almost mountainous, for it rises at one place nearly three thousand feet above the sea. The valleys and lower slopes are rich and fertile, producing good fruit and fair wine, and the views are often of great beauty. The fisheries are of some importance, especially that of the tunny. Porto Ferrajo, the chief town, is a picturesquely situated place, on the northern side, which still retains the forts built by Cosimo I. to defend his newly obtained territory, and the mansion, a very modest palace, inhabited by Napoleon.

"It must be confessed my isle is very little," was Napoleon's remark when for the first time he looked around over his kingdom from a mountain summit above Porto Ferrajo. Little it is in reality, for the island is not much more than fifteen miles long, and at the widest part ten miles across; and truly little it must have seemed to the man who had dreamed of Europe for his empire, and had half realized his vision. Nevertheless, as one of his historians remarks, "If an empire could be supposed to exist within such a brief space, Elba possesses so much both of beauty and variety as might constitute the scene of a summer night's dream of sovereignty."

At first he professed to be "perfectly resigned to his fate, often spoke of himself as a man politically dead, and claimed credit for what he said on public affairs, as having no remaining interest in them." A comment on himself in connection with Elba is amusing. He had been exploring his new domain in the company of Sir 205] Niel Campbell, and had visited, as a matter of course, the iron mines. On being informed that they were valuable, and brought in a revenue of about twenty thousand pounds per annum, "These then," he said, "are mine." But being reminded that he had conferred that revenue on the Legion of Honor, he exclaimed, "Where was my head when I made such a grant? But I have made many foolish decrees of that sort!"

He set to work at once to explore every corner of the island, and then to design a number of improvements and alterations on a scale which, had they been carried into execution with the means which he possessed, would have perhaps taken his lifetime to execute. The instinct of the conqueror was by no means dead within him; for "one of his first, and perhaps most characteristic, proposals was to aggrandize and extend his Lilliputian dominions by the occupation of an uninhabited island called Pianosa, which had been left desolate on account of the frequent descents of the corsairs. He sent thirty of his guards, with ten of the independent company belonging to the island, upon this expedition (what a contrast to those which he had formerly directed!), sketched out a plan of fortification, and remarked with complacency, 'Europe will say that I have already made a conquest.'"

He was after a short time joined on the island by his mother and his sister Pauline, and not a few of those who had once fought under his flag drifted gradually to Elba and took service in his guards. A plot was organized in France, and when all was ready Napoleon availed himself of the temporary absence of Sir Neil Campbell and of an English cruiser and set sail from Elba.

206]At four in the afternoon of Sunday, the 26th of February, "a signal gun was fired, the drums beat to arms, the officers tumbled what they could of their effects into flour-sacks, the men arranged their knapsacks, the embarkation began, and at eight in the evening they were under weigh." He had more than one narrow escape on his voyage; for he was hailed by a French frigate. His soldiers, however, had concealed themselves, and his captain was acquainted with the commander of the frigate, so no suspicions were excited. Sir Niel Campbell also, as soon as he found out what had happened, gave chase in a sloop of war, but only arrived in time to obtain a distant view of Napoleon's flotilla as its passengers landed.

Pianosa, the island mentioned above, lies to the north of Elba, and gets its name from its almost level surface; for the highest point is said to be only eighty feet above the sea. Considering its apparent insignificance, it figures more than could be expected in history. The ill-fated son of Marcus Agrippa was banished here by Augustus, at the instigation of Livia, and after a time was more effectually put out of the way, in order to secure the succession of her son Tiberius. We read also that it was afterwards the property of Marcus Piso, who used it as a preserve for peacocks, which were here as wild as pheasants with us. Some remnants of Roman baths still keep up the memory of its former masters. Long afterwards it became a bone of contention between Pisa and Genoa, and the latter State, on permitting the former to resume possession of these islands of the Tuscan Archipelago, stipulated that Pianosa should be left forever uncultivated and deserted. To secure the execution 207] of this engagement the Genoese stopped up all the wells with huge blocks of rock.

Capraja, a lovely island to the northwest of Elba, is rather nearer to Corsica than to Italy. Though less than four miles long, and not half this breadth, it rivals either in hilliness, for its ridges rise in two places more than fourteen hundred feet above the sea. Saracen, Genoese, Pisan, and Corsican have caused it in bygone times to lead a rather troubled existence, and even so late as 1796 Nelson knocked to pieces the fort which defended its harbor, and occupied the island.

"The 'stagno,' or lagoon, the sea-marsh of Strabo, is a vast expanse of stagnant salt water, so shallow that it may be forded in parts, yet never dried up by the hottest summer; the curse of the country around for the foul and pestilent vapour and the swarms of mosquitoes and other insects it generates at that season, yet compensating the inhabitants with an abundance of fish. The fishery is generally carried on at night, and in the way often practiced in Italy and Sicily, by harpooning the fish, which are attracted by a light in the prow of the boat. It is a curious sight on calm nights to see hundreds of these little skiffs or canoes wandering about with their lights, and making an ever-moving illumination on the surface of the lake."[2]

Elba seems to maintain some relation with the mainland by means of the hilly promontory which supports the houses of Piombino, a small town, chiefly interesting as being at no great distance from Populonia, an old Etruscan city of which some considerable ruins still 208]remain. Here, when the clans gathered to bring back the Tarquins to Rome, stood

"Sea-girt Populonia,
Whose sentinels descry

95

Sardinia's snowy mountain tops
Fringing the southern sky."

But long after Lars Porsenna of Clusium had retreated baffled from the broken bridge Populonia continued to be a place of some importance, for it has a castle erected in the Middle Ages. But now it is only a poor village; it retains, however, fragments of building recalling its Roman masters, and its walls of polygonal masonry carry us back to the era of the Etruscans.

It must not be forgotten that almost the whole of the coast line described in this chapter, from the river Magra to Civita Vecchia, belonged to that mysterious and, not so long since, almost unknown people, the Etruscans. Indeed, at one time their sway extended for a considerable distance north and south of these limits. Even now there is much dispute as to their origin, but they were a powerful and civilized race before Rome was so much as founded. They strove with it for supremacy in Italy, and were not finally subdued by that nation until the third century before our era. "Etruria was of old densely populated, not only in those parts which are still inhabited, but also, as is proved by remains of cities and cemeteries, in tracts now desolated by malaria and relapsed into the desert; and what is now the fen or the jungle, the haunt of the wild boar, the buffalo, the fox, and the noxious reptile, where man often dreads to stay his steps, and hurries away from a plague-stricken land, of old yielded rich harvests of corn, wine and oil, and 209] contained numerous cities mighty and opulent, into whose laps commerce poured the treasures of the East and the more precious produce of Hellenic genius. Most of these ancient sites are now without a habitant, furrowed yearly by the plough, or forsaken as unprofitable wilderness; and such as are still occupied are, with few exceptions, mere phantoms of their pristine greatness, mere villages in the place of populous cities. On every hand are traces of bygone civilization, inferior in quality, no doubt, to that which at present exists but much wider in extent and exerting far greater influence on the neighboring nations and on the destinies of the world."[3]

South of this headland the Maremma proper begins. Follonica, the only place for some distance which can be called a town, is blackened with smoke to an extent unusual in Italy, for here much of the iron ore from Elba is smelted. But the views in the neighborhood, notwithstanding the flatness of the marshy or scrub-covered plain, are not without a charm. The inland hills are often attractive; to the north lie the headland of Piombino and sea-girt Elba, to the south the promontory of Castiglione, which ends in a lower line of bluff capped by a tower, and the irregular little island of Formica. At Castiglione della Pescaia is a little harbor, once fortified, which exports wool and charcoal, the products of the neighboring hills. The promontory of Castiglione must once have been an island, for it is parted from the inland range by the level plain of the Maremma. Presently Grosseto, the picturesque capital of the Maremma, appears, perched on steeply rising ground above the enclosing plain, its sky-line relieved by a couple of low towers and a dome; it has been protected with defenses, which 210] date probably from late in the seventeenth century. Then, after the Omborne has been crossed, one of the rivers, which issue from the Apennines, the promontory of Talamone comes down to the sea, protecting the village of the same name. It is a picturesque little place, overlooked by an old castle, and the anchorage is sheltered by the island of S. Giglio, quiet enough now, but the guide-book tells us that here, two hundred and twenty-five years before the Christian era, the Roman troops disembarked and scattered an invading Gaulish army. But to the south lies another promontory on a larger scale than Tlamone; this is the Monte Argentario, the steep slopes of which are a mass of forests. The views on this part of the coast are exceptionally attractive. Indeed, it would be difficult to find anything more striking than the situation of Orbitello. The town lies at the foot of the mountain, for Argentario, since it rises full two thousand feet above the sea, and is bold in outline, deserves the name. It is almost separated from the mainland by a great salt-water lagoon, which is bounded on each side by two low and narrow strips of land. The best view is from the south, where we look across a curve of the sea to the town and to Monte Argentario with its double summit, which, as the border of the lagoon is so low, seems to be completely insulated.

Orbitello is clearly proved to have been an Etruscan town; perhaps, according to Mr. Dennis, founded by the Pelasgi, "for the foundations of the sea-wall which surrounds it on three sides are of vast polygonal blocks, just such as are seen in many ancient sites of central Italy (Norba, Segni, Palæstrina, to wit), and such as compose the walls of the neighboring Cosa." Tombs of Etruscan construction have also been found in the 211]immediate neighborhood of the city, on the isthmus of sand which connects it with the mainland. Others also have been found within the circuit of the walls. The tombs have been unusually productive; in part, no doubt, because they appear to have escaped earlier plunderers. Vases, numerous articles in bronze, and gold ornaments of great beauty have been found. Of the town itself, which from the distance has a very picturesque aspect, Mr. Dennis says: "It is a place of some size, having nearly six thousand inhabitants, and among Maremma towns is second only to Grosseto. It is a proof how much population tends to salubrity in the Maremma that Orbitello, though in the midst of a stagnant lagoon ten square miles in extent, is comparatively healthy, and has more than doubled its population in thirty years, while Telamona and other small places along the coast are almost deserted in summer, and the few people that remain become bloated like wine-skins or yellow as lizards." But the inland district is full of ruins and remnants of towns which in many cases were strongholds long before Romulus traced out the lines of the walls of Rome with his plough, if indeed that ever happened. Ansedonia, the ancient Cosa, is a very few miles away, Rusellæ, Saturnia, Sovana at a considerably greater distance; farther to the south rises another of these forest-clad ridges which, whether insulated by sea or by fen, are so characteristic of this portion of the Italian coast. Here the old walls of Corno, another Etruscan town, may be seen to rise above the olive-trees and the holm-oaks.

Beyond this the lowland becomes more undulating, and the foreground scenery a little less monotonous. Corneto now appears, crowning a gently shelving plateau at the end of a spur from the inland hills, which is 212] guarded at last by a line of cliffs. Enclosed by a ring of old walls, like Cortona, it "lifts to heaven a diadem of towers." In site and in aspect it is a typical example of one of the old cities of Etruria. Three hundred feet and more above the plain which parts it from the sea, with the gleaming water full in view on one side and the forest-clad ranges on the other, the outlook is a charming one, and the attractions within its walls are by no means slight. There are several old churches, and numerous Etruscan and Roman antiquities are preserved in the municipal museum. The town itself, however, is not of Etruscan origin, its foundation dates only from the Middle Ages; but on an opposite and yet more insulated hill the ruins of Tarquinii, one of the great cities of the Etrurian League, can still be traced; hardly less important than Veii, one of the most active cities in the endeavor to restore the dynasty of the Tarquins, it continued to flourish after it had submitted to Rome, but it declined in the dark days which followed the fall of the Empire, and never held up its head after it had been sacked by the Saracens, till at last it was deserted for Corneto, and met the usual fate of becoming a quarry for the new town. Only the remnants of buildings and of its defenses are now visible; but the great necropolis which lies to the southeast of the Corneto, and on the same spur with it, has yielded numerous antiquities. A romantic tale of its discovery, so late as 1823, is related in the guide-books. A native of Corneto in digging accidentally broke into a tomb. Through the hole he beheld the figure of a warrior extended at length, accoutred in full armour. For a few minutes he gazed astonished, then the form of the dead man vanished almost like a ghost, for it crumbled into dust under the influence of the 213] fresh air. Numerous subterranean chambers have since been opened; the contents, vases, bronzes, gems and ornaments, have been removed to museums or scattered among the cabinets of collectors, but the mural paintings still remain. They are the works of various periods from the sixth to the second or third century before the Christian era, and are indicative of the influence exercised by Greek art on the earlier inhabitants of Italy.

As the headland, crowned by the walls of Corneto, recedes into the distance a little river is crossed, which, unimportant as it seems, has a place in ecclesiastical legend, for we are informed that at the Torre Bertaldo, near its mouth, an angel dispelled St. Augustine's doubts on the subject of the Trinity. Then the road approaches the largest port on the coast since Leghorn was left. Civita Vecchia, as the name implies, is an old town, which, after the decline of Ostia, served for centuries as the port of Rome. It was founded by Trajan, and sometimes bore his name in olden time, but there is little or nothing within the walls to indicate so great an antiquity. It was harried, like so many other places near the coast, by the Saracens, and for some years was entirely deserted, but about the middle of the ninth century the inhabitants returned to it, and the town, which then acquired its present name, by degrees grew into importance as the temporal power of the Papacy increased. If there is little to induce the traveller to halt, there is not much more to tempt the artist. Civita Vecchia occupies a very low and faintly defined headland. Its houses are whitish in color, square in outline, and rather flat-topped. There are no conspicuous towers or domes. It was once enclosed by fortifications, built at various dates about the seventeenth century. These, however, have been removed on the 214] land side, but still remain fairly perfect in the neighborhood of the harbor, the entrance to which is protected by a small island, from which rises a low massive tower and a high circular pharos. There is neither animation nor commerce left in the place; what little there was disappeared when the railway was opened. It is living up to its name, and its old age cannot be called vigorous.

South of Civita Vecchia the coast region, though often monotonous enough, becomes for a time slightly more diversified. There is still some marshy ground, still some level plain, but the low and gently rolling hills which border the main mass of the Apennines extend at times down to the sea, and even diversify its coast-line, broken by a low headland. This now and again, as at Santa Marinella, is crowned by an old castle. All around much evergreen scrub is seen, here growing in tufts among tracts of coarse herbage, there expanding into actual thickets of considerable extent, and the views sometimes become more varied, and even pretty. Santa Severa, a large castle built of grey stone, with its keep-like group of higher towers on its low crag overlooking the sea, reminds us of some old fortress on the Fifeshire coast. Near this headland, so antiquarians say, was Pyrgos, once the port of the Etruscan town of Cære, which lies away among the hills at a distance of some half-dozen miles. Here and there also a lonely old tower may be noticed along this part of the coast. These recall to mind in their situation, though they are more picturesque in their aspect, the Martello Towers on the southern coast of England. Like them, they are a memorial of troublous times, when the invader was dreaded. They were erected to protect the Tuscan coast from the descents of 215] the Moors, who for centuries were the dread of the Mediterranean. Again and again these corsairs swooped down; now a small flotilla would attack some weakly defended town; now a single ship would land its boatload of pirates on some unguarded beach to plunder a neighboring village or a few scattered farms, and would retreat from the raid with a little spoil and a small band of captives, doomed to slavery, leaving behind smoking ruins and bleeding corpses. It is strange to think how long it was before perfect immunity was secured from these curses of the Mediterranean. England, whatever her enemies may say, has done a few good deeds in her time, and one of the best was when her fleet, under the command of Admiral Pellew, shattered the forts of Algiers and burnt every vessel of the pirate fleet.

The scenery for a time continues to improve. The oak woods become higher, the inland hills are more varied in outline and are forest-clad. Here peeps out a crag, there a village or a castle. At Palo a large, unattractive villa and a picturesque old castle overlook a fine line of sea-beach, where the less wealthy classes in Rome come down for a breath of fresh air in the hot days of summer. It also marks the site of Alsium, where, in Roman times, one or two personages of note, of whom Pompey was the most important, had country residences. For a time there is no more level plain; the land everywhere shelves gently to the sea, covered with wood or with coarse herbage. But before long there is another change, and the great plain of the Tiber opens out before our eyes, extending on one hand to the not distant sea, on the other to the hills of Rome. It is flat, dreary, and unattractive, at any rate in the winter season, as is the 216] valley of the Nen below Peterborough, or of the Witham beyond the Lincolnshire wolds. It is cut up by dykes, which are bordered by low banks. Here and there herds of mouse-colored oxen with long horns are feeding, and hay-ricks, round with low conical tops, are features more conspicuous than cottages. The Tiber winds on its serpentine course through this fenland plain, a muddy stream, which it was complimentary for the Romans to designate flavus, unless that word meant a color anything but attractive. One low tower in the distance marks the site of Porto, another that of Ostia and near the latter a long grove of pines is a welcome variation to the monotony of the landscape.

These two towns have had their day of greatness. The former, as its name implies, was once the port of Rome, and in the early days of Christianity was a place of note. It was founded by Trajan, in the neighborhood of a harbor constructed by Claudius; for this, like that of Ostia, which it was designed to replace, was already becoming choked up. But though emperors may propose, a river disposes, especially when its mud is in question. The port of Trajan has long since met with the same fate; it is now only a shallow basin two miles from the sea. Of late years considerable excavations have been made at Porto on the estate of Prince Tortonia, to whom the whole site belongs. The port constructed by Trajan was hexagonal in form; it was surrounded by warehouses and communicated with the sea by a canal. Between it and the outer or Claudian port a palace was built for the emperor, and the remains of the wall erected by Constantine to protect the harbor on the side of the land can still be seen. The only mediæval antiquities which

Porto contains are the old castle, which serves as the 217] episcopal palace, and the flower of the church of Santa Rufina, which is at least as old as the tenth century.

Ostia, which is a place of much greater antiquity than Porto, is not so deserted, though its star declined as that of the other rose. Founded, as some say, by Ancus Martius, it was the port of Rome until the first century of the present era. Then the silting up of its communication with the sea caused the transference of the commerce to Porto, but "the fame of the temple of Castor and Pollux, the numerous villas of the Roman patricians abundantly scattered along the coast, and the crowds of people who frequented its shores for the benefit of sea bathing, sustained the prosperity of the city for some time after the destruction of its harbor." But at last it went down hill, and then invaders came. Once it had contained eighty thousand inhabitants; in the days of the Medici it was a poor village, and the people eked out their miserable existences by making lime of the marbles of the ruined temples! So here the vandalism of peasants, even more than of patricians, has swept away many a choice relic of classic days. Villas and temples alike have been destroyed; the sea is now at a distance; Ostia is but a small village, "one of the most picturesque though melancholy sites near Rome," but during the greater part of the present century careful excavations have been made, many valuable art treasures have been unearthed, and a considerable portion of the ancient city has been laid bare. Shops and dwellings, temples and baths, the theater and the forum, with many a remnant of the ancient town, can now be examined, and numerous antiquities of smaller size are preserved in the museum at the old castle. This, with its strong bastions, its lofty circular tower and huge 218] machicolations, is a very striking object as it rises above the plain "massive and gray against the sky-line." It has been drawn by artists not a few, from Raffaelle, who saw it when it had not very long been completed, down to the present time.

219]

X

VENICE

Its early days—The Grand Canal and its palaces—Piazza of St. Mark—A Venetian funeral—The long line of islands—Venetian glass—Torcello, the ancient Altinum—Its two unique churches.

SO long as Venice is unvisited a new sensation is among the possibilities of life. There is no town like it in Europe. Amsterdam has its canals, but Venice is all canals; Genoa has its palaces, but in Venice they are more numerous and more beautiful. Its situation is unique, on a group of islands in the calm lagoon. But the Venice of to-day is not the Venice of thirty years ago. Even then a little of the old romance had gone, for a long railway viaduct had linked it to the mainland. In earlier days it could be reached only by a boat, for a couple of miles of salt water lay between the city and the marshy border of the Paduan delta. Now Venice is still more changed, and for the worse. The people seem more poverty-stricken and pauperized. Its buildings generally, especially the ordinary houses, look more dingy and dilapidated. The paint seems more chipped, the plaster more peeled, the brickwork more rotten; everything seems to tell of decadence, commercial and moral, rather than of regeneration. In the case of the more important structures, indeed, the effects of time have often 220] been more than repaired. Here a restoration, not seldom needless and ill-judged, has marred some venerable relic of olden days with crude patches of color, due to modern reproductions of the ancient and original work: the building has suffered, as it must be admitted not a few of our own most precious heirlooms have suffered, from the results of zeal untempered by discretion, and the destroyer has worked his will under the guise of the restorer.

The mosquito flourishes still in Venice as it did of yore. It would be too much to expect that the winged representative of the genus should thrive less in Italian freedom than under Austrian bondage, but something might have been done to extirpate the two-legged species. He is present in force in most towns south of the Alps, but he is nowhere so abundant or so exasperating as in Venice. If there is one place in one town in Europe where the visitor might fairly desire to possess his soul in peace and to gaze in thoughtful wonder, it is in the great piazza, in front of the façade, strange and beautiful as a dream, of the duomo of St. Mark. Halt there and try to feast on its marvels, to worship in silence and in peace. Vain illusion. There is no crowd of hurrying vehicles or throng of hurrying men to interfere of necessity with your visions (there are often more pigeons than people in the piazza), but up crawls a beggar, in garments vermin-haunted, whining for "charity"; down swoop would-be guides, volunteering useless suggestions in broken and barely intelligible English; from this side and from that throng vendors of rubbish, shell-ornaments, lace, paltry trinkets, and long ribands of photographic "souvenirs," appalling in their ugliness. He who can stand five minutes before San Marco and 221] retain a catholic love of mankind must indeed be blessed with a temper of much more than average amiability.

The death of Rome was indirectly the birth of Venice. Here in the great days of the Empire there was not, so far as we know, even a village. Invaders came, the Adriatic littoral was wrecked; its salvage is to be found among the islands of the lagoons. Aquileia went up in flames, the cities of the Paduan delta trembled before the hordes of savage Huns, but the islands of its coast held out a hope of safety. What in those days these camps of refuge must have been can be inferred from the islands which now border the mainland, low, marshy, overgrown by thickets, and fringed by reeds; they were unhealthy, but only accessible by intricate and difficult channels, and with little to tempt the spoiler. It was better to risk fever in the lagoons than to be murdered or driven off into slavery on the mainland. It was some time before Venice took the lead among these scattered settlements. It became the center of government in the year 810, but it was well-nigh two centuries before the Venetian State attained to any real eminence. Towards this, the first and perhaps the most important step was crushing the Istrian and Dalmatian pirates. This enabled the Republic to become a great "Adriatic and Oriental Company," and to get into their hands the carrying trade to the East. The men of Venice were both brave and shrewd, something like our Elizabethan forefathers, mighty on sea and land, but men of understanding also in the arts of peace. She did battle with Genoa for commercial supremacy, with the Turk for existence. She was too strong for the former, but the latter at last wore her out, and Lepanto was one of her latest and least fruitful triumphs. Still, it was not till the end of the 222] sixteenth century that a watchful eye could detect the symptoms of senile decay. Then Venice tottered gradually to its grave. Its slow disintegration occupied more than a century and a half; but the French Revolution indirectly caused the collapse of Venice, for its last doge abdicated, and the city was occupied by Napoleon in 1797. After his downfall Venetia was handed over to Austria, and found in the Hapsburg a harsh and unsympathetic master. It made a vain struggle for freedom in 1848, but was at last ceded to Italy after the Austro-Prussian war in 1866.

The city is built upon a group of islands; its houses are founded on piles, for there is no really solid ground. How far the present canals correspond with the original channels between small islands, how far they are artificial, it is difficult to say; but whether the original islets were few or many, there can be no doubt that they were formerly divided by the largest, or the Grand Canal, the Rio Alto or Deep Stream. This takes an S-like course, and parts the city roughly into two halves. The side canals, which are very numerous, for the town is said to occupy one hundred and fourteen islands, are seldom wider, often rather narrower than a by-street in the City of London. In Venice, as has often been remarked, not a cart or a carriage, not even a coster's donkey-cart, can be used. Streets enough there are, but they are narrow and twisting, very like the courts in the heart of London. The carriage, the cab, and the omnibus are replaced by the gondolas. These it is needless to describe, for who does not know them? One consequence of this substitution of canals for streets is that the youthful Venetian takes to the water like a young duck to a pond, and does not stand much on ceremony, in the matter of taking off 223] his clothes. Turn into a side canal on a summer's day, and one may see the younger members of a family all bathing from their own doorstep, the smallest one, perhaps, to prevent accidents, being tied by a cord to a convenient ring; nay, sometimes as we are wandering through one of the narrow calle (alleys) we hear a soft patter of feet, something damp brushes past, and a little Venetian lad, lithe and black-eyed, bare-legged, bare-backed, and all but bare-breeched, shoots past as he makes a short cut to his clothes across a block of buildings, round which he cannot yet manage to swim.

In such a city as Venice it is hard to praise one view above another. There is the noble sweep of the Grand Canal, with its palaces; there are many groups of buildings on a less imposing scale, but yet more picturesque, on the smaller canals, often almost every turn brings some fresh surprise; but there are two views which always rise up in my mind before all others whenever my thoughts turn to Venice, more especially as it used to be. One is the view of the façade of San Marco from the Piazza. I shall make no apology for quoting words which describe more perfectly than my powers permit the impressions awakened by this dream-like architectural conception. "Beyond those troops of ordered arches there rises a vision out of the earth, and all the great square seems to have opened from it in a kind of awe, that we may see it far away: a multitude of pillars and white domes clustered into a long, low pyramid of colored light, a treasure-heap, as it seems, partly of gold and partly of opal and mother-of-pearl, hollowed beneath into five great vaulted porches, ceiled with fair mosaic and beset with sculptures of alabaster, clear as amber and delicate as ivory; sculpture fantastic and involved, of 224] palm-leaves and lilies, and grapes and pomegranates, and birds clinging and fluttering among the branches, all twined together into an endless network of buds and plumes, and, in the midst of it, the solemn forms of angels, sceptered and robed to the feet, and leaning to each other across the gates, their features indistinct among the gleaming of the golden ground through the leaves beside them, interrupted and dim, like the morning light as it faded back among the branches of Eden when first its gates were angel-guarded long ago. And round the walls of the porches there are set pillars of variegated stones, jasper and porphyry, and deep-green serpentine, spotted with flakes of snow, and marbles that half refuse and half yield to the sunshine, Cleopatra-like, 'their bluest veins to kiss,' the shadow as it steals back from them revealing line after line of azure undulation, as a receding tide leaves the waved sand: their capitals rich with interwoven tracery, rooted knots of herbage, and drifting leaves of acanthus and vine, and mystical signs all beginning and ending in the Cross: and above them in the broad archivolts a continuous chain of language and of life, angels and the signs of heaven and the labors of men, each in its appointed season upon the earth; and above them another range of glittering pinnacles, mixed with white arches edged with scarlet flowers, a confusion of delight, among which the breasts of the Greek horses are seen blazing in their breadth of golden strength, and the St. Mark's lion, lifted on a blue field covered with stars, until at last, as if in ecstasy, the crests of the arches break into a marble foam, and toss themselves far into the blue sky in flashes and wreaths of sculptured spray, as if the breakers on the Lido shore 225] had been frost-bound before they fell, and the sea-nymphs had inlaid them with coral and amethyst."[4]

This is San Marco as it was. Eight centuries had harmed it little; they had but touched the building with a gentle hand and had mellowed its tints into tender harmony; now its new masters, cruel in their kindness, have restored the mosaics and scraped the marbles; now raw blotches and patches of crude color glare out in violent contrast with those parts which, owing to the intricacy of the carved work, or some other reason, it has been found impossible to touch. To look at St. Mark's now is like listening to some symphony by a master of harmony which is played on instruments all out of tune.

Photographs, pictures, illustrations of all kinds, have made St. Mark's so familiar to all the world that it is needless to attempt to give any description of its details.

It may suffice to say that the cathedral stands on the site of a smaller and older building, in which the relics of St. Mark, the tutelary saint of Venice, had been already enshrined. The present structure was begun about the year 976, and occupied very nearly a century in building. But it is adorned with the spoils of many a classic structure: with columns and slabs of marble and of porphyry and of serpentine, which were hewn from quarries in Greece and Syria, in Egypt and Libya, by the hands of Roman slaves, and decked the palaces and the baths, the temples and the theaters of Roman cities.

The inside of St. Mark's is not less strange and impressive, but hardly so attractive as the exterior. It is plain in outline and almost heavy in design, a Greek cross in plan, with a vaulted dome above the center and each 226] arm. Much as the exterior of St. Mark's owes to marble, porphyry, and mosaic, it would be beautiful if constructed only of grey limestone. This could hardly be said of the interior: take away the choice stones from columns and dado and pavement, strip away the crust of mosaic, those richly robed figures on ground of gold, from wall and from vault (for the whole interior is veneered with marbles or mosaics), and only a rather dark, massive building would remain, which would seem rather lower and rather smaller than one had been led to expect.

The other view in Venice which seems to combine best its peculiar character with its picturesque beauty may be obtained at a very short distance from St. Mark's. Leave the façade of which we have just spoken, the three great masts, with their richly ornamented sockets of bronze, from which, in the proud days of Venice, floated the banners of Candia, Cyprus, and the Morea; turn from the Piazza into the Piazzetta; leave on the one hand the huge Campanile, more huge than beautiful (if one may venture to whisper a criticism), on the other the sumptuous portico of the Ducal Palace; pass on beneath the imposing façade of the palace itself, with its grand colonnade; on between the famous columns, brought more than seven centuries since from some Syrian ruins, which bear the lion of St. Mark and the statue of St. Theodore, the other patron of the Republic; and then, standing on the Molo at the head of the Riva degli Schiavoni, look around; or better still, step down into one of the gondolas which are in waiting at the steps, and push off a few dozen yards from the land: then look back on the façade of the Palace and the Bridge of Sighs, along the busy quays of the Riva, towards the green trees of the Giardini Publici, look up the Piazzetta, between 227]the twin columns, to the glimpses of St. Mark's and the towering height of the Campanile, along the façade of the Royal Palace, with the fringe of shrubbery below contrasting pleasantly with all these masses of masonry, up the broad entrance to the Grand Canal, between its rows of palaces, across it to the great dome of Santa Maria della Salute and the Dogana della Mare, with its statue of Fortune (appropriate to the past rather than to the present) gazing out from its seaward angle. Beyond this, yet farther away, lies the Isola San Giorgio, a group of plain buildings only, a church, with a dome simple in outline and a brick campanile almost without adornment, yet the one thing in Venice, after the great group of St. Mark; this is a silent witness to its triumphs in presses itself on the mind. From this point of view Venice rises before our eyes in its grandeur and in its simplicity, in its patrician and its plebeian aspects, as "a sea Cybele, fresh from ocean, throned on her hundred isles ... a ruler of the waters and their powers."

But to leave Venice without a visit to the Grand Canal would be to leave the city with half the tale untold. Its great historic memories are gathered around the Piazza of St. Mark; this is a silent witness to its triumphs in peace and in war, to the deeds noble and brave, of its rulers. But the Grand Canal is the center of its life, commercial and domestic; it leads from its quays to its Exchange, from the Riva degli Schiavoni and the Dogana della Mare to the Rialto. It is bordered by the palaces of the great historic families who were the rulers and princes of Venice, who made the State by their bravery and prudence, who destroyed it by their jealousies and self-seeking. The Grand Canal is a genealogy of Venice, illustrated and engraved on stone. As one 228] glides along in a gondola, century after century in the history of domestic architecture, from the twelfth to the eighteenth, slowly unrolls itself before us. There are palaces which still remain much as they were of old, but here and there some modern structure, tasteless and ugly, has elbowed for itself a place among them; not a few, also, have been converted into places of business, and are emblazoned with prominent placards proclaiming the trade of their new masters, worthy representatives of an age that is not ashamed to daub the cliffs of the St. Gothard with the advertisements of hotels and to paint its boulders for the benefit of vendors of chocolate!

But in the present era one must be thankful for anything that is spared by the greed of wealth and the vulgarity of a "democracy." Much of old Venice still remains, though little steamers splutter up and down the Grand Canal, and ugly iron bridges span its waters, both, it must be admitted, convenient, though hideous; still the gondolas survive; still one hears at every corner the boatman's strange cry of warning, sometimes the only sound except the knock of the oar that breaks the silence of the liquid street. Every turn reveals something quaint and old-world. Now it is a market-boat, with its wicker panniers hanging outside, loaded with fish or piled with vegetables from one of the more distant islets; now some little bridge, now some choice architectural fragment, a doorway, a turret, an oriel, or a row of richly ornate windows, now a tiny piazzetta leading up to the façade and campanile of a more than half-hidden church; now the marble enclosure of a well. Still the water-carriers go about with buckets of hammered copper hung at each end of a curved pole; still, though more rarely, some quaint costume may be seen in the calle; still the dark 229] shops in the narrow passages are full of goods strange to the eye, and bright in their season with the flowers and fruits of an Italian summer; still the purple pigeons gather in scores at the wonted hour to be fed on the Piazza of St. Mark, and, fearless of danger, convert the distributor of a pennyworth of maize into a walking dovecot.

Still Venice is delightful to the eyes (unhappily not always so to the nose in many a nook and corner) notwithstanding the pressure of poverty and the wantonness of restorers. Perchance it may revive and yet see better days (its commerce is said to have increased since 1866); but if so, unless a change comes over the spirit of the age, the result will be the more complete destruction of all that made its charm and its wonder; so this chapter may appropriately be closed by a brief sketch of one scene which seems in harmony with the memories of its departed greatness, a Venetian funeral. The dead no longer rest among the living beneath the pavement of the churches: the gondola takes the Venetian "about the streets" to the daily business of life; it bears him away from his home to the island cemetery. From some narrow alley, muffled by the enclosing masonry, comes the sound of a funeral march; a procession emerges on to the piazzetta by the water-side; the coffin is carried by long-veiled acolytes and mourners with lighted torches, accompanied by a brass band with clanging cymbals. A large gondola, ornamented with black and silver, is in waiting at the nearest landing place; the band and most of the attendants halt by the water-side; the coffin is placed in the boat, the torches are extinguished; a wilder wail of melancholy music, a more resonant clang of the cymbals, sounds the last farewell to home and its 230]pleasures and its work; the oars are dipped in the water, and another child of Venice is taken from the city of the living to the city of the dead.

A long line of islands completely shelters Venice from the sea, so that the waters around its walls are very seldom ruffled into waves. The tide also rises and falls but little, not more than two or three feet, if so much. Thus no banks of pestiferous mud are laid bare at low water by the ebb and flow, and yet some slight circulation is maintained in the canals, which, were it not for this, would be as intolerable as cesspools. Small boats can find their way over most parts of the lagoon, where in many places a safe route has to be marked out with stakes, but for large vessels the channels are few. A long island, Malamocco by name, intervenes between Venice and the Adriatic, on each side of which are the chief if not the only entrances for large ships. At its northern end is the sandy beach of the Lido, a great resort of the Venetians, for there is good sea-bathing. But except this, Malamocco has little to offer; there is more interest in other parts of the lagoon. At the southern end, some fifteen miles away, the old town of Chioggia is a favorite excursion. On the sea side the long fringe of narrow islands, of which Malamocco is one, protected by massive walls, forms a barrier against the waves of the Adriatic. On the land side is the dreary fever-haunted region of the Laguna Morta, like a vast fen, beyond which rise the serrate peaks of the Alps and the broken summits of the Euganean Hills. The town itself, the Roman Fossa Claudia, is a smaller edition of Venice, joined like it to the mainland by a bridge. If it has fewer relics of architectural value it has suffered less from modern changes, and has retained much more of its old-world character.

231]Murano, an island or group of islands, is a tiny edition of Venice, and a much shorter excursion, for it lies only about a mile and a half away to the north of the city. Here is the principal seat of the workers in glass; here are made those exquisite reproductions of old Venetian glass and of ancient mosaic which have made the name of Salviati noted in all parts of Europe. Here, too, is a cathedral which, though it has suffered from time, neglect and restoration, is still a grand relic. At the eastern end there is a beautiful apse enriched by an arcade and decorated with inlaid marbles, but the rest of the exterior is plain. As usual in this part of Italy (for the external splendor of St. Mark's is exceptional) all richness of decoration is reserved for the interior. Here columns of choice stones support the arches; there is a fine mosaic in the eastern apse, but the glory of Murano is its floor, a superb piece of opus Alexandrinum, inlaid work of marbles and porphyries, bearing date early in the eleventh century, and richer in design than even that at St. Mark's, for peacocks and other birds, with tracery of strange design, are introduced into its patterns.

But there is another island beyond Murano, some half-dozen miles away from Venice, which must not be left unvisited. It is reached by a delightful excursion over the lagoon, among lonely islands thinly inhabited, the garden grounds of Venice, where they are not left to run wild with rank herbage or are covered by trees. This is Torcello, the ancient Altinum. Here was once a town of note, the center of the district when Venice was struggling into existence. Its houses now are few and ruinous; the ground is half overgrown with populars and acacias and pomegranates, red in summer-time with scarlet flowers. But it possesses two churches which, 232] though small in size are almost unique in their interest, the duomo, dedicated to St. Mary, and the church of Sta. Fosca. They stand side by side, and are linked together by a small cloister. The former is a plain basilica which retains its ancient plan and arrangement almost intact. At one end is an octagonal baptistry, which, instead of being separated from the cathedral by an atrium or court, is only divided from it by a passage. The exterior of the cathedral is plain; the interior is not much more ornate. Ancient columns, with quaintly carved capitals supporting stilted semicircular arches, divide the aisles from the nave. Each of these has an apsidal termination. The high altar stands in the center of the middle one, and behind it, against the wall, the marble throne of the bishop is set up on high, and is approached by a long flight of marble steps. On each side, filling up the remainder of the curve, six rows of steps rise up like the seats of an amphitheater, the places of the attendant priests. The chancel, true to its name, is formed by enclosing a part of the nave with a low stone wall and railing. Opinions differ as to the date of this cathedral. According to Fergusson it was erected early in the eleventh century, but it stands on the site of one quite four centuries older, and reproduces the arrangement of its predecessor if it does not actually

106

incorporate portions of it. Certainly the columns and capitals in the nave belong, as a rule, to an earlier building. Indeed, they have probably done duty more than once, and at least some of them were sculptured before the name of Attila had been heard of in the delta of the North Italian rivers.

The adjoining church of Sta. Fosca is hardly less interesting. An octagonal case, with apses at the eastern end, supports a circular drum, which is covered by a low 233] conical roof, and a cloister or corridor surrounds the greater part of the church. This adds much to the beauty of the design, the idea, as Fergusson remarks, being evidently borrowed from the circular colonnades of the Roman temples. He also justly praises the beauty of the interior. In this church also, which in its present condition is not so old as the cathedral, the materials of a much older building or buildings have been employed. But over these details or the mosaics in the cathedral we must not linger, and must only pause to mention the curious stone chair in the adjacent court which bears the name of the throne of Attila; perhaps, like the chair of the Dukes of Corinthia, it was the ancient seat of the chief magistrate of the island.

234]

XI

ALEXANDRIA

The bleak and barren shores of the Nile Delta—Peculiar shape of the city—Strange and varied picture of Alexandrian street life—The Place Mehemet Ali—Glorious panorama from the Cairo citadel—Pompey's Pillar—The Battle of the Nile—Discovery of the famous inscribed stone at Rosetta—Port Said and the Suez Canal.

IT is with a keen sense of disappointment that the traveller first sights the monotonous and dreary-looking Egyptian sea-board. The low ridges of desolate sandhills, occasionally broken by equally unattractive lagunes, form a melancholy contrast to the beautiful scenery of the North African littoral farther west, which delighted his eyes a short time before, while skirting the Algerian coast. What a change from the thickly-wooded hills gently sloping upwards from the water's edge to the lower ridges of the Atlas range, whose snow-clad peaks stand out clear in the brilliant atmosphere, the landscape diversified with cornfields and olive groves, and thickly studded with white farmhouses, looking in the distance but white specks, and glittering like diamonds under the glowing rays of the sun. Now, instead of all this warmth of color and variety of outline, one is confronted by the bleak and barren shores of the Nile Delta.

If the expectant traveller is so disenchanted with his 235] first view of Egypt from the sea, still greater is his disappointment as the ship approaches the harbor. This bustling and painfully modern-looking town—the city of the great Alexander, and the gate of that land of oriental romance and fascinating association—might, but for an occasional palm-tree or minaret standing out among the mass of European buildings, be mistaken for some flourishing European port, say a Marseilles or Havre plumped down on the Egyptian plain.

But though we must not look for picturesque scenery and romantic surroundings in this thriving port, there is yet much to interest the antiquarian and the "intelligent tourist" in this classic district. The Delta sea-board was for centuries the battle-ground of the Greek and Roman Empires, and the country between Alexandria and Port Said is strewed with historic sites.

Alexandria itself, though a much Europeanized and a hybrid sort of city, is not without interest. It has been rather neglected by Egyptian travel writers, and consequently by the tourist, who rarely strikes out a line for himself. It is looked upon too much as the port of Cairo, just as Leghorn is of Pisa and Florence, and visitors usually content themselves with devoting to it but one day, and then rushing off by train to Cairo.

It would be absurd, of course, to compare Alexandria, in point of artistic, antiquarian, and historical interest, to this latter city; though, as a matter of fact, Cairo is a modern city compared to the Alexandria of Alexander; just as Alexandria is but of mushroom growth contrasted with Heliopolis, Thebes, Memphis, or the other dead cities of the Nile Valley of which traces still remain. It has often been remarked that the ancient city has bequeathed nothing but its ruins and its name to 236] Alexandria of to-day. Even these ruins are deplorably scanty, and most of the sites are mainly conjectural. Few vestiges remain of the architectural splendor of the Ptolemaic dynasty. Where are now the 4,000 palaces, the 4,000 baths, and the 400 theaters, about which the conquering general Amru boasted to his master, the Caliph Omar? What now remains of the magnificent temple of Serapis, towering over the city on its platform of one hundred steps? Though there are scarcely any traces of the glories of ancient Alexandria, once the second city of the Empire, yet the recollection of its splendors has not died out, and to the thoughtful traveller this city of memories has its attractions. Here St. Mark preached the Gospel and suffered martyrdom, and here Athanasius opposed in warlike controversy the Arian heresies. Here for many centuries were collected in this center of Greek learning and culture the greatest intellects of the civilized world. Here Cleopatra, "vainqueur des vainqueurs du monde," held Antony willing captive, while Octavius was preparing his legions to crush him. Here Amru conquered, and here Abercrombie fell. Even those whose tastes do not incline them to historical or theological researches are familiar, thanks to Kingsley's immortal romance, with the story of the noble-minded Hypatia and the crafty and ambitious Cyril, and can give rein to their imagination by verifying the sites of the museum where she lectured, and the Cæsarum where she fell a victim to the atrocious zeal of Peter the Reader and his rabble of fanatical monks.

The peculiar shape of the city, built partly on the Pharos Island and peninsula, and partly on the mainland, is due, according to the chroniclers, to a patriotic whim 237] of the founder, who planned the city in the form of a chlamys, the short cloak or tunic worn by the Macedonian soldiers. The modern city, though it has pushed its boundaries a good way to the east and west, still preserves this curious outline, though to a non-classical mind it rather suggests a star-fish. Various legends are extant to account for the choice of this particular spot for a Mediterranean port. According to the popular version, a

108

venerable seer appeared to the Great Conqueror in a dream, and quoted those lines of the Odyssey which describe the one sheltered harbor on the northern coast of Egypt:—"a certain island called Pharos, that with the high-waved sea is washed, just against Egypt." Acting on this supernatural hint, Alexander decided to build his city on that part of the coast to which the Pharos isle acted as a natural breakwater, and where a small Greek fishing settlement was already established, called Rhacotis. The legend is interesting, but it seems scarcely necessary to fall back on a mythical story to account for the selection of this site. The two great aims of Alexander were the foundation of a center for trade, and the extension of commerce, and also the fusion of the Greek and Roman nations. For the carrying out of these objects, the establishment of a convenient sea-port with a commanding position at the mouth of the Nile was required. The choice of a site a little west of the Nile mouths was, no doubt, due to his knowledge of the fact that the sea current sets eastward, and that the alluvial soil brought down by the Nile would soon choke a harbor excavated east of the river, as had already happened at Pelusium. It is this alluvial wash which has rendered the harbors of Rosetta and Damietta almost useless for vessels of any draught, 238] and at Port Said the accumulation of sand necessitates continuous dredging in order to keep clear the entrance of the Suez Canal.

A well-known writer on Egypt has truly observed that there are three Egypts to interest the traveller. The Egypt of the Pharoahs and the Bible, the Egypt of the Caliphates and the "Arabian Nights," and the Egypt of European commerce and enterprise. It is to this third stage of civilization that the fine harbor of Alexandria bears witness. Not only is it of interest to the engineer and the man of science, but it is also of great historic importance. It serves as a link between ancient and modern civilization. The port is Alexander the Great's best monument—"si quæris monumentum respice." But for this, Alexandria might now be a little fishing port of no more importance than the little Greek fishing village, Rhacotis, whose ruins lie buried beneath its spacious quays. It is not inaccurate to say that the existing harbor is the joint work of Alexander and English engineers of the present century. It was originally formed by the construction of a vast mole (Heptastadion) joining the island of Pharos to the mainland; and this stupendous feat of engineering, planned and carried out by Alexander, has been supplemented by the magnificent breakwater constructed by England in 1872, at a cost of over two and a half millions sterling. After Marseilles, Malta, and Spezzia, it is perhaps the finest port in the Mediterranean, both on account of its natural advantages as a haven, and by reason of the vast engineering works mentioned above. The western harbor (formerly called Eunostos or "good home sailing") of which we are speaking—for the eastern, or so-called new harbor, is choked with sand and given up to native craft—has only 239] one drawback in the dangerous reef at its entrance, and which should have been blasted before the breakwater and the other engineering works were undertaken. The passage through the bar is very intricate and difficult, and is rarely attempted in very rough weather. The eastern harbor will be of more interest to the artist, crowded as it is with the picturesque native craft and dahabyehs with their immense lateen sails. The traveller, so disgusted with the modern aspect of the city from the western harbor, finds some consolation here, and begins to feel that he is really in the East. Formerly this harbor was alone available for foreign ships, the bigoted Moslems objecting to the "Frankish dogs" occupying their best haven. This restriction has, since the time of Mehemet Ali, been removed, greatly to the advantage of Alexandrian trade.

109

During the period of Turkish misrule—when Egypt under the Mamelukes, though nominally a vilayet of the Ottoman Empire, was practically under the dominion of the Beys—the trade of Alexandria had declined considerably, and Rosetta had taken away most of its commerce. When Mehemet Ali, the founder of the present dynasty, rose to power, his clear intellect at once comprehended the importance of this ancient emporium, and the wisdom of Alexander's choice of a site for the port which was destined to become the commercial center of three continents.

Mehemet is the creator of modern Alexandria. He deepened the harbor, which had been allowed to be choked by the accumulation of sand, lined it with spacious quays, built the massive forts which protect the coast, and restored the city to its old commercial importance, by putting it into communication with the Nile through the medium of the Mahmoudiyeh Canal. This vast 240] undertaking was only effected with great loss of life. It was excavated by the forced labor of 250,000 peasants, of whom some 20,000 died from the heat and the severe toil.

On landing from the steamer the usual scrimmage with Arab porters, Levantine hotel touts, and Egyptian donkey boys, will have to be endured by the traveller. He may perhaps be struck, if he has any time or temper left for reflection at all, with the close connection between the English world of fashion and the donkey, so far at least as nomenclature is concerned, each animal being named after some English celebrity. The inseparable incidents of disembarkation at an Eastern port are, however, familiar to all who have visited the East; and the same scenes are repeated at every North African port, from Tangier to Port Said, and need not be further described.

The great thoroughfare of Alexandria, a fine street running in a straight line from the western gate of the city to the Place Mehemet Ali, is within a few minutes of the quay. A sudden turn and this strange mingling of Eastern and Western life bursts upon the spectator's astonished gaze. This living diorama, formed by the brilliant and ever-shifting crowd, is in its way unique. A greater variety of nationalities is collected here than even in Constantinople or cosmopolitan Algiers. Let us stand aside and watch this motley collection of all nations, kindreds, and races pouring along this busy highway. The kaleidoscopic variety of brilliant color and fantastic costume seems at first a little bewildering. Solemn and impassive-looking Turks gently ambling past on gaily caparisoned asses, grinning negroes from the Nubian hills, melancholy-looking fellahs in their scanty blue kaftans, cunning-featured Levantines, green-turbaned 241]Shereefs, and picturesque Bedouins from the desert stalking along in their flowing bernouses, make up the mass of this restless throng. Interspersed, and giving variety of color to this living kaleidoscope, gorgeously-arrayed Jews, fierce-looking Albanians, their many-colored sashes bristling with weapons, and petticoated Greeks. Then, as a pleasing relief to this mass of color, a group of Egyptian ladies glide past, "a bevy of fair damsels richly dight," no doubt, but their faces, as well as their rich attire, concealed under the inevitable yashmak surmounting the balloon-like trousers. Such are the elements in this mammoth masquerade which make up the strange and varied picture of Alexandrian street life. And now we may proceed to visit the orthodox sights, but we have seen the greatest sight Alexandria has to show us.

The Place Mehemet Ali, usually called for the sake of brevity the Grand Square, is close at hand. This is the center of the European quarter, and round it are collected the banks, consular offices, and principal shops. This square, the focus of the life of modern Alexandria, is appropriately named after the founder of the present dynasty, and the creator of the Egypt of to-day. To this great ruler, who at one time bid fair to become the founder, not only of an independent kingdom, but of a great Oriental Empire, Alexandria owes much of its prosperity and commercial importance. The career of Mehemet Ali is interesting and romantic. There is a certain similarity between his history and that of Napoleon I., and the coincidence seems heightened when we remember that they were born in the same year. Each, rising from an obscure position, started as an adventurer on foreign soil, and each rose to political eminence by force of arms. Unlike Napoleon, however, in one important 242] point, Mehemet Ali founded a dynasty which still remains in power, in spite of the weakness and incapacity of his successors. To Western minds, perhaps, his great claim to hold a high rank in the world's history lies in his efforts to introduce European institutions and methods of civilization, and to establish a system of government opposed to Mohammedan instincts. He created an army and navy which were partly based on European models, stimulated agriculture and trade, and organized an administrative and fiscal system which did much towards putting the country on a sound financial footing. The great blot of his reign was no doubt the horrible massacre of the Mameluke Beys, and this has been the great point of attack by his enemies and detractors. It is difficult to excuse this oriental example of a coup d'état, but it must be remembered that the existence of this rebellious element was incompatible with the maintenance of his rule, and that the peace of the country was as much endangered by the Mameluke Beys as was that of the Porte by the Janissaries a few years later, when a somewhat similar atrocity was perpetrated.

In the middle of the square stands a handsome equestrian statue of Mehemet Ali which is, in one respect, probably unique. The Mohammedan religion demands the strictest interpretation of the injunction in the decalogue against making "to thyself any craven image," and consequently a statue to a follower of the creed of Mahomet is rarely seen in a Mohammedan country. The erection of this particular monument was much resented by the more orthodox of the Mussulman population of Alexandria, and the religious feelings of the mob manifested themselves in riots and other hostile demonstrations. Not only representations in stone or metal, but any kind of 243] likeness of the human form is thought impious by Mohammedans. They believe that the author will be compelled on the Resurrection Day to indue with life the sacrilegious counterfeit presentment. Tourists in Egypt who are addicted to sketching, or who dabble in photography, will do well to remember these conscientious scruples of the Moslem race, and not let their zeal for bringing back pictorial mementoes of their travels induce them to take "snapshots" of mosque interiors, for instance. In Egypt, no doubt, the natives have too wholesome a dread of the Franks to manifest their outraged feelings by physical force, but still it is ungenerous, not to say unchristian, to wound people's religious prejudices. In some other countries of North Africa, notably in the interior of Morocco or Tripoli, promiscuous photography might be attended with disagreeable results, if not a certain amount of danger. A tourist would find a Kodak camera, even with all the latest improvements, a somewhat inefficient weapon against a mob of fanatical Arabs.

That imposing pile standing out so prominently on the western horn of Pharos is the palace of Ras-et-Teen, built by Mehemet Ali, and restored in execrable taste by his grandson, the ex-Khedive Ismail. Seen from the ship's side, the palace has a rather striking appearance. The exterior, however, is the best part of it, as the ornate and gaudy interior contains little of interest. From the upper balconies there is a good view of the harbor, and the gardens are well worth visiting. They are prettily laid out, and among many other trees, olives may be seen, unknown in any other part of the Delta. The decorations and appointments of the interior are characterized by a tawdry kind of magnificence. The incongruous mixture of modern French embellishments and oriental splendor 244] gives the saloons a meretricious air, and the effect is bizarre and unpleasing. It is a relief to get away from such obtrusive evidences of the ex-Khedive's decorative tastes, by stepping out on the balcony. What a forest of masts meets the eye as one looks down on the vast harbor; the inner one, a "sea within a sea," crowded with vessels bearing the flags of all nations, and full of animation and movement.

The view is interesting, and makes one realize the commercial importance of this great emporium of trade, the meeting-place of the commerce of three continents, yet it does not offer many features to distinguish it from a view of any other thriving port.

For the best view of the city and the surrounding country we must climb the slopes of Mount Caffarelli to the fort which crowns the summit, or make our way to the fortress Kom-el-Deek on the elevated ground near the Rosetta Gate. Alexandria, spread out like a map, lies at our feet. At this height the commonplace aspect of a bustling and thriving seaport, which seems on a close acquaintance to be Europeanized and modernized out of the least resemblance to an oriental city, is changed to a prospect of some beauty. At Alexandria, even more than at most cities of the East, distance lends enchantment to the view. From these heights the squalid back streets and the bustling main thoroughfares look like dark threads woven into the web of the city, relieved by the white mosques, with their swelling domes curving inward like fan palms towards the crescents flashing in the rays of the sun, and their tall graceful minarets piercing the smokeless and cloudless atmosphere. The subdued roar of the busy streets and quays is occasionally varied by the melodious cry of the muezzin. Then looking northward 245] one sees the clear blue of the Mediterranean, till it is lost in the hazy horizon. To the west and south the placid waters of the Mareotis Lake, in reality a shallow and insalubrious lagoon, but to all appearances a smiling lake, which, with its water fringed by the low-lying sand dunes, reminds the spectator of the peculiar beauties of the Norfolk Broads.

Looking south beyond the lake lies the luxuriant plain of the Delta. The view may not be what is called picturesque, but the scenery has its special charm. The country is no doubt flat and monotonous, but there is no monotony of color in this richly cultivated plain.

Innumerable pens have been worn out in comparison and simile when describing the peculiar features of this North African Holland. To some this huge market garden with its network of canals, simply suggests a chess-board. Others are not content with these prosaic comparisons, and their more fanciful metaphor likens the country to a green robe interwoven with silver threads, or to a seven-ribbed fan, the ribs being of course the seven mouths of the Nile. Truth to tell, though, the full force of this fanciful image would be more felt by a spectator who is enjoying that glorious panorama from the Cairo citadel, as the curious triangular form of the Delta is much better seen from that point than from Alexandria at the base of the triangle.

One may differ as to the most appropriate metaphors, but all must agree that there are certain elements of beauty about the Delta landscape. Seen, as most tourists do see it, in winter or spring, the green fields of waving corn and barley, the meadows of water-melons and cucumbers, the fields of pea and purple lupin one mass of colors, interspersed with the palm-groves and white 246] minarets, which mark the site of the almost invisible mud villages, and intersected thickly with countless canals and trenches that in the distance look like silver threads, and suggest Brobdignagian filigree work, or the delicate tracery of King Frost on our window-panes, the view is impressive and not without beauty.

In the summer and early autumn, especially during August and September when the Nile is at its height, the view is more striking though hardly so beautiful. Then it is that this Protean country offers its most impressive aspect. The Delta becomes an inland archipelago studded with green islands, each island crowned with a white-mosqued village, or conspicuous with a cluster of palms. The Nile and its swollen tributaries are covered with huge-sailed dahabyehs, which give life and variety to the watery expanse.

Alexandria can boast of few "lions" as the word is usually understood, but of these by far the most interesting is the column known by the name of Pompey's Pillar. Everyone has heard of the famous monolith, which is as closely associated in people's minds with Alexandria as the Colosseum is with Rome, or the Alhambra with Granada. It has, of course, no more to do with the Pompey of history (to whom it is attributed by the unlettered tourist) than has Cleopatra's Needle with that famous Queen, the "Serpent of Old Nile"; or Joseph's Well at Cairo with the Hebrew Patriarch. It owes its name to the fact that a certain prefect, named after Cæsar's great rival, erected on the summit of an existing column a statue in honor of the horse of the Roman Emperor Diocletian. There is a familiar legend which has been invented to account for the special reason of its erection, which guide-book compilers are very fond of. 247] According to this story, this historic animal, through an opportune stumble, stayed the persecution of the Alexandrian Christians, as the tyrannical emperor had sworn to continue the massacre till the blood of the victims reached his horse's knees. Antiquarians and Egyptologists are, however, given to scoffing at the legend as a plausible myth.

In the opinion of many learned authorities, the shaft of this column was once a portion of the Serapeum, that famous building which was both a temple of the heathen god Serapis and a vast treasure-house of ancient civilization. It has been suggested—in order to account for its omission in the descriptions of Alexandria, given by Pliny and Strabo, who had mentioned the two obelisks of Cleopatra—that the column had fallen, and that the Prefect Pompey had merely re-erected it in honor of Diocletian, and replaced the statue of Serapis with one of the Emperor—or of his horse, according to some chroniclers. This statute, if it ever existed, has now disappeared. As it stands, however, it is a singularly striking and beautiful monument, owing to its great height, simplicity of form, and elegant proportions. It reminds the spectator a little of Nelson's Column in Trafalgar Square, and perhaps the absence of a statue is not altogether to be regretted considering the height of the column, as it might suggest to the irrepressible tourists who scoff at Nelson's statue as the "Mast-headed Admiral," some similar witticism at the expense of Diocletian.

With the exception of this monolith, which, "a solitary column, mourns above its prostrate brethren," only a few fragmentary and scattered ruins of fallen columns mark the site of the world-renowned Serapeum. Nothing else remains of the famous library, the magnificent 248]portico with its hundred steps, the vast halls, and the four hundred marble columns of that great building designed to perpetuate the glories of the Ptolemies. This library, which was the forerunner of the great libraries of modern times, must not be confounded with the equally famous one that was attached to the Museum, whose exact site is still a bone of contention among antiquarians. The latter was destroyed by accident, when Julius Cæsar set fire to the Alexandrian fleet. The Serapeum collection survived for six hundred years, till its wanton destruction through the fanaticism of the Caliph Omar. The Arab conqueror is said to have justified this barbarism with a fallacious epigram, which was as unanswerable, however logically faulty, as the famous one familiar to students of English history under the name of Archbishop Morton's Fork. "If these writings," declared the uncompromising conqueror, "agree with the Book of God, they are useless, and need not be preserved; if they disagree, they are pernicious, and ought to be destroyed." Nothing could prevail against this flagrant example of a petitio principii, and for six months the three hundred thousand parchments supplied fuel for the four thousand baths of Alexandria.

Hard by Pompey's Pillar is a dreary waste, dotted with curiously carved structures. This is the Mohammedan cemetery. As in most Oriental towns, the cemetery is at the west end of the town, as the Mohammedans consider that the quarter of the horizon in which the sun sets is the most suitable spot for their burying-places.

In this melancholy city of the dead are buried also many of the ruins of the Serapeum, and scattered about among the tombs are fragments of columns and broken pedestals. On some of the tombs a green turban is roughly painted, 249] strangely out of harmony with the severe stone carving. This signifies that the tomb holds the remains of a descendant of the prophet, or of a devout Moslem, who had himself, and not vicariously as is so often done, made the pilgrimage to the sacred city of Mecca. Some of the head-stones are elaborately carved, but most are quite plain, with the exception of a verse of the Koran cut in the stone. The observant tourist will notice on many of the tombs a curious little round hole cut in the stone at the head, which seems to be intended to form a passage to the interior of the vault, though the aperture is generally filled up with earth. It is said that this passage is made to enable the Angel Israfel at the Resurrection to draw out the occupant by the hair of his head; and the custom which obtains among the lower class Moslems of shaving the head with the exception of a round tuft of hair in the middle—a fashion which suggests an incipient pigtail or an inverted tonsure—is as much due to this superstition as to sanitary considerations.

Of far greater interest than this comparatively modern cemetery are the cave cemeteries of El-Meks. These catacombs are some four miles from the city. The route along the low ridge of sand-hills is singularly unpicturesque, but the windmills which fringe the shore give a homely aspect to the country, and serve at any rate to break the monotony of this dreary and prosaic shore. We soon reach Said Pacha's unfinished palace of El-Meks, which owes its origin to the mania for building which helped to make the

114

reign of that weak-minded ruler so costly to his over-taxed subjects. One glimpse at the bastard style of architecture is sufficient to remove any feeling of disappointment on being told that the building is not open to the public. The catacombs, which spread 250] for a long distance along the seashore, and of which the so-called Baths of Cleopatra are a part, are very extensive, and tourists are usually satisfied with exploring a part. There are no mummies, but the niches can be clearly seen. The plan of the catacombs is curiously like the wards of a key.

There are few "sights" in Alexandria of much interest besides those already mentioned. In fact, Alexandria is interesting more as a city of sites than sights. It is true that the names of some of the mosques, such as that of the One Thousand and One Columns, built on the site of St. Mark's martyrdom, and the Mosque of St. Athanasius, are calculated to arouse the curiosity of the tourist: but the interest is in the name alone. The Mosque of many Columns is turned into a quarantine station, and the Mosque of St. Athanasius has no connection with the great Father except that it stands on the site of a church in which he probably preached.

Then there is the Coptic Convent of St. Mark, which, according to the inmates, contains the body of the great Evangelist—an assertion which would scarcely deceive the most ignorant and the most credulous tourist that ever entrusted himself to the fostering care of Messrs. Cook, as it is well known that St. Mark's body was removed to Venice in the ninth century. The mosque, with the ornate exterior and lofty minaret, in which the remains of Said Pacha are buried, is the only one besides those already mentioned which is worth visiting.

The shores of the Delta from Alexandria to Rosetta are singularly rich in historical associations, and are thickly strewn with historic landmarks. The plain in which have been fought battles which have decided the fate of the whole western world, may well be called the 251] "Belgium of the East." In this circumscribed area the empires of the East and West struggled for the mastery, and many centuries later the English here wrested from Napoleon their threatened Indian Empire. In the few miles' railway journey between Alexandria and the suburban town of Ramleh the passenger traverses classic ground. At Mustapha Pacha the line skirts the Roman camp, where Octavius defeated the army of Antony, and gained for Rome a new empire. Unfortunately there are now few ruins left of this encampment, as most of the stones were used by Ismail Pacha in building one of his innumerable palaces, now converted into a hospital and barracks for the English troops. Almost on this very spot where Octavius conquered, was fought the battle of Alexandria, which gave the death-blow to Napoleon's great scheme of founding an Eastern Empire, and converting the Mediterranean into "un lac français." This engagement was, as regards the number of troops engaged, an insignificant one; but as the great historian of modern Europe has observed, "The importance of a triumph is not always to be measured by the number of men engaged. The contest of 12,000 Britons with an equal number of French on the sands of Alexandria, in its remote effect, overthrew a greater empire than that of Charlemagne, and rescued mankind from a more galling tyranny than that of the Roman Emperors."[5] A few minutes more and the traveller's historical musings are interrupted by the shriek of the engine as the train enters the Ramleh station. This pleasant and salubrious town, with its rows of trim villas standing in their own well-kept grounds and gardens, the residences of Alexandrian merchants, suggests a fashionable or "rising" 252] English watering place rather than an Oriental town. As a residence it has no doubt many advantages, including a good and sufficient water supply, and frequent communication by train with Alexandria. But these are not the attractions which appeal to the traveller or tourist. The only objects of interest are the ruins of the Temple of Arsenoe, the wife of Ptolemy Philadelphus. Concerning this temple there is an interesting and romantic legend, which no doubt suggested to Pope his fanciful poem, "The Rape of the Lock":—

"Not Berenice's hair first rose so bright,
The heavens bespangling with dishevelled light."

This pretty story, which has been immortalized by Catullus, is as follows:—When Ptolemy Euergetes left for his expedition to Syria, his wife Berenice vowed to dedicate her hair to Venus Zephyrites should her husband return safe and sound. Her prayer was answered, and in fulfilment of her vow she hung within the Temple of Arsenoe the golden locks that had adorned her head. Unfortunately they were stolen by some sacrilegious thief. The priests were naturally troubled, the King was enraged, and the Queen inconsolable. However, the craft of Conon, the Court astronomer, discovered a way by which the mysterious disappearance could be satisfactorily explained, the priests absolved of all blame, and the vanity of the Queen gratified. The wily astronomer-courtier declared that Jupiter had taken the locks and transformed them into a constellation, placing it in that quarter of the heavens (the "Milky Way") by which the gods, according to tradition, passed to and from Olympus. This pious fraud was effected by annexing the group of stars which formed the tail of the constellation 253] Leo, and declaring that this cluster of stars was the new constellation into which Berenice's locks had been transformed. This arbitrary modification of the celestial system is known by the name of Coma Berenices, and is still retained in astronomical charts.

"I 'mongst the stars myself resplendent now,
I, who once curled on Berenice's brow,
The tress which she, uplifting her fair arm,
To many a god devoted, so from harm
They might protect her new-found royal mate,
When from her bridal chamber all elate,
With its sweet triumph flushed, he went in haste
To lay the regions of Assyria waste."[6]

A few miles northwest of Ramleh, at the extremity of the western horn of Aboukir Bay, lies the village of Aboukir. The railway to Rosetta skirts that bay of glorious memory, and as the traveller passes by those silent and deserted shores which fringe the watery arena whereon France and England contended for the Empire of the East, he lives again in those stirring times, and the dramatic episodes of that famous Battle of the Nile crowd upon the memory. That line of deep blue water, bounded on the west by the rocky islet, now called Nelson's Island, and on the east by Fort St. Julien on the Rosetta headland, marks the position of the French fleet on the 1st of August, 1798. The fleet was moored in the form of a crescent close along the shore, and was covered by the batteries of Fort Aboukir. So confident was Bruèys, the French Admiral, in the strength of his position, and in his superiority in guns and men (nearly as three to two) over Nelson's fleet, that he sent that famous despatch to Paris, declaring that the enemy was purposely avoiding 254] him. Great must have been his dismay when the English fleet, which had been scouring the Mediterranean with bursting sails for six long weeks in search of him, was signaled, bearing down unflinchingly upon its formidable foe—that foe with which Nelson had vowed he would do battle, if above water, even if he had to sail to the Antipodes. "By to-morrow I shall have gained a peerage or Westminster Abbey," were the historic words uttered by the English Admiral when the French fleet was sighted, drawn up in order of battle in Aboukir Bay. The soundings of this dangerous roadstead were unknown to him, but declaring that "where there was room for the enemy to swing, there must be room for us to anchor," he ordered his leading squadron to take up its position to the landward of the enemy. The remainder of the English fleet was ordered to anchor on the outside of the enemy's line, but at close quarters, thus doubling on part of the enemy's line, and placing it in a defile of fire. In short, the effect of this brilliant and masterly disposition of the English fleet was to surround two-thirds of the enemy's ships, and cut them off from the support of their consorts, which were moored too far off to injure the enemy or aid their friends. The French Admiral, in spite of his apparently impregnable position, was consequently out-manœuvred from the outset, and the victory of Nelson virtually assured.

Evening set in soon after Nelson had anchored. All through the night the battle raged fiercely and unintermittently, "illuminated by the incessant discharge of over two thousand cannon," and the flames which burst from the disabled ships of the French squadron. The sun had set upon as proud a fleet as ever set sail from the shores 255] of France, and morning rose upon a strangely altered scene. Shattered and blackened hulks now only marked the position they had occupied but a few hours before. On one ship alone, the Tonnant, the tricolor was flying. When the Theseus drew near to take her as prize, she hoisted a flag of truce, but kept her colors flying. "Your battle flag or none!" was the stern reply, as her enemy rounded to and prepared to board. Slowly and reluctantly, like an expiring hope, that pale flag fluttered down her lofty spars, and the next that floated there was the standard of Old England. "And now the battle was over— India was saved upon the shores of Egypt—the career of Napoleon was checked, and his navy was annihilated. Seven years later that navy was revived, to perish utterly at Trafalgar—a fitting hecatomb for the obsequies of Nelson, whose life seemed to terminate as his mission was then and thus accomplished." The glories of Trafalgar, immortalized by the death of Nelson, have no doubt obscured to some extent those of the Nile. The latter engagement has not, indeed, been enshrined in the memory of Englishmen by popular ballads—those instantaneous photographs, as they might be called, of the highest thoughts and strongest emotions inspired by patriotism—but hardly any great sea-fight of modern times has been more prolific in brilliant achievements of heroism and deeds of splendid devotion than the Battle of the Nile. The traditions of this terrible combat have not yet died out among the Egyptians and Arabs, whose forefathers had lined the shores of the bay on that memorable night, and watched with mingled terror and astonishment the destruction of that great armament. It was with some idea of the moral effect the landing of English troops on 256] the shores of this historic bay would have on Arabi's soldiery, that Lord Wolseley contemplated disembarking there the English expeditionary force in August, 1882.

On the eastern horn of Aboukir Bay, on the Rosetta branch of the Nile, and about five miles from its mouth, lies the picturesque town of Rosetta. Its Arabic name is Rashid, an etymological coincidence which has induced some writers to jump to the conclusion that it is the birthplace of Haroun Al Rashid. To some persons no doubt the town would be shorn of much of its interest if dissociated from our old friend of "The Thousand and One Nights;" but the indisputable fact remains that Haroun Al Rashid died some seventy years before the foundation of the town in a. d. 870. Rosetta was a port of some commercial importance until the opening of the Mahmoudiyeh Canal in 1819 diverted most of its trade to Alexandria. The town is not devoid of architectural interest, and many fragments of ruins may be met with in the half-deserted streets, and marble pillars, which bear signs of considerable antiquity, may be noticed built into the doorways of the comparatively modern houses. One of the most interesting architectural features of Rosetta is the North Gate, flanked with massive towers of a form unusual in Egypt, each tower being crowned with a conical-shaped roof. Visitors will probably have noticed the curious gabled roofs and huge projecting windows of most of the houses. It was from these projecting doorways and latticed windows that such fearful execution was done to the British troops at the time of the ill-fated English expedition to Egypt in 1807. General Wauchope had been sent by General Fraser, who was in command of the troops, with an absurdly inadequate force of 1,200 men to take the strongly-garrisoned town. Mehemet 257] Ali's Albanian troops had purposely left the gates open in order to draw the English force into the narrow and winding streets. Their commander, without any previous examination, rushed blindly into the town with all his men. The Albanian soldiery waited till the English were confined in this infernal labyrinth of narrow, crooked streets, and then from every window and housetop rained down on them a perfect hail of musket-shot and rifle-ball. Before the officers could extricate their men from this terrible death-trap a third of the troops had fallen. Such was the result of this rash and futile expedition, which dimmed the lustre of their arms in Egypt, and contributed a good deal to the loss of their military prestige. That this crushing defeat should have taken place so near the scene of the most glorious achievement of their arms but a few years before, was naturally thought a peculiar aggravation of the failure of this ill-advised expedition.

To archæological students and Egyptologists Rosetta is a place of the greatest interest, as it was in its neighborhood that the famous inscribed stone was found which furnished the clue—sought in vain for so many years by Egyptian scholars—to the hieroglyphic writings of Egypt. Perhaps none of the archæological discoveries made in Egypt since the land was scientifically exploited by the savants attached to Napoleon's expedition, not even that of the mummified remains of the Pharaohs, is more precious in the eyes of Egyptologists and antiquarians than this comparatively modern and ugly-looking block of black basalt, which now reposes in the Egyptian galleries of the British Museum. The story of its discovery is interesting. A certain Monsieur Bouchard, a French Captain of Engineers, while making some excavations 258] at Fort St. Julien, a small fortress in the vicinity of Rosetta, discovered this celebrated stone in 1799. The interpretation of the inscription for many years defied all the efforts of the most learned French savants and English scholars, until, in 1822, two well-known Egyptologists, Champollion and Dr. Young, after independent study and examination, succeeded in deciphering that part of the inscription which was in Greek characters. From this they learnt that the inscription was triplicate and trilingual: one in Greek, the other in the oldest form of hieroglyphics, the purest kind of "picture-writing," and the third in demotic characters—the last being the form of hieroglyphics used by the people, in which the symbols are more obscure than in the pure hieroglyphics used by the priests. The inscription, when finally deciphered, proved to be one of comparatively recent date, being a decree of Ptolemy V., issued in the year 196 b. c. The Rosetta stone was acquired by England as part of the spoils of war in the Egyptian expedition of 1801.

At Rosetta the railway leaves the coast and goes south to Cairo.

If the traveller wishes to see something of the agriculture of the Delta, he would get some idea of the astonishing fertility of the country by merely taking the train to Damanhour, the center of the cotton-growing district. The journey does not take more than a couple of hours. The passenger travelling by steamer from Alexandria to Port Said, though he skirts the coast, can see no signs of the agricultural wealth of Egypt, and for him the whole of Egypt might be an arid desert instead of one of the most fertile districts in the whole world. The area of cultivated lands, which, however, extends yearly seawards, is separated from the coast by a belt composed of 259] strips of sandy desert, marshy plain, low sandhills, and salt lagunes, which varies in breadth from fifteen to thirty miles. A line drawn from Alexandria to Damietta, through the southern shore of Lake Boorlos, marks approximately the limit of cultivated land in this part of the Delta. The most unobservant traveller in Egypt cannot help perceiving that its sole industry is agriculture, and that the bulk of its inhabitants are tillers of the soil. Egypt seems, indeed, intended by nature to be the granary and market-garden of North Africa, and the prosperity of the country depends on its being allowed to retain its place as a purely agricultural country. The ill-advised, but fortunately futile, attempts which have been made by recent rulers to develop manufactures at the expense of agriculture, are the outcome of a short-sighted policy or perverted ambition. Experience has proved that every acre diverted from its ancient and rational use as a bearer of crops is a loss to the national wealth.

That "Egypt is the gift of the Nile" has been insisted upon with "damnable iteration" by every writer on Egypt, from Herodotus downwards. According to the popular etymology,[7] the very name of the Nile (Νεῖλος, from νέα ἰλὺς, new mud) testifies to its peculiar fertilizing properties. The Nile is all in all to the Egyptian, and can we wonder that Egyptian mythologists recognized in it the Creative Principle waging eternal warfare with Typhon, the Destructive Principle, represented by the encroaching desert? As Mr. Stanley Lane-Poole has well observed, "without the Nile there would be no 260] Egypt; the great African Sahara would spread uninterruptedly to the Red Sea. Egypt is, in short, a long oasis worn in the rocky desert by the ever-flowing stream, and made green and fertile by its waters."

At Cairo the Nile begins to rise about the third week in June, and the beginning of the overflow coincides with the heliacal rising of the Dog Star. The heavens have been called the clocks of the Ancients, and, according to some writers, it was the connection between the rise of the Nile and that of the Dog Star that first opened the way to the study of astronomy among the ancient Egyptians, so that not only was the Nile the creator of their country, but also of their science. The fellahs, however, still cherish a lingering belief in the supernatural origin of the overflow. They say that a miraculous drop of water falls into the Nile on the 17th of June, which causes the river to swell. Till September the river continues to rise, not regularly, but by leaps and bounds. In this month it attains its full height, and then gradually subsides till it reaches its normal height in the winter months.

As is well known, the quality of the harvest depends on the height of the annual overflow—a rise of not less than eighteen feet at Cairo being just sufficient, while a rise of over twenty-six feet, or thereabouts, would cause irreparable damage. It is a common notion that a very high Nile is beneficial; whereas an excessive inundation would do far more harm to the country than an abnormal deficiency of water. Statistics show

119

conclusively that most of the famines in Egypt have occurred after an exceptionally high Nile. Shakespeare, who, we know, is often at fault in matters of natural science, is perhaps partly accountable for this popular error:—"The higher 261]Nilus swells, the more it promises," he makes Antony say, when describing the wonders of Egypt to Cæsar.

The coast between Rosetta and Port Said is, like the rest of the Egyptian littoral, flat and monotonous. The only break in the dreary vista is afforded by the picturesque-looking town of Damietta, which, with its lofty houses, looking in the distance like marble palaces, has a striking appearance seen from the sea. The town, though containing some spacious bazaars and several large and well-proportioned mosques, has little to attract the visitor, and there are no antiquities or buildings of any historic interest. The traveller, full of the traditions of the Crusades, who expects to find some traces of Saladin and the Saracens, will be doomed to disappointment. Damietta is comparatively modern, the old Byzantine city having been destroyed by the Arabs early in the thirteenth century, and rebuilt—at a safer distance from invasion by sea—a few miles inland, under the name of Mensheeyah. One of the gateways of the modern town, the Mensheeyah Gate, serves as a reminder of its former name. Though the trade of Damietta has, in common with most of the Delta sea-ports, declined since the construction of the Mahmoudiyeh Canal, it is still a town of some commercial importance, and consular representatives of several European powers are stationed here. To sportsmen Damietta offers special advantages, as it makes capital headquarters for the wild-fowl shooting on Menzaleh Lake, which teems with aquatic birds of all kinds. Myriads of wild duck may be seen feeding here, and "big game"—if the expression can be applied to birds—in the shape of herons, pelicans, storks, flamingoes, etc., is plentiful. In the marshes which abut on the lake, specimens 262] of the papyrus are to be found, this neighborhood being one of the few habitats of this rare plant. Soon after rounding the projecting ridge of low sand-hills which fringe the estuary of the Damietta Branch of the Nile, the noble proportions of the loftiest lighthouse of the Mediterranean come into view. It is fitted with one of the most powerful electric lights in the world, its penetrating rays being visible on a clear night at a distance of over twenty-five miles. Shortly afterwards the forest of masts, apparently springing out of the desert, informs the passenger of the near vicinity of Port Said.

There is, of course, nothing to see at Port Said from a tourist's standpoint. The town is little more than a large coaling station, and is of very recent growth. It owes its existence solely to the Suez Canal, and to the fact that the water at that part of the coast is deeper than at Pelusium, where the isthmus is narrowest. The town is built partly on artificial foundations on the strip of low sand-banks which forms a natural sea-wall protecting Lake Menzaleh from the Mediterranean. In the autumn at high Nile it is surrounded on all sides by water. An imaginative writer once called Port Said the Venice of Africa—not a very happy description, as the essentially modern appearance of this coaling station strikes the most unobservant visitor. The comparison might for its inappositeness rank with the proverbial one between Macedon and Monmouth. Both Venice and Port Said are land-locked, and that is the only feature they have in common.

The sandy plains in the vicinity of the town are, however, full of interest to the historian and archæologist. Here may be found ruins and remains of antiquity which recall a period of civilization reaching back more 263]centuries than Port Said (built in 1859) does years. The ruins of Pelusium (the Sin of the Old Testament), the key of Northeastern Egypt in the Pharaonic period, are only eighteen miles distant, and along the shore may still be traced a few vestiges of the great highway—the oldest road in the world of which remains exist—constructed by Rameses II., in 1350 b. c., when he undertook his expedition for the conquest of Syria.

To come to more recent history. It was on the Pelusiac shores that Cambyses defeated the Egyptians, and here some five centuries later Pompey the Great was treacherously murdered when he fled to Egypt, after the Battle of Pharsalia.

To the southwest of Port Said, close to the wretched little fishing village of Sais, situated on the southern shore of Lake Menzaleh, are the magnificent ruins of Tanis (the Zoan of the Old Testament). These seldom visited remains are only second to those of Thebes in historical and archæological interest. It is a little curious that while tourists flock in crowds to distant Thebes and Karnak, few take the trouble to visit the easily accessible ruins of Tanis. The ruins were uncovered at great cost of labor by the late Mariette Bey, and in the great temple were unearthed some of the most notable monuments of the Pharaohs, including over a dozen gigantic fallen obelisks—a larger number than any Theban temple contains. This vast building, restored and enlarged by Rameses II., goes back to over five thousand years. As Thebes declined Tanis rose in importance, and under the kings of the Twenty-first Dynasty it became the chief seat of Government. Mr. John Macgregor (Rob Roy), who was one of the first of modern travellers to call attention to these grand ruins, declares that of all the 264]celebrated remains he had seen none impressed him "so deeply with the sense of fallen and deserted magnificence" as the ruined temple of Tanis.

The Suez Canal is admittedly one of the greatest undertakings of modern times, and has perhaps effected a greater transformation in the world's commerce, during the thirty years that have elapsed since its completion, than has been effected in the same period by the agency of steam. It was emphatically the work of one man, and of one, too, who was devoid of the slightest technical training in the engineering profession. Monsieur de Lesseps cannot, of course, claim any originality in the conception of this great undertaking, for the idea of opening up communication between the Mediterranean and the Red Sea by means of a maritime canal is almost as old as Egypt itself, and many attempts were made by the rulers of Egypt from Sesostris downwards to span the Isthmus with "a bridge of water." Most of these projects proved abortive, though there was some kind of water communication between the two seas in the time of the Ptolemies, and it was by this canal that Cleopatra attempted to escape after the battle of Actium. When Napoleon the Great occupied Egypt, he went so far as to appoint a commission of engineers to examine into a projected scheme for a maritime canal, but owing to the ignorance of the commissioners, who reported that there was a difference of thirty feet in the levels of the two seas—though there is really scarcely more than six inches—which would necessitate vast locks, and involve enormous outlay of money, the plan was given up.

121

The Suez Canal is, in short, the work of one great man, and its existence is due to the undaunted courage, the indomitable energy, to the intensity of conviction, and to 265] the magnetic personality of M. de Lesseps, which influenced everyone with whom he came in contact, from Viceroy down to the humblest fellah. This great project was carried out, too, not by a professional engineer, but by a mere consular clerk, and was executed in spite of the most determined opposition of politicians and capitalists, and in the teeth of the mockery and ridicule of practical engineers, who affected to sneer at the scheme as the chimerical dream of a vainglorious Frenchman.

The Canal, looked at from a purely picturesque standpoint, does not present such striking features as other great monuments of engineering skill—the Forth Bridge, the Mont Cenis Tunnel, or the great railway which scales the highest peaks of the Rocky Mountains. This "huge ditch," as it has been contemptuously called, "has not indeed been carried over high mountains, nor cut through rock-bound tunnels, nor have its waters been confined by Titanic masses of masonry." In fact, technically speaking, the name canal as applied to this channel is a misnomer. It has nothing in common with other canals—no locks, gates, reservoirs, nor pumping engines. It is really an artificial strait, or a prolongation of an arm of the sea. We can freely concede this, yet to those of imaginative temperament there are elements of romance about this great enterprise. It is the creation of a nineteenth-century wizard who, with his enchanter's wand—the spade—has transformed the shape of the globe, and summoned the sea to flow uninterruptedly from the Mediterranean to the Indian Ocean. Then, too, the most matter-of-fact traveller who traverses it can hardly fail to be impressed with the genius loci. Every mile of the Canal passes through a region enriched by the memories of events which had their birth in the remotest ages of 266] antiquity. Across this plain four thousand years ago Abraham wandered from far-away Ur of the Chaldees. Beyond the placid waters of Lake Menzaleh lie the ruins of Zoan, where Moses performed his miracles. On the right lies the plain of Pelusium, across which Rameses II. led his great expedition for the conquest of Syria; and across this sandy highway the hosts of Persian, Greek, and Roman conquerors successively swept to take possession of the riches of Egypt. In passing through the Canal at night—the electric light seeming as a pillar of fire to the steamer, as it swiftly, but silently, ploughs its course through the desert—the strange impressiveness of the scene is intensified. "The Canal links together in sweeping contrast the great Past and the greater Present, pointing to a future which we are as little able to divine, as were the Pharaohs or Ptolemies of old to forecast the wonders of the twentieth century."

267]

XII

MALTA

"England's Eye in the Mediterranean"—Vast systems of fortifications—Sentinels and martial music—The Strada Reale of Valletta—Church of St. John—St. Elmo—The Military Hospital, the "very glory of Malta"—Citta Vecchia—Saint Paul and his voyages.

THERE is a difference of opinion among voyagers as to whether it is best to approach Malta by night or by day; whether there is a greater charm in tracing the outline of "England's Eye in the Mediterranean" by the long, undulating lines of light along its embattled front, and then, as the sun rises, to permit the details to unfold themselves, or to see the entire mass of buildings and sea walls and fortifications take shape according to the rapidity with which the ship nears the finest of all the British havens in the Middle Sea. Much might be said for both views, and if by "Malta" is meant its metropolis, then the visitor would miss a good deal who did not see the most picturesque portion of the island in both of these aspects. And by far the majority of those who touch at Valletta, on their way to or from some other place, regard this city as "the colony" in miniature. Many, indeed, are barely aware that it has a name apart from that of the island on which it is built; still fewer that the "Villa" of La Valletta is only one of four fortified towns all run 268] into one, and that over the surface of this thickly populated clump are scattered scores of villages, while their entire coasts are circled by a ring of forts built wherever the cliffs are not steep enough to serve as barriers against an invader. On the other hand, while there is no spot in the Maltese group half so romantic, or any "casal" a tithe as magnificent as Valletta and its suburbs, it is a little unfortunate for the scenic reputation of the chief island-fortress that so few visitors see any other part of it than the country in the immediate vicinity of its principal town. For, if none of the islands are blessed with striking scenery, that of Malta proper is perhaps the least attractive.

Though less than sixty miles from Sicily, these placid isles oft though they have been shaken by earthquakes, do not seem to have ever been troubled by the volcanic outbursts of Etna. Composed of a soft, creamy rock, dating from the latest geological period, the elephants and hippopotami disinterred from their caves show that, at a time when the Mediterranean stretched north and south over broad areas which are now dry land, these islands were still under water, and that at a date comparatively recent, before the Straits of Gibraltar had been opened, and when the contracted Mediterranean was only a couple of lakes Malta was little more than a peninsula of Africa. Indeed, so modern is the group as we know it, that within the human era Comino seems to have been united with the islands on each side of it. For, as the deep wheel-ruts on the opposite shores of the two nearer islands, even at some distance in the water, demonstrate, the intervening straits have either been recently formed, or were at one period so shallow as to be fordable.

269]But if it be open to doubt whether night or day is the best time to make our first acquaintance with Malta, there can be none as to the season of the year when it may be most advantageously visited; for if the tourist comes to Malta in spring, he will find the country bright with flowers, and green with fields of wheat and barley, and cumin and "sulla" clover, or cotton, and even with plots of sugar-cane, tobacco, and the fresh foliage of vineyards enclosed by hedges of prickly pears ready to burst into gorgeous blossom. Patches of the famous Maltese potatoes flourish cheek by jowl with noble crops of beans and melons. Figs and pomegranates, peaches, pears, apricots, and medlars are in blossom; and if the curious pedestrian peers over the orchard walls, he may sight oranges and lemons gay with the flowers of which the fragrance is scenting the evening air. But in autumn, when the birds of passage arrive for the winter, the land has been burnt into barrenness by the summer sun of the scorching sirocco. The soil, thin, but amazingly fertile, and admirably suited by its spongy texture to retain the moisture, looks white and parched as it basks in the hot sunshine; and even the gardens, enclosed by high stone walls to shelter them from the torrid winds from Africa, or the wild "gregale" from the north, or the Levanter which sweeps damp and depressing towards the Straits of Gibraltar, fail to relieve the dusty, chalk-like aspect of the landscape. Hills there are—they are called the "Bengemma mountains" by the proud Maltese—but they are mere hillocks to the scoffer from more Alpine regions, for at Ta-l'aghlia, the highest elevation in Malta, 750 feet is the total tale told by the barometer, while it is seldom that the sea cliffs reach half that height. The valleys in the undulating surface 270] are in proportion, and even they and the little glens worn by the watercourses are bald, owing to the absence of wood; for what timber grew in ancient times has long ago been hewn down, and the modern Maltee has so inveterate a prejudice against green leaves which are not saleable that he is said to have quietly uprooted the trees which a paternal Government planted for the supposed benefit of unappreciative children. Hence, with the exception of a bosky grove around some ancient palace of the knights, or a few carob trees, so low that the goats in lack of humble fodder can, as in Morocco, climb into them for a meal, the rural districts of Malta lack the light and shade which forests afford, just as its arid scenery is unrelieved either by lake, or river, or by any brook worthy of the name. However, as the blue sea, running into inlet and bay, or ending the vista of some narrow street, or driving the spray before the "tempestuous" wind, called "Euroklydon," is seldom out of sight, the sparkle of inland water is less missed than it would be were the country larger.

But Malta proper is only one of the Maltese group. As the geography books have it, there are three main islands, Malta, Gozo, and between them the little one of Comino, which with Cominetto, a still smaller islet close by, seems to have been the crest of a land of old, submerged beneath the sea. The voyager is barely out of sight of Sicily before the faint outlines of these isles are detected, like sharply defined clouds against a serenely blue sky. Yet, undeniably, the first view of Malta is disappointing; for with Etna fresh in the memory of the visitor from one direction, and the great Rock of Gibraltar vivid in the recollection of those arriving from the other end of the Mediterranean, there is little in any 271] of the three islands to strike the imagination. For most of the picturesqueness of Malta is due to the works of man, and all of its romance to the great names and mighty events with which its historic shores are associated. But there are also around the coasts of this major member of the Maltese clump the tiny Filfla, with its venerable church; the Pietro Negro, or Black Rock; Gzeier sanctified by the wreck of St. Paul; and Scoglio Marfo, on which a few fishermen encamp, or which grow grass enough for some rabbits or a frugal goat or two; and, great in fame though small in size, the Hagra tal General, or Fungus Rock, on which still flourishes that curious parasitic plant, the Fungus Melitensis of the old botanists, the Cynomorium coccineum of latter-day systematists. The visitor who has the curiosity to land on the rock in April or May will find it in full flower, and perhaps, considering its ancient reputation, may be rather disappointed with the appearance of a weed which at one time enjoyed such a reputation as a stauncher of blood and a sovereign remedy for a host of other diseases that the Knights of Malta stored it carefully as a gift for friendly monarchs and to the hospitals of the island. It is less valued in our times, though until very recently the keeper of the rock on which it flourishes most abundantly was a permanent official in the colonial service. The place indeed is seldom profaned nowadays by human feet; for the box drawn in a pulley by two cables, which was the means of crossing the hundred and fifty feet of sea between the rocks and the shore of Dueira, was broken down some years ago, and has not since been renewed. But, apart from these scientific associations of this outlier of Gozo, the second largest island of the Maltese group is worthy of being more 272] frequently examined than it is, albeit the lighthouse of Ta Giurdan is familiar enough to every yachtsman in the "Magnum Mare." For it is the first bit of Malta seen from the west, and the last memory of it which the home-coming exile sights as he returns with a lighter heart from the East. Yet except for its classical memories (it was the fable isle of Calypso, the Gaulos of the Greeks, the Gaulum of the Romans, and the Ghaudex of the Arabs, a name still in use among the natives), the tourist in search of the picturesque will not find a great deal to gratify him in Gozo, with its bay-indented shore, rugged in places, but except in the southern and western coast rarely attaining a height of three hundred feet above the sea. Still, its pleasing diversity of hill and dale, its occasional groves of trees, and the flourishing gardens from which Valletta market is supplied with a great portion of its vegetables, lend an appearance of rural beauty to Gozo seldom seen or altogether lacking in the rest of the group. Gozo appears to have suffered less from foreign invasions than Malta or even Comino. Its goat cheese still preserves something of the reputation that comestible obtained in days when the world had a limited acquaintance with dairy produce, and the "Maltese jacks," potent donkeys (the very antipodes of their tiny kindred on the Barbary coast) are mostly exported from this spot. But, like the peculiar dogs and cats of the group, they are now getting scarce.

The appearance of the Gozitans also is somewhat different from that of their countrymen elsewhere, and they speak the Maltese tongue with a closer approach to the Arabic than do the inhabitants of the other islands, whose speech has become intermingled with that of every Mediterranean race, from the Tyrians to the Italians, 273] though the basis of it is unquestionably Phœnician, and is gradually getting dashed with the less sonorous language of their latest rulers. Indeed, the lamps in daily use are identical in shape with the earthenware ones disinterred from the most ancient of Carthaginian tombs, and until lately a peculiar jargon, allied to Hebrew, and known as "Braik," was spoken at Casal Garbo, an inland village not far from the bay off which lies the General's Rock. But the Gozo folk nowadays trade neither in tin nor in purple, their gaily-painted boats crossing the Straits of Freghi with no more romantic cargoes than cabbages and cucumbers for His Majesty's ships; and the swarthy damsels who sit at the half-doors of the white houses are intent on nothing so much as the making of the famous Maltese lace. Except, however, in the strength, industry, and thrift of the Gozitans, there is little in this island to remind the visitor of their Phœnician forefathers, and in a few years, owing to the steady intercourse which daily steam communication has brought about between them and their less sophisticated countrymen, the "Giant's Tower" (the ruins of a temple of Astarte) at Casal Xghara will be about the only remnant of these pre-historic settlers. But Casal Nadur, with its robust men and handsome women, the Tierka Zerka or Azure Window, a natural arch on the seashore, and Rabato, the little capital in the center of the island, which, in honor of the Jubilee year, changed its name for that of Victoria, are all worthy of a walk farther afield than Migiarro, or the "carting place," off which the Valletta steamer anchors. From the ruined walls of the citadel the visitor can survey Gozo with its conical hills, flattened at the top owing to the wearing away of the upper limestone by the action of the weather 274] and sinking of the underlying greensand, the whole recalling a volcano-dotted region. Then, if he cares to tarry so long, the sightseer may from this pleasant center tramp or drive to the Bay of Ramla, in a rock overhanging which is another "Grotto of Calypso," or to the Bay of Marsa-il-Forno, or to the Bay of Xlendi, through a well-watered ravine filled with fruit-trees, a walk which offers an opportunity of seeing the best cliff scenery in the island; or, finally, to the Cala Dueira, hard by which is the General's Rock, which (as we already know) forms one of the chief lions of Gozo. Comino with its caves will not detain the most eager of sightseers very long, and its scanty industries, incapable of supporting more than forty people, are not calculated to arouse much enthusiasm.

The shortest route to Valletta from Migiarro is to Marfa; but most people will prefer to land at once at Valletta. Here the change from the quiet islands to the busy metropolis of the group is marked. Everything betokens the capital of a dependency which, if not itself wealthy, is held by a wealthy nation, and a fortress upon which money has been lavished by a succession of military masters without any regard to the commercial aspects of the outlay. For if Malta has been and must always continue to be a trading center, it has for ages never ceased to be primarily a place of arms, a stronghold to the defensive strength of which every other interest must give way. All the public buildings are on a scale of substantiality which, to the voyager hitherto familiar only with Gibraltar, is rather striking. Even the residences of the officials are finer than one would expect in a "colony" (though there are no colonists, and no room for them) with a population less than 275]170,000, and a revenue rarely exceeding £250,000 per annum. Dens, vile beyond belief, there are no doubt in Valletta. But these are for the most part in narrow bye-lanes, which have few attractions for the ordinary visitor, or in the Manderaggio, a quasi-subterranean district, mostly below sea-level, where the houses are often without windows and conveniences even more important; so that there is an unconscious grimness in the prophetic humor which has dubbed this quarter of Valletta (two-and-a-half acres in area, peopled by 2,544 persons) "the place of cattle." Yet though the ninety-five square miles of the Maltese islands are about the most densely populated portions of the earth, the soil is so fertile, and the sources of employment, especially since the construction of the Suez Canal, so plentiful, that extreme penury is almost unknown, while the rural population seem in the happy mean of being neither rich nor poor.

But the tourist who for the first time surveys Valletta from the deck of a steamer as she anchors in the Quarantine Harbor, or still better from the Grand Harbor on the other side of the peninsula on which the capital is built, sees little of this. Scarcely is the vessel at rest before she is surrounded by a swarm of the peculiar high-prowed "dghaisas," or Maltese boats, the owners of which, standing while rowing, are clamorous to pull the passenger ashore; for Malta, like its sister fortress at the mouth of the Mediterranean, does not encourage wharves and piers, alongside of which large craft may anchor and troublesome crews swarm when they are not desired. Crowds of itinerant dealers, wily people with all the supple eagerness of the Oriental, and all the lack of conscience which is the convenient heritage of the trader of the Middle Sea, establish themselves on deck, ready 276] to part with the laces, and filigrees, and corals, and shells, and apocryphal coins of the Knights of St. John, for any ransom not less than twice their value. But in Malta, as elsewhere in the Mediterranean ports, there are always two prices, the price for which the resident obtains anything, and the price which the stranger is asked to pay. To these tariffs a new one has of late years been added, and this is that paradisaical figure, that fond legend of a golden age invoked only when the buyer is very eager, or very verdant, or very rich, "the price that Lady Brassey paid." However, even when the sojourner fancies that he has made a fair bargain (and the appraisements fall suddenly as the last bell begins to ring), the pedler is well in pocket, so well, indeed, that it has been calculated every steamer leaves behind it something like two hundred pounds in cash.

But if the rubbish sold in Valletta can be bought quite as good and rather more cheaply in London, Valletta itself must be seen in situ. The entrance to either of the harbors enables one to obtain but a slight idea of the place. It seems all forts and flat-roofed buildings piled one above the other in unattractive terraces. There are guns everywhere, and, right and left, those strongholds which are the final purposes of cannon. As the steamer creeps shrieking into "Port Marsa-Musciet" (the "Port" is superfluous, since the Arabic "Marsa" means the same thing) or Quarantine Harbor, it passes Dragut Point, with Fort Tigne on the right and Fort St. Elmo on the left, in addition to Fort Manoel and the Lazaretto on an island straight ahead. Had our destination been the Grand Harbor on the other side of Valletta, Fort Ricasoli and Fort St. Angelo would have been equally in evidence, built on two of the various projections which 277]intersect the left side of that haven. But the forts are, as it were, only the ganglia of the vast systems of fortifications which circle every creek and bay and headland of Valletta and its offshoots. Ages of toil, millions of money, and the best talent of three centuries of engineers have been lavished on the bewildering mass of curtains and horn-works, and ravelins and demilunes, and ditches and palisades, and drawbridges and bastions, and earthworks, which meet the eye in profusion enough to have delighted the soul of Uncle Toby. Sentinels and martial music are the most familiar of sights and sounds, and after soldiers and barracks, sailors and war-ships, the most frequent reminders that Malta, like Gibraltar, is a great military and naval station. But it is also in possession of some civil rights unknown to the latter. Among these is a legislature with limited power and boundless chatter, and, what is of more importance to the visitor, the citizens can go in and out of Valletta at all hours of the day and night, no raised drawbridge or stolid portcullis barring their movements in times of peace. The stranger lands without being questioned as to his nationality, and in Malta the Briton is bereft of the Civis-Romanus-sum sort of feeling he imbibes in Gibraltar; for here the alien can circulate as freely as the lords of the soil. But the man who wishes to explore Valletta must be capable of climbing; for from the landing place to the chief hotel in the main street the ascent is continuous, and for the first part of the way is by a flight of stairs. Indeed, these steps are so often called into requisition that one can sympathize with the farewell anathema of Bryon as he limped up one of these frequent obstacles to locomotion,

278] "Adieu! ye cursed streets of stairs!
(How surely he who mounts you swears)."

The reason of this peculiar construction is that Valletta is built on the ridge of Mount Scebarras, so that the ascent from the harbor to the principal streets running along the crest of the hill is necessarily steep. The result is, however, a more picturesque town than would have been the case had the architect who laid out the town when Jean de La Valette, Grand Master of the Knights, resolved in 1566 to transfer the capital here from the center of the island, been able to find funds to form a plateau by leveling down the summit of the mound. Hence Valletta is composed of streets running longitudinally and others crossing the former at right angles. Most of these are eked out by steps; one, the

Strada Santa Lucia, is made up of flights of them, and none are level from end to end. The backbone of the town and the finest of its highways is the Strada Reale, or Royal Street, which in former days was known as the Strada San Georgio, and during the brief French occupation as "the Street of the Rights of Man." Seven main streets run parallel with it, while eleven at right angles extend in straight lines across the promontory from harbor to harbor. The Strada Reale, with the Strada Mercanti alongside of it are, however, the most typical bits of the capital, and the visitor who conscientiously tramps through either, with a peep here and there up or down the less important transverse "strade," obtains a fair idea of the city of La Valette, whose statue stands with that of L'Isle Adam over the Porta Reale at the farther end of the street bearing that name. Here the first barrier to an invasion from the landward 279] side is met with in the shape of a deep ditch hewn through the solid rock, right across the peninsula from the one harbor to the other, cutting off if necessary the suburb of Floriana from the town proper, though Floriana, with its rampart gardens, parade ground, and barracks, is again protected on the inland aspect by other of the great fortifications which circle the seashore everywhere.

However, the drawbridge is down at present, and a long stream of people, civil and military, are crossing and recrossing it, to and from the Strada Reale. For this street is the chief artery through which is ever circulating the placid current of Valletteese life. Soldiers in the varied uniforms of the regiments represented in the garrison are marching backwards and forwards, to or from parade, or to keep watch on the ramparts, or are taking their pleasure afoot, or in the neat little covered "carrozzellas" or cabs of the country, in which, unlike those of Gibraltar of a similar build, a drive can be taken at the cost of the coin which, according to Sydney Smith, was struck to enable a certain thrifty race to be generous. Sailors from the war-ships in the Grand Harbor, and merchant seamen on a run ashore, are utilizing what time they can spare from the grog shops in the lower town to see the sights of the place. Cabmen and carmen driving cars without sides, and always rushing at the topmost speed of their little horses, scatter unwary pedestrians. Native women, with that curious "faldetta," or one-sided hood to their black cloaks which is a characteristic of Malta as the mantilla is of Spain, pass side by side with English ladies in the latest of London fashions, or sturdy peasant women, returning from market, get sadly in the way of the British nursemaid dividing her attention in unequal proportions between 280] her infantile charges and the guard marching for "sentry-go" to the ramparts. Flocks of goats, their huge udders almost touching the ground, are strolling about to be milked at the doors of customers. Maltese laborers, brown little men, bare-footed, broad-shouldered, and muscular, in the almost national dress of a Glengarry cap, cotton trousers, and flannel shirt, with scarlet sash, coat over one arm, and little earrings, jostle the smart officers making for the Union Club, or the noisy "globe-trotter" just landed from the steamer which came to anchor an hour ago. A few snaky-eyed Hindoos in gaily embroidered caps invite you to inspect their stock of ornamental wares, but except for an Arab or two from Tunis, or a few hulking Turks from Tripoli with pilot jackets over their barracans, the Strada Reale of Valletta has little of that human picturesqueness imparted to the Water-port Street of Gibraltar by the motley swarms of Spaniards, and Sicilians, and negroes, and Moors, and English who fill it at all periods between morning gun-fire to the hour when the stranger is ousted from within the gates. Malta being a most religiously Roman Catholic country, priests and robe-girded Carmelites are everywhere plentiful, and all day long the worshipers entering and leaving the numerous churches, with the eternal "jingle-jingle" of their bells, remind one of Rabelais's description of England in his day. At every turning the visitor is accosted by whining beggars whose pertinacity is only equaled by that of the boot-blacks and cabmen, who seem to fancy that the final purpose of man in Malta is to ride in carrozzellas with shining shoes. In Gibraltar we find a relief to the eye in the great rock towering overhead, the tree-embosomed cottages nestling on its slopes, or the occasional clumps of 281] palms in the hollows. These are wanting to the chief strada of Valletta. In architectural beauty the two streets cannot, however, be compared. The Water-port is lined with houses, few of which are handsome and most of which are mean, while the scarcity of space tends to crowd the narrow "ramps" as thickly as any lane in Valletta. It is seldom that the shops are better than those of a petty English town, and altogether the civil part of the rock fortresses has not lost the impress of having been reared by a people with but little of the world's wealth to spare, and kept alive by a population who have not a great deal to spend.

The main street of Valletta on the other hand is lined by good, and in most cases by handsome, houses, frequently with little covered stone balconies which lend a peculiar character to the buildings. The yellow limestone is also pleasant to look upon, while the many palaces which the comfort-loving knights erected for their shelter, impart to Valletta the appearance of a "a city built by gentlemen for gentlemen." Here on the right is the pretty Opera House (open, in common with the private theaters, on Sunday and Saturday alike), and on the other side of the road the Auberge of the Language of Provence, now occupied by the Union Club. A little farther on, in an open space shaded with trees, is the Church of St. John, on which the knights lavished their riches, and still, notwithstanding the pillage of the French troops in 1798, rich in vessels of gold and silver, crosses, pixes, jewels, monuments chivalric emblazonments, paintings, carven stone and other ecclesiastical embellishments, though like the wealthy order of military monks, whose pride it was, the Church of St. John is ostentatiously plain on the outside. The Auberge d'Auvergne, 282] now the Courts of Justice, is on the other side of the street, and hard by, a building which was formerly the Treasury of the Knights, the storehouse into which was gathered the contributions of the Commanderies throughout Europe. The Public Library fronted by some trees a little way back from the road is interesting from its containing the books of the Bailiff Louis de Tencin, the Grand Master de Rohan (who erected it), and of many of the more lettered knights, besides a good collection of the island antiquities. Close to it is the palace of the Grand Master, now the residence of the Governor, or in part utilized as Government offices. The courtyards, planted with oranges, euphorbias, hibiscus, and other greenery, and the walls covered with Bougainvillia, have a delightfully cool appearance to the pedestrian who enters from the hot street; while the broad marble staircase, the corridors lined with portraits and men-at-arms, and pictures representing the warlike exploits of the knightly galleys, the armory full of ancient weapons, and majolica vases from the Pharmacy, and the numerous relics of the former rulers of the island, are worthy of a long study by those interested in art or antiquity. The Council Chamber also merits a visit, for there may be seen the priceless hangings of Brussels tapestry. And last of all, the idlest of tourists is not likely to neglect the Hall of St. Michael and St. George, the frescoes celebrating the famous deeds of the Order of St. John, and the quaint clock in the interior court, which, according to Maltese legend, was brought from Rhodes when that island was abandoned after a resistance only less glorious than a victory. For, as Charles V. exclaimed when he heard of the surrender which led to Malta becoming the home of the knights, "there has been nothing 283] in the world so well lost as Rhodes." The main guard, with its pompous Latin inscription recording how "Magnæ et invictæ Britanniæ Melitensium Amor et Europæ vox Has insulas confirmant An mdcccxiv," is exactly opposite the palace. But when the visitor sees the wealth of art which the knights were forced to leave behind them, he is apt to be puzzled how the Maltese, who contributed not one baiocco to buy it, or to build these palaces or fortifications, could either through "Amor," or that necessity which knows no law, make them over us to us, or how "Magna et invicta Britannia" could accept without compensation the property of the military monks, whose Order, bereft of wealth and influence, still exists and claims with the acquiescence of at least one court to rank among the sovereign Powers of Christendom. The knights are, however, still the greatest personalities in Malta. We come upon them, their eight-pointed cross and their works at every step. Their ghosts still walk the highways. The names of the Grand Masters are immortalized in the cities they founded and in the forts they reared. Their portraits in the rude art of the Berlin lithographer hang on even the walls of the hotels. Their ecclesiastical side is in evidence by the churches which they reared, by the hagiological names which they gave to many of the streets, by the saintly figures with which, in spite of three-fourths of a century of Protestant rulers, still stand at the corners, and by the necessity which we have only recently found to come to an understanding with the Pope as to the limits of the canon law in this most faithful portion of his spiritual dominions.

On the other hand, the secular side of the Order is quite as prominent. Here, for instance, after descending 284] some steps which serve as a footpath, we come to the Fort of St. Elmo, which terminates the Strada Reale. But long before there was any regular town on Monte Sceberras, when the capital was in the center of the island, this fortress on the point midway between the two harbors was a place round which the tide of battle often swirled, when Paynim and Christian fought for the mastery of the island. Of all these sieges the greatest is that of 1565, a year before the town of Valletta was laid out. Twice previously, in 1546 and 1551, the Turks had endeavored to expel the knights, but failed to effect a landing. But in the year mentioned Sultan Solyman, The Magnificent, the same Solyman who thirty-four years before had driven them from Rhodes, determined to make one supreme effort to dislodge the Order from their new home. The invading fleet consisted of a hundred and thirty-eight vessels under the Renegade Piali, and an army of thirty-three thousand men under the orders of Mustafa Pasha. These sea and land forces were soon afterwards increased by the arrival of two thousand five hundred resolute old Corsairs brought from Algiers by Hassan Pasha, and eighteen ships containing sixteen hundred men under the still more famous Dragut, the Pirate Chief of Tripoli, who, by the fortunes of war, was in a few years later fated to toil as a galley-slave in this very harbor. The siege lasted for nearly four months. Every foot of ground was contested with heroic determination until it was evident that Fort St. Elmo could no longer hold out. Then the knights, worn and wounded, and reduced to a mere remnant of their number, received the viaticum in the little castle chapel, and embracing each other went forth on the ramparts to meet whatever lot was in store for 285] them. But St. Angelo and Senglea, at the end of the peninsula on which Isola is now built, held out until, on the arrival of succor from Sicily, the Turks withdrew. Of the forty thousand men who on the 18th of May had sat down before the Castle, not ten thousand re-embarked; whilst of the eight or nine thousand defenders, barely six hundred were able to join in the Te Deum of thanks for the successful termination of what was one of the greatest struggles in ancient or modern times. Then it was that "the most illustrous and most Reverend Lord, Brother John de la Valette," to quote his titles inscribed over the Porta Reale, determined to lay out the new city, so that, before twelve months passed, the primeval prophecy that there would be a time when every foot of land in Monte Sceberras would be worth an ounce of silver bade fair to come true. St. Elmo is still the chief of the island fortresses, and the little chapel which the knights left to fall under the Turkish scimitars is again in good preservation, after having been long forgotten under a pile of rubbish. But though churchmen and soldiers, the masters of Malta were, if all tales are true, a good deal more militaires than monks. Eye-witnesses describe the knights as they sailed on a warlike expedition waving their hands to fair ladies on the shore. In their albergos or barracks the "Languages" lived luxuriously, and though dueling was strictly prohibited, there is a narrow street, the Strada Stretta, running parallel with the Reale, in which this extremely unecclesiastical mode of settling disputes was winked at. For by a pleasant fiction, any encounter within its limits was regarded as simply a casual difficulty occasioned by two fiery gentlemen accidentally jostling each other!

Turning into the Strada Mercanti, the San Giacomio 286] of a former nomenclature, we come upon more reminders of this picturesque brotherhood. For close by the Hospital for Incurables is the site of their cemetery, and farther up the steep street is the Military Hospital, which was founded by the Grand Master, Fra Luis de Vasconçelos. This infirmary, as an old writer tells us, was in former days "the very glory of Malta." Every patient had two beds for change, and a closet with lock and key to himself. No more than two people were put in one ward, and these were waited upon by the "Serving Brothers," their food being brought to them on silver dishes, and everything else ordered with corresponding magnificence. Nowadays, though scarcely so sumptuous, the hospital is still a noble institution, one of the rooms, four hundred and eighty feet in length, being accounted the longest in Europe. But there are no silver dishes, and the nurses have ceased to be of knightly rank. The University, an institution which turns out doctors with a celerity which accounts for the number of them in the island, is an even less imposing building than the public pawnbroking establishment hard by, and neither is so noteworthy as the market, which is remarkable from a literary point of view as being perhaps the only edifice in Valletta the founder of which has been content to inscribe his merits in the vulgar tongue. On the top of the hill, for we have been climbing all the time, is a house with a fine marble doorway, which also is the relic of the knights. For this building was the Castellania, or prison, and the pillory in which prisoners did penance, and the little window from above which prisoners were suspended by the hands, are still, with the huge hook to which the rope was attached, to be seen by those who are curious in such disciplinary matters. But like the 287] rock-hewn dungeons in which the knights kept their two thousand galley-slaves, in most cases Turks and Moors who had fallen in the way of their war-ships, which still exist in the rear of the Dockyard Terrace, such reminders of a cruel age and a stern Order are depressing to the wanderer in search of the picturesque. He prefers to look at the Auberge of the Language of Italy, where the Royal Engineers have their quarters, or at the Palazzo Parisi, opposite (it is a livery stable at present), where General Bonaparte resided during that brief stay in Malta which has served ever since to make the French name abhorred in the island, or at the Auberge de Castille, the noblest of all the knights' palaces, where the two scientific corps hold their hospitable mess.

We have now tramped the entire length of the two chief longitudinal streets of Malta, and have seen most of the buildings of much general interest. But in the Strade Mezzodi and Britannica there are many private dwellings of the best description, and even some public ones, like the Auberge de France (devoted to the head of the Commissariat Department), warrant examination from a historical if not from an architectural, point of view. All of these knightly hotels are worthy of notice. Most of them are now

131

appropriated to the needs of Government offices or, like the Auberge d'Arragon (an Episcopal residence), to the housing of local dignitaries. But where the Auberge d'Allemagne once stood the collegiate church of St. Paul has been built, and if there ever was an Auberge d'Angleterre (for the language of England was suppressed when Henry VIII. confiscated the English Commanderies and was early succeeded by that of Bavaria), the building which bore her name was leveled when the new theater was built. It is nevertheless 288] certain that the Turcopolier or General of the Horse was, until the Reformation, selected from the Language of England, just as that of Provence always furnished the Grand Commander, France the Grand Hospitaller, Italy the Admiral, Arragon the Drapier, Auvergne the Commander, Germany the Grand Bailiff, and Castile the Grand Chancellor of the Sovereign Order, whose Grand Master held among other titles those of Prince of Malta and Gozo.

We are now at the Upper Barracca, one of those arcades erected as promenades by the knights, and still the favorite walk of the citizens in the cool of morning and evening. From this point also is obtained a good bird's-eye view of Valletta and much of the neighboring country, and if the visitor continues his walk to St. Andrew's Bastion he may witness a panorama of both harbors; one, which the Maltese affirm (and we are not called upon to contradict them), is surpassed by the Bosphorus alone. It is at all events the most picturesque of the island views. There at a glance may be seen the two chief harbors alive with boats, sailing vessels, and steamers, from the huge ironclad to the noisy little launch. We then see that beside the main peninsula upon which Valletta is built, and which divides the Quarantine from the Grand Harbor, there are several other headlands projecting into these ports in addition to the island occupied by Fort Manoel and the Lazaretto. These narrow peninsulas cut the havens into a host of subsidiary basins, bays, and creeks, while Valletta itself has overflowed into the suburbs of Floriana, Sliema, and St. Julian, and may by-and-by occupy Tasbiesch and Pieta; Bighi, where the Naval Hospital is situated, and Corradino, associated with gay memories of the racecourse, and the more sombre 289] ones which pertain to the cemeteries and the prisons, all of which are centered in this quarter, where in former days the knights had their horse-breeding establishments and their game preserves.

But there are certain suburbs of Valletta which no good Maltese will describe by so humble a name. These are the "Three Cities" of Vittoriosa and Senglea, built on the two peninsulas projecting into the Grand Harbor, and separated by the Dockyard Creek, and Burmola or Cosspicua, stretching back from the shore. These three "cities" are protected by the huge Firenzuola and Cottonera lines of fortifications, and as Fort Angelo, the most ancient of the Maltese strongholds, and Fort Ricasoli, recalling the name of its builder, are among their castles, they hold their heads very high in Malta. Indeed, long before Valletta was thought of, and when Notabile was seen to be unfitted for their purpose, the knights took up their residence in Borgo or the Burgh, which, as the Statue of Victory still standing announces, was dignified by the name of Citta Vittoriosa after their victory over the Turks. Strada Antico Palazzo del Governatore recalls the old Palace which once stood in this street, and indeed until 1571 this now poor town was the seat of Government. Antique buildings, like the Nunnery of Santa Scolastica, once a hospital, and the Inquisitor's Palace, now the quarters of the English garrison, are witnesses to its fatten dignity. Burmola is also a city of old churches, and Senglea named after the Grand Master De la Sengle, though at present a place of little consequence, contains plenty of architectural proofs that when its old name of "Chersoneso," or the Peninsula, was changed to Isola, or "The Unconquered," this "city," with Fort Michael to do its fighting, played 290] in Malta militant a part almost as important as it does nowadays when its dockyard and arsenal are its chief titles to fame.

Turning our survey inland, we see from the Barracca a rolling country, whitish, dry, and uninviting, dotted with white rocks projecting above the surface; white little villages, each with its church and walled fields; and topping all, on the summit of a rising ground, a town over which rise the spires of a cathedral. This is Citta Vecchia, the "old city" as it was called when the capital was transferred to Valletta, though the people round about still call it by the Saracenic name of "Medina," (the town), the more modern designation of "Notabile" being due to a complimentary remark of Alfonso the Magnanimous, King of Castile. No town in Malta is more ancient. Here, we know from the famous oration of Cicero, that Verres, Prætor of Sicily, established some manufactories for cotton goods, out of which were made women's dresses of extraordinary magnificence, and here also the same voluptuous ruler did a reprehensible amount of plundering from temples and the "abodes of wealthy and honorable citizens." In their time-honored capital the Grand Masters had to be inaugurated, and in its cathedral every Bishop of Malta must still be consecrated. But the glory of Notabile is its memories, for in all Christendom there is no more silent city than the one towards which we creep by means of the island railway which has of late years shortened the eight miles between it and Valletta. Every rood, after leaving the cave-like station hollowed out of the soft solid rock, and the tunnels under the fortifications, seems sleepier and sleepier. Every few minutes we halt at a white-washed shed hard by a white-washed "casal." And all the "casals" seem 291] duplicates of each other. The white streets of these villages are narrow, and the people few. But the church is invariably disproportionately large, well built, and rich in decorations, while the shops in the little square are much poorer than people who support so fine a church ought to patronize. There is Hamrun, with its Apostolic Institute directed by Algerian missionaries, Misada in the valley, and Birchircara. Casal Curmi, where the cattle market is held, is seen in the distance, and at Lia and Balzan we are among the orange and lemon gardens for which these villages are famous. The San Antonio Palace, with its pleasant grounds, forms a relief to the eye. At Attard, "the village of roses," the aqueduct which supplies Valletta with the water of Diar Handur comes in sight, and then, at San Salvador, the train begins the steep pull which ends at the base of the hill on which Notabile is built.

On this slope are little terraced fields and remains of what must at one time have been formidable fortifications. But all is crumbling now. A few of the Valletta merchants are taking advantage of the railway by building country houses, and some of the old Maltese nobility cling to the town associated with their quondam glory. But its decaying mansions with their mouldering coats of arms, palaces appropriated to prosaic purposes, ramparts from which for ages the clash of arms has departed, and streets silent except for the tread of the British soldiers stationed there or the mumble of the professional beggar, tell a tale of long-departed greatness. A statue of Juno is embedded in the gateway, and in the shed-like museum have been collected a host of Phœnician, Roman, and other remains dug out of the soil of the city. Maltese boys pester us to buy copper coins of the knights which 292] are possibly honest, and their parents produce silver ones which are probably apocryphal.

In Notabile itself there is not, however, a great deal to look at, though from the summit of the Sanatorium, of old the Courts of Justice (and there are dreadful dungeons underneath it still), a glance may be obtained over the entire island. To the prosaic eye it looks rather dry to be the "Fior del Mondo," the flower of the world, as the patriotic Maltese terms the land which he leaves with regret and returns to with joy. There to the south lies Verdala Palace, and the Boschetto, a grove in much request for picnic parties from Valletta, and beyond both, the Inquisitor's summer palace, close to where the sea spray is seen flying against the rugged cliffs. The Bingemma hills, thick with Phœnician tombs, are seen to the west, and if the pedestrian cares he may visit the old rock fortress of Kala ta Bahria, Imtarfa, where stood the temple of Proserpine, and Imtahleb near the seashore, where in the season wild strawberries abound. Musta, with its huge domed church, is prominent enough to the northeast, while with a glass it is not difficult to make out Zebbar and Zeitun, Zurrico, Paola, and other villages of the southeastern coast scattered through a region where remains of the past are very plentiful. For here are the ruins of the temples of Hagiar Khim and Mnaidra, rude prehistoric monuments, and on the shore of the Marsa Scirocco (a bay into which the hot wind of Africa blows direct), is a megalithic wall believed to be the last of the temple of Melkarte, the Tyrian Hercules.

But in Notabile, far before Apollo and Proserpine, whose marble temples stood here, before even the knights, whose three centuries of iron rule have a singular fascination for the Maltese, there is a name very often in many 293] mouths. And that is "San Paolo." Saint Paul is in truth the great man of Malta, and the people make very much of him. He is almost as popular a personage as Sir Thomas Maitland, the autocratic "King Tom," of whose benevolent despotism and doughty deeds also one is apt in time to get a little tired. Churches and streets and cathedrals are dedicated to the Apostle of the Gentiles, and from the summit of the Sanatorium a barefooted Maltese points out "the certain creek with a shore" in which he was wrecked, the island of Salmun, on which there is a statue of him, and the church erected in his honor. It is idle to hint to this pious son of Citta Vecchia that it is doubtful whether Paul was ever wrecked in Malta at all, that not unlikely the scene of that notable event was Melita, in the Gulf of Ragusa. Are there not hard by serpents turned into stone, if no living serpents to bite anybody, and a miraculous fountain which bursts forth at the Apostle's bidding? And is not "the tempestuous wind called Euroklydon" blowing at this very moment? And in the cathedral we learn for the first time that Publius, on the site of whose house it is built, became the first bishop of Malta. For is not his martyrdom sculptured in marble, and painted on canvas? And by-and-by we see the grotto in which St. Paul did three months' penance, though the reason is not explained, and over it the chapel raised to the memory of the converted Roman Governor, and not far away the Catacombs in which the early Christians sheltered themselves, though whether there is an underground passage from there to Valletta, as historians affirm, is a point in which our barefooted commentator is not agreed.

All these are to him irreverent doubts. Notabile, with its cathedral, and convents, and monasteries, its church 294] of St. Publius, the "stone of which never grows less," the seminary for priests, the Bishop's Palace and the Bishop's Hospital, is no place for scepticism touching Saint Paul and his voyages. Any such unbeliefs we had better carry elsewhere. The day is hot and the old city is somnolent, and the talk is of the past. At the wicket gate of the little station at the hill foot the engine is, at least, of the present. And as we slowly steam into Valletta, and emerge into the busy street, we seem to have leapt in an hour from the Middle Ages into the Twentieth Century. The band is playing in the Palace Square, and the politicians are in procession over some event with which we as seekers after the picturesque are not concerned. But in Valletta we are in the land of living men. Behind us is a city of the dead, and around it lie villages which seem never to have been alive.

XIII

SICILY

Scylla and Charybdis—Messina, the chief commercial center of Sicily—The magnificent ruins of the Greek Theater at Taormina—Omnipresence of Mt. Etna—Approach to Syracuse—The famous Latomia del Paradiso—Girgenti, the City of Temples—Railway route to Palermo—Mosaics—Cathedral and Abbey of Monreale—Monte Pellegrino at the hour of sunset.

TO the traveller who proposes to enter Sicily by the favorite sea-route from Naples to Messina the approach to the island presents a scene of singular interest and beauty. A night's voyage from the sunny bay which sleeps at the foot of Vesuvius suffices to bring him almost within the shadow of Etna. By daybreak he has just passed the Punta del Faro, the lighthoused promontory at the extreme northeastern angle of this three-cornered isle, the Trinacria of the ancients, and is steaming into the Straits. Far to his left he can see, with the eye of faith at any rate, the rock of Scylla jutting out from the Calabrian coast, while the whirlpool of Charybdis, he will do well to believe, is eddying and foaming at the foot of the Pharos a few hundred yards to his right. Here let him resolutely locate the fabled monster of the gaping jaws into which were swept those luckless mariners of old whose dread of Scylla drove them too near to the Sicilian shore. Modern geographers may maintain (as what will they not 296]maintain?) that Charybdis should be identified with the Garofalo, the current which sweeps round the breakwater of Messina seven miles to the south; but Circe distinctly told Ulysses that the two monsters were not a "bowshot apart"; and the perfectly clear and straightforward account given of the matter by Æneas to Dido renders it impossible to doubt that Scylla and Charybdis faced each other at the mouth of the Straits. The traveller will be amply justified in believing that he has successfully negotiated the passage between these two terrors as soon as he has left the Pharos behind him and is speeding along the eastern coast of the island towards the city of Messina.

Very bold and impressive grows the island scenery under the gradually broadening daylight. Tier on tier above him rise the bare, brown hill-slopes, spurs of the great mountain pyramid which he is approaching. These tumbled masses of the mountains, deepening here where the night shadow still lingers into downright black, and reddening there where they "take the morning" to the color of rusty iron, proclaim their volcanic character, to all who are familiar with the signs thereof, unmistakably enough. Just such a ferruginous face does Nature turn towards you as you drop down at twilight past the Isleta of Las Palmas, in Gran Canaria, or work your way from the eastern to the western coast of Teneriffe, round the spreading skirts of the Peak. Rock scenery of another character is visible on the left, among the Calabrian mountains, dwarfed somewhat by the nearer as well as loftier heights of the island opposite, but bearing no mean part in the composition of the land- and sea-scape, nevertheless. Mile after mile the view maintains its rugged beauty, and when at last the town and harbor 297] of Messina rise in sight, and the fort of Castellaccio begins to fill the eye, to the exclusion of the natural ramparts of the hills, the traveller will be fain to admit that few islands in the world are approached through scenery so romantic and so well attuned to its historic associations.

There are those who find Messina disappointing, and there is no doubt that to quit the waters of a rock-embosomed strait for the harbor of a large commercial seaport possessing no special claim to beauty of situation, is to experience a certain effect of disenchantment. It would not be fair, however, to hold the town, as a town, responsible for this. It is only some such jewel as Naples or as Algiers that could vie with such a setting. Messina is not an Algiers or a Naples; it is only an honest, ancient, prosperous, active, fairly clean, and architecturally unimpressive town. The chief commercial center of Sicily, with upwards of eighty thousand inhabitants, a Cathedral, an Archbishop, and a University, it can afford, its inhabitants perhaps believe, to dispense with æsthetic attractions. But its spacious quays, its fine and curiously shaped port, the Harbor of the Sickle as it was called by the ancients when after it they named the city "Zancle," have an interest of their own if they are without much claim to the picturesque; and the view from the Faro Grande on the curve of the Sickle, with the Sicilian mountains behind, the Calabrian rocks in front, and the Straits to the right and left of the spectator, is not to be despised.

Still, Messina is not likely to detain any pleasure-tourist long, especially with Taormina, the gem of the island, and one might almost say, indeed, of all Italy, awaiting him at only the distance of a railway journey of some sixty to a hundred miles. The line from Messina 298] to Giardini, the station for Taormina, and the spot whence Garibaldi crossed to Calabria in the autumn of 1860, skirts the sea-coast, burrowing under headlands and spanning dry river-beds for a distance of thirty miles, amid the scenery which has been already viewed from the Straits, but which loses now from its too close neighborhood to the eye. The rock-built town of ancient Taormina is perched upon a steep and craggy bluff some four hundred feet above the railway line, and is approached by an extremely circuitous road of about three miles in length. Short cuts there are for the youthful, the impetuous, and the sound in wind; but even these fortunate persons might do worse than save their breath and restrain their impatience to reach their destination, if only for the sake of the varying panorama which unfolds itself as they ascend from level to level on their winding way. There can be no denying that Taormina stands nobly and confronts the Straits with a simple dignity that many greater and even higher cities might well envy. To see it from a favoring angle of the battlemented road, with the southern sunlight bathing its bright white walls and broken lines of housetops, with the tower of Sant' Agostino traced against the cone of Etna, and the wall that skirts it almost trembling on the utmost verge of the cliff, while at the foot of the declivity the Straits trend southward in "tender, curving lines of creamy spray," to see this is at least to admit that some short cuts are not worth taking, and that the bridle-path up the hillside might well be left to those animals for whose use it was constructed, and who are generally believed

136

to prefer an abridgment of their journey to any conceivable enhancement of its picturesque attractions.

At Taormina one may linger long. The pure, inspiriting 299] air of its lofty plateau, and the unequaled beauty of the prospect which it commands, would alone be sufficient to stay the hurried footsteps of even the most time-pressed of "globe-trotters"; but those who combine a love of scenery with a taste for archæology and the classical antique will find it indeed a difficult place to leave. For, a little way above the town, and in the center of an exquisite landscape stand the magnificent ruins of the Greek Theater, its auditorium, it is true, almost leveled with the plain, but more perfect as to the remains of its stage and proscenium than any other in Sicily, and, with one exception, in the world. But there is no need to be a scholar or an antiquarian to feel the extraordinary fascination of the spot. Nowhere among all the relics of bygone civilizations have Time and Nature dealt more piously with the work of man. Every spring and summer that have passed over those mouldering columns and shattered arches have left behind them their tribute of clasping creeper and clambering wild flower and softly draping moss. Boulder and plinth in common, the masonry alike of Nature and of man, have mellowed into the same exquisite harmony of greys and greens; and the eye seeks in vain to distinguish between the handiwork of the Great Mother and those monuments of her long-dead children which she has clothed with an immortality of her own.

Apart, however, from the indescribable charm of its immediate surroundings, the plateau of the theater must fix itself in the memory of all who have entered Sicily by way of Messina as having afforded them their first "clear" view of Etna, their first opportunity, that is to say, of looking at the majestic mountain uninterrupted at any point of its outline or mass by objects on a lower 300] level. The whole panorama indeed from this point is magnificent. To the left, in the foreground, rise the heights of Castiglione from the valley of the Alcantara; while, as the eye moves round the prospect from left to right, it lights in succession on the hermitage of S. Maria della Rocca, the Castle of Taormina, the overhanding hill of Mola, and Monte Venere towering above it. But, dominating the whole landscape, and irresistibly recalling to itself the gaze which wanders for a moment to the nearer chain of mountains or the blue Calabrian hills across the Strait, arises the never-to-be-forgotten pyramid of Etna, a mountain unrivaled in its combination of majesty and grace, in the soft symmetry of its "line," and the stern contrast between its lava-scarred sides, with their associations of throe and torture, and the eternal peace of its snow-crowned head. It will be seen at a closer view from Catania, and, best of all, on the journey from that place to Syracuse; but the first good sight of it from Taormina, at any rate when weather and season have been favorable, is pretty sure to become an abiding memory.

Twenty miles farther southwards along the coast lie the town and baths of Aci Reale, a pleasant resort in the "cure" season, but to others than invalids more interesting in its associations with Theocritus and Ovid, with "Homer the Handel of Epos, and Handel the Homer of song;" in a word, with Acis and Galatea, and Polyphemus, and the much-enduring Ulysses. Aci Castello, a couple of miles or so down the coast, is, to be precise, the exact spot which is associated with these very old-world histories, though Polyphemus's sheep-run probably extended far along the coast in both directions, and the legend of the giant's defeat and discomfiture by the hero 301] of the Odyssey is preserved in the nomenclature of the rocky chain which juts out at this point from the Sicilian shore. The Scogli dei Ciclopi are a fine group of basaltic rocks, the biggest of them some two hundred feet in height and two thousand feet in circumference, no doubt "the stone far greater than the first" with which Polyphemus took his shot at the retreating Wanderer, and which "all but struck the end of the rudder." It is a capital "half-brick" for a giant to "heave" at a stranger, whether the Cyclops did, in fact, heave it or not; and, together with its six companions, it stands out bravely and with fine sculpturesque effect against the horizon. A few miles farther on is Catania, the second city in population and importance of Sicily, but, except for one advantage which would give distinction to the least interesting of places, by no means the second in respect of beauty. As a town, indeed, it is commonplace. Its bay, though of ample proportions, has no particular grace of contour; and even the clustering masts in its busy harbor scarcely avail to break the monotony of that strip of houses on the flat seaboard, which, apart from its surroundings, is all that constitutes Catania. But with Etna brooding over it day and night, and the town lying outstretched and nestling between the two vast arms which the giant thrusts out towards the sea on each side, Catania could not look wholly prosaic and uninteresting even if she tried.

We must again return to the mountain, for Etna, it must be remembered, is a persistent feature, is the persistent feature of the landscape along nearly the whole eastern coast of Sicily from Punta di Faro to the Cape of Santa Croce, if not to the promontory of Syracuse. Its omnipresence becomes overawing as one hour of 302] travel succeeds another and the great mountain is as near as ever. For miles upon miles by this southward course it haunts the traveller like a reproving conscience. Each successive stage on his journey gives him only a different and not apparently more distant view. Its height, ten thousand feet, although, of course, considerable, seems hardly sufficient to account for this perpetual and unabating prominence, which, however, is partly to be explained by the outward trend taken by the sea-coast after we pass Catania, and becoming more and more marked during the journey from that city to Syracuse. There could be no better plan of operations for one who wishes to view the great mountain thoroughly, continuously, protractedly, and at its best, than to await a favorable afternoon, and then to take the journey in question by railway, so timing it as to reach the tongue of Santa Croce about sunset. From Catania to Lentini the traveller has Etna, wherever visible, on his right; at Lentini the line of railway takes a sharp turn to the left, and, striking the coast at Agnone, hugs it all along the northern shore of the promontory, terminating with Cape Santa Croce, upon approaching which point it doubles back upon itself, to follow the "re-entering angle" of the cape, and then, once more turning to the left, runs nearly due southward along the coast to Syracuse. Throughout the twenty miles or so from Lentini to Augusta, beneath the promontory of Santa Croce, Etna lies on the traveller's left, with the broad blue bay fringed for part of the way by a mile-wide margin of gleaming sand between him and it. Then the great volcanic cone, all its twenty miles from summit to sea-coast foreshortened into nothingness by distance, seems to be rising from the very sea; its long-cooled lava streams might 303]almost be mingling with the very waters of the bay. As the rays of the westering sun strike from across the island upon silver-gray sand and blue-purple sea and russet-iron mountain slopes, one's first impulse is to exclaim with

Wordsworth, in vastly differing circumstances, that "earth hath not anything to show more fair." But it has. For he who can prolong his view of the mountain until after the sun has actually sunk will find that even the sight he has just witnessed can be surpassed. He must wait for the moment when the silver has gone out of the sand, and the purple of the sea has changed to gray, and the russet of Etna's lava slopes is deepening into black; for that is also the moment when the pink flush of the departed sunset catches its peak and closes the symphony of color with a chord more exquisitely sweet than all.

From Cape Santa Croce to Syracuse the route declines a little perhaps in interest. The great volcano which has filled the eye throughout the journey is now less favorably placed for the view, and sometimes, as when the railway skirts the Bay of Megara in a due southward direction, is altogether out of sight. Nor does the approach to Syracuse quite prepare one for the pathetic charm of this most interesting of the great, dead, half-deserted cities of the ancient world, or even for the singular beauty of its surroundings. You have to enter the inhabited quarter itself, and to take up your abode on that mere sherd and fragment of old Greek Syracuse, the Island of Ortygia, to which the present town is confined (or rather, you have to begin by doing this, and then to sally forth on a long walk of exploration round the contorni, to trace the line of the ancient fortifications, and to map out as best you may the four other quarters, each 304] far larger than Ortygia, which, long since given over to orange-gardens and scattered villas and farmhouses, were once no doubt well-peopled districts of the ancient city), ere you begin either to discover its elements of material beauty or to feel anything of its spiritual magic. It is hard to believe that this decayed and apparently still decaying little island town was once the largest of the Hellenic cities, twenty miles, according to Strabo, in circumference, and even in the time of Cicero containing in one of its now deserted quarters "a very large Forum, most beautiful porticoes, a highly decorated Town Hall, a most spacious Senate House, and a superb Temple of Jupiter Olympius." A spoiler more insatiable than Verres has, alas! carried off all these wonders of art and architecture, and of most of them not even a trace of the foundations remains. Of the magnificent Forum a single unfluted column appears to be the solitary relic. The porticoes, the Town Hall, the Senate House, the Temple of the Olympian Jove are irrecoverable even by the most active architectural imagination. But the west wall of the district which contained these treasures is still partially traceable, and in the adjoining quarter of the ancient city we find ourselves in its richest region both of the archæological and the picturesque.

For here is the famous Latomia del Paradiso, quarry, prison, guard-house, and burial-place of the Syracusan Greek, and the yet more famous Theater, inferior to that of Taormina in the completeness of the stage and proscenium, but containing the most perfectly preserved auditorium in the world. The entrance to the Latomia, that gigantic, ear-shaped orifice hewn out of the limestone cliff, and leading into a vast whispering-chamber, the acoustic properties of which have caused it to be 305] identified with the (historic or legendary) Ear of Dionysius, has a strange, wild impressiveness of its own. But in beauty though not in grandeur it is excelled by another abandoned limestone quarry in the neighborhood, which has been converted by its owner into an orangery. This lies midway between the Latomia del Paradiso and the Quarry of the Cappuccini, and is in truth a lovely retreat. Over it broods the perfect stillness that never seems so deep as in those deserted places which have once been haunts of busy life. It is rich in the spiritual charm of natural beauty and the sensuous luxury of sub-tropical culture: close at hand the green and gold of orange trees, in the middle distance the solemn plumes of the cypresses,

139

and farther still the dazzling white walls of the limestone which the blue sky bends down to meet.

To pass from the quarries to the remains of the Greek Theater hard by is in some measure to exchange the delight of the eye for the subtler pleasures of mental association. Not that the concentric curves of these moldering and moss-lined stone benches are without their appeal to the senses. On the contrary, they are beautiful in themselves, and, like all architectural ruins, than which no animate things in nature more perfectly illustrate the scientific doctrine of "adaptation to environment," they harmonize deliciously in line and tone with their natural surroundings. Yet to most people, and especially so to those of the contemplative habit, the Greek Theater at Syracuse, like the Amphitheaters of Rome and Verona, will be most impressive at moments when the senses are least active and the imagination busiest. It is when we abstract the mind from the existing conditions of the ruin; it is when we "restore" it by those processes of mental architecture which can never blunder into Vandalism; it is 306] when we re-people its silent, time-worn benches with the eager, thronging life of twenty centuries ago, that there is most of magic in its spell. And here surely imagination has not too arduous a task, so powerfully is it assisted by the wonderful completeness of these remains. More than forty tiers of seats shaped out of the natural limestone of the rock can still be quite distinctly traced; and though their marble facings have of course long moldered into dust, whole cunei of them are still practically as uninjured by time, still as fit for the use for which they were intended, as when the Syracusans of the great age of Attic Drama flocked hither to hear the tragedies of that poet whom they so deeply reverenced that to be able to recite his verse was an accomplishment rewarded in the prisoners who possessed it by liberation from bondage. To the lover of classical antiquity Syracuse will furnish "moments" in abundance; but at no other spot either in Ortygia itself or in these suburbs of the modern city, not at the Fountain of Arethusa on the brink of the great port; not in the Temple of Minerva, now the Cathedral, with its Doric columns embedded in the ignominy of plaster; not in that wildest and grandest of those ancient Syracusan quarries, the Latomia dei Cappuccini, where the ill-fated remnant of the routed army of Nicias is supposed to have expiated in forced labor the failure of the Sicilian Expedition, will he find it so easy to rebuild the ruined past as here on this desolate plateau, with these perfect monuments of the immortal Attic stage around him, and at his feet the town, the harbor, the promontory of Plemmyrium, the blue waters of the Ionian Sea.

It is time, however, to resume our journey and to make for that hardly less interesting or less beautifully situated 307] town of Sicily which is usually the next halting-place of the traveller. The route to Girgenti from Syracuse is the most circuitous piece of railway communication in the island. To reach our destination it is necessary to retrace our steps almost the whole way back to Catania. At Bicocca, a few miles distant from that city, the line branches off into the interior of the country for a distance of some fifty or sixty miles, when it is once more deflected, and then descends in a southwesterly direction towards the coast. At a few miles from the sea, within easy reach of its harbor, Porto Empedocle, lies Girgenti. The day's journey will have been an interesting one. Throughout its westward course the line, after traversing the fertile Plain of Catania, the rich grain-bearing district which made Sicily the granary of the Roman world, ascends gradually into a mountainous region and plunges between Calascibetta and Castrogiovanni into a tortuous ravine, above which rise towering the two last-named heights. The latter of the two is planted on the site of the plain of Enna, the scene of the earliest abduction recorded in history. Flowers no longer flourish in the same abundance on the meads from which Persephone was carried off by the Dark King of Hades; but the spot is still fair and fertile, truly a "green navel of the isle," the central Omphalos from which the eye ranges northward, eastward, and south-westward over each expanse of Trinacria's triple sea. But those who do not care to arrest their journey for the sake of sacrificing to Demeter, or of enjoying the finest, in the sense of the most extensive, view in Sicily, may yet admire the noble situation of the rock-built town of Castrogiovanni, looking down upon the railway from its beetling crag.

Girgenti, the City of Temples, the richest of all places 308] in the world save one in monuments of Pagan worship, conceals its character effectually enough from him who enters it from the north. Within the precincts of the existing city there is little sign to be seen of its archæological treasures, and, to tell the truth, it has but few attractions of its own. Agrigentum, according to Pindar "the most beautiful city of mortals," will not so strike a modern beholder; but that, no doubt, is because, like Syracuse and other famous seats of ancient art and religious reverence, it has shrunk to dimensions so contracted as to leave all the riches of those stately edifices to which it owed the fame of its beauty far outside its present boundaries. Nothing, therefore, need detain the traveller in the town itself (unless, indeed, he would snatch a brief visit to the later-built cathedral, remarkable for nothing but the famous marble sarcophagus with its relief of the Myth of Hippolytus), and he will do well to mount the Rupe Atenea without delay. The view, however, in every direction is magnificent, the town to the right of the spectator and behind him, the sea in front, and the rolling, ruin-dotted plain between. From this point Girgenti itself looks imposing enough with the irregular masses of its roofs and towers silhouetted against the sky. But it is the seaward view which arrests and detains the eye. Hill summit or hotel window, it matters little what or where your point of observation is, you have but to look from the environs of Girgenti towards Porto Empedocle, a few miles to the south, and you bring within your field of vision a space of a few dozen acres in extent which one may reasonably suppose to have no counterpart in any area of like dimensions on the face of the globe. It is a garden of moldering shrines, a positive orchard of shattered porticoes 309] and broken column-shafts, and huge pillars prostrate at the foot of their enormous plinths. You can count and identify and name them all even from where you stand. Ceres and Proserpine, Juno Lacinia, Concord, Hercules, Æsculapius, Jupiter Olympius, Castor and Pollux, all are visible at once, all recognizable and numerable from east to west in their order as above. It is a land of ruined temples, and, to all appearance, of nothing else. One can just succeed, indeed, in tracing the coils of the railway as it winds like a black snake towards Porto Empedocle, but save that there are no signs of life. One descries no wagon upon the roads, no horse in the furrows, no laborer among the vines. Girgenti itself, with its hum and clatter, lies behind you; no glimpse of life or motion is visible on the quays of the port. All seems as desolate as those gray and moldering fanes of the discrowned gods, a solitude which only changes in character without deepening in intensity as the eye travels across the foam-fringed coast-line out on the sailless sea. There is a strange beauty in this silent Pantheon of dead deities, this landscape which might almost seem to be still echoing the last wail of the dying Pan; and it is a beauty of death and desolation to which the like of nature, here especially abounding, contributes not a little by contrast. For nowhere in Sicily is the country-side more lavishly enriched by the olive. Its contorted stem and quivering, silvery foliage are everywhere. Olives climb the hill-slopes in straggling files; olives cluster in twos and threes and larger groups upon the level plain; olives trace themselves against the broken walls of the temples, and one

141

catches the flicker of their branches in the sunlight that streams through the roofless peristyles. From Rupe Atenea out across the plain to where the eye lights upon 310] the white loops of the road to Porto Empedocle one might almost say that every object which is not a temple or a fragment of a temple is an olive tree.

By far the most interesting of the ruins from the archæologist's point of view is that of the Temple of Concord, which, indeed, is one of the best-preserved in existence, thanks, curiously enough, to the religious Philistinism which in the Middle Ages converted it into a Christian church. It was certainly not in the spirit of its tutelary goddess that it was so transformed: nothing, no doubt, was farther from the thoughts of those who thus appropriated the shrine of Concord than to illustrate the doctrine of the unity of religion. But art and archæology, if not romance, have good reason to thank them that they "took over" the building on any grounds, for it is, of course, to this circumstance that we owe its perfect condition of preservation, and the fact that all the details of the Doric style as applied to religious architecture can be studied in this temple while so much of so many of its companion fanes has crumbled into indistinguishable ruin. Concordia has remained virtually intact through long centuries under the homely title of "the Church of St. Gregory of the Turnips," and it rears its stately façade before the spectator in consequence with architrave complete, a magnificent hexastyle of thirty-four columns, its lateral files of thirteen shafts apiece receding in noble lines of perspective. Juno Lacinia, or Juno Lucinda (for it may have been either as the "Lacinian Goddess" or as the Goddess of Childbed that Juno was worshipped here), an older fane than Concordia, though the style had not yet entered on its decline when the latter temple was built, is to be seen hard by, a majestic and touching ruin. It dates from the fifth century 311] b. c., and is therefore Doric of the best period. Earthquakes, it seems, have co-operated with time in the work of destruction, and though twenty-five whole pillars are left standing, the façade, alas! is represented only by a fragment of architrave. More extensive still have been the ravages inflicted on the Temple of Hercules by his one unconquerable foe. This great and famous shrine, much venerated of old by the Agrigentines, and containing that statue of the god which the indefatigable "collector" Verres vainly endeavored to loot, is now little more than a heap of tumbled masonry, with one broken column-shaft alone still standing at one extremity of its site. But it is among the remains of the ancient sanctuary of Zeus, all unfinished, though that edifice was left by its too ambitious designers, that we get the best idea of the stupendous scale on which those old-world religious architects and masons worked. The ruin itself has suffered cruelly from the hand of man; so much so, indeed, that little more than the ground plan of the temple is to be traced by the lines of column bases, vast masses of its stone having been removed from its site to be used in the construction of the Mole. But enough remains to show the gigantic scale on which the work was planned and partially carried out. The pillars which once stood upon those bases were twenty feet in circumference, or more than two yards in diameter and each of their flutings forms a niche big enough to contain a man! Yon Caryatid, who has been carefully and skillfully pieced together from the fragments doubtless of many Caryatids, and who now lies, hands under head, supine and staring at the blue sky above him, is more than four times the average height of a man. From the crown of his bowed head to his stony soles he measures 312]twenty-five feet, and to watch a tourist sitting by or on him and gazing on Girgenti in the distance is to be visited by a touch of that feeling of the irony of human things to which Shelley gives expression in his "Ozymandias."

The railway route from Girgenti to Palermo is less interesting than that from Catania to Girgenti. It runs pretty nearly due south and north across the island from shore to shore, through a country mountainous indeed, as is Sicily everywhere, but not marked by anything particularly striking in the way of highland scenery. At Termini we strike the northern coast, and the line branches off to the west. Another dozen miles or so brings us to Santa Flavia, whence it is but half an hour's walk to the ruins of Soluntum, situated on the easternmost hill of the promontory of Catalfano. The coast-view from this point is striking, and on a clear day the headland of Cefalu, some twenty miles away to the eastward, is plainly visible. Ten more miles of "westing" and we approach Palermo, the Sicilian capital, a city better entered from the sea, to which it owes its beauty as it does its name.

To the traveller fresh from Girgenti and its venerable ruins, or from Syracuse with its classic charm, the first impressions of Palermo may very likely prove disappointing. Especially will they be so if he has come with a mind full of historic enthusiasm and a memory laden with the records of Greek colonization, Saracen dominion, and Norman conquest, and expecting to find himself face to face with the relics and remainder of at any rate the modern period of the three. For Palermo is emphatically what the guide-books are accustomed to describe as "a handsome modern city"; which means, as most people familiar with the Latin countries are but too well aware, 313] a city as like any number of other Continental cities, built and inhabited by Latin admirers and devotees of Parisian "civilization," as "two peas in a pod." In the Sicilian capital the passion for the monotonous magnificence of the boulevard has been carried to an almost amusing pitch. Palermo may be regarded from this point of view as consisting of two most imposing boulevards of approximately equal length, each bisecting the city with scrupulous equality from east to west and from north to south, and intersecting each other in its exact center at the mathematically precise angle of ninety degrees. You stand at the Porta Felice, the water-gate of the city, with your back to the sea, and before you, straight as a die, stretches the handsome Via Vittorio Emanuele for a mile or more ahead. You traverse the handsome Via Vittorio Emanuele for half its length and you come to the Quattro Canti, a small octagonal piazza which boasts itself to be the very head of Palermo, and from this intersection of four cross-roads, you see stretching to right and left of you the equally handsome Via Macqueda. Walk down either of these two great thoroughfares, the Macqueda or the Vittorio Emanuele, and you will be equally satisfied with each; the only thing which may possibly mar your satisfaction will be your consciousness that you would be equally satisfied with the other, and, indeed, that it requires an effort of memory to recollect in which of the two you are. There is nothing to complain of in the architecture or decoration of the houses. All is correct, regular, and symmetrical in line, bright and cheerful in color, and, as a whole, absolutely wanting in individuality and charm.

It is, however, of course impossible to kill an ancient and interesting city altogether with boulevards. Palermo, 314] like every other city, has its "bits," to be found without much difficulty by anyone who will quit the beaten track of the two great thoroughfares and go a-questing for them himself. He may thus find enough here and there to remind him that he is living on the "silt" of three, nay, four civilizations, on a fourfold formation to which Greek and Roman, Saracen and Norman, have each contributed its successive layer. It need hardly be said that the latter has left the deepest traces of any. The Palazzo Reale, the first of the Palermitan sights to which the traveller is likely to bend his way, will afford the best illustration of this. Saracenic in origin, it has received successive additions

143

from half-a-dozen Norman princes, from Robert Guiscard downwards, and its chapel, the Cappella Palatina, built by Roger II. in the early part of the twelfth century, is a gem of decorative art which would alone justify a journey to Sicily to behold. The purely architectural beauties of the interior are impressive enough, but the eye loses all sense of them among the wealth of their decoration. The stately files of Norman arches up the nave would in any other building arrest the gaze of the spectator, but in the Cappella Palatina one can think of nothing but mosaics. Mosaics are everywhere, from western door to eastern window, and from northern to southern transept wall. A full-length, life-sized saint in mosaic grandeur looks down upon you from every interval between the arches of the nave, and medallions of saints in mosaic, encircled with endless tracery and arabesque, form the inner face of every arch. Mosaic angels float with outstretched arms above the apse. A colossal Madonna and Bambino, overshadowed by a hovering Père Eternel, peer dimly forth in mosaic across the altar through the darkness of the chancel. 315] The ground is golden throughout, and the somber richness of the effect is indescribable. In Palermo and its environs, in the Church of Martorana, and in the Cathedral of Monreale, no less than here, there is an abundance of that same decoration, and the mosaics of the latter of the two edifices above mentioned are held to be the finest of all; but it is by those of the Cappella Palatina, the first that he is likely to make the acquaintance of, that the visitor, not being an expert or connoisseur in this particular species of art-work, will perhaps be the most deeply impressed.

The Palazzo Reale may doubtless too be remembered by him, as affording him the point of view from which he has obtained his first idea of the unrivaled situation of Palermo. From the flat roof of the Observatory, fitted up in the tower of S. Ninfa, a noble panorama lies stretched around us. The spectator is standing midway between Amphitrite and the Golden Shell that she once cast in sport upon the shore. Behind him lies the Conca d'Oro, with the range of mountains against which it rests, Grifone and Cuccio, and the Billieni Hills, and the road to Monreale winding up the valley past La Rocca; in front lies the noble curve of the gulf, from Cape Mongerbino to the port, the bold outlines of Monte Pellegrino, the Bay of Mondello still farther to the left, and Capo di Gallo completing the coast-line with its promontory dimly peering through the haze. Palermo, however, does not perhaps unveil the full beauty of its situation elsewhere than down at the sea's edge, with the city nestling in the curve behind one and Pellegrino rising across the waters in front.

But the environs of the city, which are of peculiar interest and attraction, invite us, and first among these is 316] Monreale, at a few miles' distance, a suburb to which the traveller ascends by a road commanding at every turn some new and striking prospect of the bay. On one hand as he leaves the town, lies the Capuchin Monastery, attractive with its catacombs of mummified ex-citizens of Palermo to the lover of the gruesome rather than of the picturesque. Farther on is the pretty Villa Tasca, then La Rocca, whence by a winding road of very ancient construction we climb the royal mount crowned by the famous Cathedral and Benedictine Abbey of Monreale. Here more mosaics, as has been said, as fine in quality and in even greater abundance than those which decorate the interior of the Cappella Palatina; they cover, it is said, an area of seventy thousand four hundred square feet. From the Cathedral we pass into the beautiful cloisters, and thence into the fragrant orange-garden, from which another delightful view of the valley towards Palermo is obtained. San Martino, the site of a suppressed Benedictine monastery, is the next spot of interest. A steep path branching off to the right from Monreale leads to a deserted fort, named Il Castellaccio, from which the road descends as far as S. Martino, whence a pleasant journey back to Palermo is made through the picturesque valley of Bocca di Falco.

The desire to climb a beautiful mountain is as strong as if climbing it were not as effectual a way of hiding its beauties as it would be to sit upon its picture; and Monte Pellegrino, sleeping in the sunshine, and displaying the noble lines of what must surely be one of the most picturesque mountains in the world, is likely enough to lure the traveller to its summit. That mass of gray limestone, which takes such an exquisite flush under the red rays of the evening, is not difficult to climb. The 317]zigzag path which mounts its sides is plainly visible from the town, and though steep at first, it grows gradually easier of ascent on the upper slopes of the mountain. Pellegrino was originally an island, and is still separated by the plain of the Conca d'Oro from the other mountains near the coast. Down to a few centuries ago it was clothed with underwood, and in much earlier times it grew corn for the soldiers of Hamilcar Barca, who occupied it in the first Punic War. Under an overhanging rock on its summit is the Grotto of Sta. Rosalia, the patron saint of the city, the maiden whom tradition records to have made this her pious retreat several centuries ago, and the discovery of whose remains in 1664 had the effect of instantaneously staying the ravages of the plague by which Palermo was just then being desolated. The grotto has since been converted, as under the circumstances was only fitting, into a church, to which many pilgrimages are undertaken by the devout. A steep path beyond the chapel leads to the survey station on the mountain top, from which a far-stretching view is commanded. The cone of Etna, over eighty miles off as the crow flies, can be seen from here, and still farther to the north, among the Liparæan group, the everlasting furnaces of Stromboli and Vulcano. There is a steeper descent of the mountain towards the southwest, and either by this or by retracing our original route we regain the road, which skirts the base of the mountain on the west, and, at four miles' distance from the gate of the town, conducts to one of the most charmingly situated retreats that monarch ever constructed for himself, the royal villa-chateau of La Favorita, erected by Ferdinand IV. (Ferdinand I. of the Two Sicilies), otherwise not the least uncomfortable of the series of uncomfortable 318] princes whom the Bourbons gave to the South Italian peoples.

Great as are the attractions of Palermo, they will hardly avail to detain the visitor during the rest of his stay in Sicily. For him who wishes to see Trinacria thoroughly, and who has already made the acquaintance of Messina and Syracuse, of Catania and Girgenti, the capital forms the most convenient of head-quarters from which to visit whatever places of interest remain to be seen in the western and southwestern corner of the island. For it is hence that, in the natural order of things, he would start for Marsala (famous as the landing-place of "the Thousand," under Garibaldi, in 1860, and the commencement of that memorable march which ended in a few weeks in the overthrow of the Bourbon rule) and Trapani (from drepanon), another sickle-shaped town, dear to the Virgilian student as the site of the games instituted by Æneas to the memory of the aged Anchises, who died at Eryx, a poetically appropriate spot for a lover of Aphrodite to end his days in. The town of the goddess on the top of Monte San Giuliano, the ancient Eryx, is fast sinking to decay. Degenerate descendants, or successors would perhaps be more correct, of her ancient worshippers prefer the plain at its foot, and year by year migrations take place thither which threaten to number this immemorial settlement of pagan antiquity among the dead cities of the past, and to leave its grass-grown streets and moldering cathedral alone with the sea and sky. There are no remains of the world-famed shrine of Venus Erycina now save a few traces of its foundation and an ancient reservoir, once a fountain dedicated to the goddess. One need not linger on San Giuliano longer than is needful to survey the mighty 319] maritime panorama which surrounds the spectator, and to note Cape Bon in Africa rising faintly out of the southward haze.

For Selinunto has to be seen, and Segesta, famous both for the grandeur and interest of their Greek remains. From Castelvetrano station, on the return route, it is but a short eight miles to the ruins of Selinus, the westernmost of the Hellenic settlements of Sicily, a city with a history of little more than two centuries of active life, and of upwards of two thousand years of desolation. Pammilus of Megara founded it, so says legend, in the seventh century b. c. In the fifth century of that era the Carthaginians destroyed it. Ever since that day it has remained deserted except as a hiding-place for the early Christians in the days of their persecution, and as a stronghold of the Mohammedans in their resistance to King Roger. Yet in its short life of some two hundred and twenty years it became, for some unknown reason of popular sanctity, the site of no fewer than seven temples, four of them among the largest ever known to have existed. Most of them survive, it is true, only in the condition of prostrate fragments, for it is supposed that earthquake and not time has been their worst foe, and the largest of them, dedicated to Hercules, or as some hold, to Appollo, was undoubtedly never finished at all. Its length, including steps, reaches the extraordinary figure of three hundred and seventy-one feet; its width, including steps, is a hundred and seventy-seven feet; while its columns would have soared when completed to the stupendous height of fifty-three feet. It dates from the fifth century b. c., and it was probably the appearance of the swarthy Carthaginian invaders which interrupted the masons at their work. It now lies a colossal heap of 320] mighty, prostrate, broken columns, their flutings worn nearly smooth by time and weather, and of plinths shaped and rounded by the same agencies into the similitude of gigantic mountain boulders.

It is, however, the temples of Selinunto rather than their surroundings which command admiration and in this respect they stand in marked contrast to that site of a single unnamed ruin, which is, perhaps, taking site and ruin together, the most "pathetic" piece of the picturesque in all Sicily, the hill and temple of Segesta. From Calatafimi, scene of one of the Garibaldian battles, to Segesta the way lies along the Castellamare road, and through a beautiful and well-watered valley. The site of the town itself is the first to be reached. Monte Barbaro, with the ruins of the theater, lies to the north, to the west the hill whereon stands the famous Temple. No one needs a knowledge of Greek archæology or Greek history, or even a special love for Greek art, in order to be deeply moved by the spectacle which the spot presents. He needs no more than the capacity of Virgil's hero to be touched by "the sense of tears in mortal things." The Temple itself is perfect, except that its columns are still unfluted; but it is not the simple and majestic outline of the building, its lines of lessening columns, or its massive architraves upborne upon those mighty shafts, which most impress us, but the harmony between this great work of man and its natural surroundings. In this mountain solitude, and before this deserted shrine of an extinct worship we are in presence of the union of two desolations, and one had well-nigh said of two eternities, the everlasting hills and the imperishable yearnings of the human heart. No words can do justice to the lonely grandeur of the Temple of Segesta. It is 321] unlike any other in Sicily in this matter of unique position. It has no rival temple near it, nor are there even the remains of any other building, temple or what not, to

146

challenge comparison, within sight of the spectator. This ruin stands alone in every sense, alone in point of physical isolation, alone in the austere pathos which that position imparts to it.

In the Museum of Palermo, to which city the explorer of these ruined sanctuaries of art and religion may now be supposed to have returned, the interesting metopes of Selinus will recall the recollection of that greater museum of ruins which he just visited at Selinunto; but the suppressed monastery, which has been now turned into a Museo Nazionale, has not much else besides its Hellenic architectural fragments to detain him. And it may be presumed, perhaps, that the pursuit of antiquities, which may be hunted with so much greater success in other parts of the islands, is not precisely the object which leads most visitors to Sicily to prolong their stay in this beautifully seated city. Its attraction lies, in effect and almost wholly, in the characteristic noted in the phrase just used. Architecturally speaking, Palermo is naught: it is branded, as has been already said, with the banality and want of distinction of all modern Italian cities of the second class. And, moreover, all that man has ever done for her external adornment she can show you in a few hours; but days and weeks would not more than suffice for the full appreciation of all she owes to nature. Antiquities she has none, or next to none, unless, indeed, we are prepared to include relics of the comparatively modern Norman domination, which of course abound in her beautiful mosaics, in that category. The silt of successive ages, and the detritus of a life which from the 322] earliest times has been a busy one, have irrecoverably buried almost all vestiges of her classic past. Her true, her only, but her all-sufficient attraction is conveyed in her ancient name. She is indeed "Panormus"; it is as the "all harbor city" that she fills the eye and mind and lingers in the memory and lives anew in the imagination. When the city itself and its environs as far as Monreale and San Martino and La Zisa have been thoroughly explored; when the imposing Porta Felice has been duly admired; when the beautiful gardens of La Flora, with its wealth of sub-tropical vegetation, has been sufficiently promenaded on; when La Cala, a quaint little narrow, shallow harbor, and the busy life on its quays have been adequately studied; then he who loves nature better than the works of man, and prefers the true eternal to the merely figurative "immortal," will confess to himself that Palermo has nothing fairer, nothing more captivating, to show than that chef-d' œuvre which the Supreme Artificer executed in shaping those noble lines of rock in which Pellegrino descends to the city at its foot, and in tracing that curve of coast-line upon which the city has sprung up under the mountain's shadow. The view of this guardian and patron height, this tutelary rock, as one might almost fancy it, of the Sicilian capital is from all points and at all hours beautiful. It dominates the city and the sea alike from whatever point one contemplates it, and the bold yet soft beauty of its contours has in every aspect a never-failing charm. The merest lounger, the most frivolous of promenaders in Palermo, should congratulate himself on having always before his eyes a mountain, the mere sight of which may be almost described as a "liberal education" in poetry and art. He should haunt the Piazza Marina, however, not merely at 323] the promenading time of day, but then also, nay, then most of all, when the throng has begun to thin, and, as Homer puts it, "all the ways are shadowed," at the hour of sunset. For then the clear Mediterranean air is at its clearest, the fringing foam at its whitest, the rich, warm background of the Conca d'Oro at its mellowest, while the bare, volcanic-looking sides of Monte Pellegrino seem fusing into ruddy molten metal beneath the slanting rays. Gradually, as you watch the color die out of it, almost as it dies out of a snow-peak at the fading of the Alpen-gluth, the shadows begin to creep up the mountain-sides, forerunners of the night which has already fallen upon the streets of the city, and through which its lights are beginning to peer. A little longer, and the body of the mountain will be a dark, vague mass, with only its cone and graceful upper ridges traced faintly against pale depths of sky.

Thus and at such an hour may one see the city, bay, and mountain at what may be called their æsthetic or artistic best. But they charm, and with a magic of almost equal potency, at all hours. The fascination remains unabated to the end, and never, perhaps, is it more keenly felt by the traveller than when Palermo is smiling her God-speed upon the parting guest, and from the deck of the steamer which is to bear him away he waves his last farewell to the receding city lying couched, the loveliest of Ocean's Nereids, in her shell of gold.

If his hour of departure be in the evening, when the rays of the westering sun strike athwart the base of Pellegrino, and tip with fire the summits of the low-lying houses of the seaport, and stream over and past them upon the glowing waters of the harbor the sight is one which will not be soon forgotten. Dimmer and dimmer 324] grows the beautiful city with the increasing distance and the gathering twilight. The warm rose-tints of the noble mountain cool down into purple, and darken at last into a heavy mass of somber shadows; the sea changes to that spectral silver which overspreads it in the gloaming. It is a race between the flying steamer and the falling night to hide the swiftly fading coast-line altogether from the view; and so close is the contest that up to the last it leaves us doubtful whether it be darkness or distance that has taken it from us. But in a few more minutes, be it from one cause or from the other, the effacement is complete. Behind us, where Palermo lay a while ago, there looms only a bank of ever-darkening haze, and before the bows of our vessel the gray expanse of Mediterranean waters which lie between us and the Bay of Naples.

325]

XIV

NAPLES

The Bay of Naples—Vesuvius—Characteristic scenes of street life—The alfresco restaurants—Chapel of St. Januarius—Virgil's Tomb—Capri, the Mecca of artists and lovers of the picturesque—The Emperor Tiberius—Description of the Blue Grotto—The coast-road from Castellamare to Sorrento—Amalfi—Sorrento, "the village of flowers and the flower of villages"—The Temples of Pæstum.

NAPLES in itself, apart from its surroundings, is not of surpassing beauty. Its claim to be "the most beautiful city in Europe" rests solely on the adventitious aid of situation. When the fictitious charm which distance gives is lost by a near approach, it will be seen that the city which has inspired the poets of all ages is little more than a huge, bustling, commonplace commercial port, not to be compared for a moment, æsthetically speaking, with Genoa, Florence, Venice, or many other Italian towns equally well known to the traveller. This inherent lack is, however, more than compensated for by the unrivaled natural beauties of its position, and of its charming environs. No town in Europe, not Palermo with its "Golden Shell," Constantinople with its "Golden Horn," nor Genoa, the "Gem of the Riviera," can boast of so magnificent a situation. The traveller who approaches Naples by sea may well be excused for any exuberance of language. As the ship 326] enters the Gulf, passing between the beautiful isles of Ischia and Capri, which seem placed like twin outposts to guard the entrance of this watery paradise, the scene is one which will not soon fade from the memory. All around stretches the bay in its azure immensity, its sweeping curves bounded on the right by the rocky Sorrentine promontory, with Sorrento, Meta, and a cluster of little fishing villages nestling in the olive-clad precipices, half hidden by orange groves and vineyards, and the majestic form of Monte Angelo towering above. Farther along the coast, Vesuvius, the tutelary genius of the scene, arrests the eye, its vine-clad lower slopes presenting a startling contrast to the dark cone of the volcano belching out fire and smoke, a terrible earnest of the hidden powers within. On the left the graceful undulations of the Camaldoli hills descend to the beautifully indented bay of Pozzuoli, which looks like a miniature replica of the parent gulf with the volcano of Monte Nuovo for its Vesuvius. Then straight before the spectator lies a white mass like a marble quarry; this, with a white projecting line losing itself in the graceful curve of Vesuvius, resolves itself, as the steamer draws nearer, into Naples and its suburbs of Portici and Torre del Greco. Beyond, in the far background, the view is shut in by a phantom range of snowy peaks, an offshoot of the Abruzzi Mountains, faintly discerned in the purple haze of the horizon. All these varied prospects unite to form a panorama which, for beauty and extent, is hardly to be matched in Europe.

This bald and inadequate description may perhaps serve to explain one reason for the pre-eminence among the many beautiful views in the South of Europe popularly allowed to the Bay of Naples. One must attribute 327] the æsthetic attraction of the Bay a good deal to the variety of beautiful and striking objects comprised in the view. Here we have not merely a magnificent bay with noble, sweeping curves (the deeply indented coasts of the Mediterranean boast many more extensive), but in addition we have in this comparatively circumscribed area an unequaled combination of sea, mountain, and island scenery. In short, the Gulf of Naples, with its islands, capes, bays, straits, and peninsulas, is an epitome of the principal physical features of the globe, and might well serve as an object lesson for a child making its first essay at geography. Then, too, human interest is not lacking. The mighty city of Naples, like a huge octopus, stretches out its feelers right and left, forming the straggling towns and villages which lie along the eastern and western shores of the bay. A more plausible, if prosaic, reason for the popularity of the Bay of Naples may, however, be found in its familiarity. Naples and Vesuvius are as well known to us in prints, photographs, or engravings as St. Paul's Cathedral or the Houses of Parliament. If other famous bays, Palermo or Corinth, for instance, were equally well known, that of Naples would have many rivals in popular estimation.

The traveller feels landing a terrible anticlimax. The noble prospect of the city and the bay has raised his expectations to the highest pitch, and the disenchantment is all the greater. The sordid surroundings of the port, the worst quarter of the city, the squalor and filth of the streets, preceded by the inevitable warfare with the rapacious rabble of yelling

149

boatmen, porters, and cab drivers, make the disillusionized visitor inclined to place a sinister interpretation on the equivocal maxim, Vedi Napoli e poi mori; and Goethe's aphorism, that a man 328] can never be utterly miserable who retains the recollection of Naples, seems to him the hollowest mockery and the cruellest irony.

The streets of Naples are singularly lacking in architectural interest. Not only are there few historic buildings or monuments, which is curious when we consider the important part Naples played in the mediæval history of the South of Europe, but there are not many handsome modern houses or palaces of any pretensions. Not that Naples is wanting in interest. The conventional sight-seer, who calls a place interesting in proportion to the number of pages devoted to its principal attractions in the guide-books, may, perhaps, contemptuously dismiss this great city as a place which can be sufficiently well "done" in a couple of days; but to the student of human nature Naples offers a splendid field in its varied and characteristic scenes of street life. To those who look below the surface, this vast hive of humanity, in which Italian life can be studied in all its varied phases and aspects, cannot be wholly commonplace.

It is a truism that the life of Naples must be seen in the streets. The street is the Neapolitan's bedroom, dining-room, dressing-room, club, and recreation ground. The custom of making the streets the home is not confined to the men. The fair sex are fond of performing al fresco toilettes, and may frequently be seen mutually assisting each other in the dressing of their magnificent hair in full view of the passers-by.

As in Oriental cities, certain trades are usually confined to certain streets or alleys in the poorer quarters of the town. The names at street corners show that this custom is a long-established one. There are streets solely for cutlers, working jewelers, second-hand bookstalls, 329] and old clothes shops, to name a few of the staple trades. The most curious of these trading-streets is one not far from the Cathedral, confined to the sale of religious wares; shrines, tawdry images, cheap crucifixes, crosses, and rosaries make up the contents of these ecclesiastical marine stores. This distinctive local character of the various arts and crafts is now best exemplified in the Piazza degli Orefici. This square and the adjoining streets are confined to silversmiths and jewelers, and here the characteristic ornaments of the South Italian peasant women can still be bought, though they are beginning to be replaced by the cheap, machine-made abominations of Birmingham. Apart from the thronging crowds surging up and down, these narrow streets and alleys are full of dramatic interest. The curious characteristic habits and customs of the people may best be studied in the poor quarters round the Cathedral. He who would watch this shifting and ever-changing human kaleidoscope must not, however, expect to do it while strolling leisurely along. This would be as futile as attempting to stem the ebb and flow of the street currents, for the streets are narrow and the traffic abundant. A doorway will be found a convenient harbor of refuge from the long strings of heavily laden mules and donkeys which largely replace vehicular traffic. A common and highly picturesque object is the huge charcoal-burner's wagon, drawn usually by three horses abreast. The richly decorated pad of the harness is very noticeable, with its brilliant array of gaudy brass flags and the shining repoussé plates, with figures of the Madonna and the saints, which, together with the Pagan symbols of horns and crescents, are supposed to protect the horses from harm. Unfortunately these talismans do not seem 330] able to protect them from the brutality of their masters. The Neapolitan's cruelty to animals is proverbial. This characteristic is especially noticeable on Festas and Sundays. A Neapolitan driver apparently considers the seating capacity of a vehicle and the carrying power of a horse to be limited only by the number of passengers who can contrive to hang on, and with anything less than a dozen perched on the body of the cart, two or three in the net, and a couple on the shafts, he will think himself weakly indulgent to his steed. It is on the Castellamare Road on a Festa that the visitor will best realize the astonishing elasticity of a Neapolitan's notions as to the powers of a beast of burden. A small pony will often be seen doing its best to drag uphill a load of twelve or fifteen hulking adults, incited to its utmost efforts by physical suasion in the form of sticks and whips, and moral suasion in the shape of shrill yells and oaths. Their diabolical din seems to give some color to the saying that "Naples is a paradise inhabited by devils."

The al fresco restaurants of the streets are curious and instructive. That huge jar of oil simmering on a charcoal fire denotes a fried-fish stall, where fish and "oil-cakes" are retailed at one sou a portion. These stalls are much patronized by the very poor, with whom macaroni is an almost unattainable luxury. At street corners a snail-soup stall may often be seen, conspicuous by its polished copper pot. The poor consider snails a great delicacy; and in this they are only following ancient customs, for even in Roman times snails were in demand, if we may judge from the number of snail-shells found among the Pompeii excavations. A picturesque feature are the herds of goats. These ambulating dairies stream through the town in the early morning. The intelligent 331] beasts know their customers, and each flock has its regular beat, which it takes of its own accord. Sometimes the goats are milked in the streets, the pail being let down from the upper floors of the houses by a string, a pristine type of ascenseur. Generally, though, the animal mounts the stairs to be milked, and descends again in the most matter-of-fact manner.

The gaudily painted stalls of the iced-water and lemonade dealers give warmth of color to the streets. There are several grades in the calling of acquaiolo (water-seller). The lowest member of the craft is the peripatetic acquaiolo, who goes about furnished simply with a barrel of iced water strapped on his back, and a basket of lemons slung to his waist, and dispenses drinks at two centesimi a tumbler. It was thought that the completion of the Serino aqueduct, which provides the whole of Naples with excellent water at the numerous public fountains, would do away with the time-honored water-seller; but it seems that the poorer classes cannot do without a flavoring of some sort, and so this humble fraternity continue as a picturesque adjunct of the streets. These are only a few of the more striking objects of interest which the observer will not fail to notice in his walks through the city. But we must leave this fascinating occupation and turn to some of the regulation sights of Naples.

Though, in proportion to its size, Naples contains fewer sights and specific objects of interest than any other city in Italy, there are still a few public buildings and churches which the tourist should not neglect. There are quite half-a-dozen churches out of the twenty-five or thirty noticed by the guide-books which fully repay the trouble of visiting them. The Cathedral is in the old 332] part of the town. Its chief interest lies in the gorgeous Chapel of St. Januarius, the patron saint of Naples. In a silver shrine under the richly decorated altar is the famous phial containing the coagulated blood of the saint. This chapel was built at the beginning of the seventeenth century, in fulfilment of a vow by the grateful populace in honor of the saint who had saved their city "from the fire of Vesuvius by the intercession of his precious blood." St. Januarius is held in the highest veneration by the lower classes of Naples, with whom the liquefaction ceremony, which

151

takes place twice a year, is an article of faith in which they place the most implicit reliance. The history of the holy man is too well known to need repetition here. The numerous miracles attributed to him, and the legends which have grown round his name, would make no inconsiderable addition to the hagiological literature of Italy.

Of the other churches, Sta. Chiara, S. Domenico Maggiore, and S. Lorenzo are best worth visiting. In building Sta. Chiara the architect would seem to have aimed at embodying, as far as possible, the idea of the church militant, the exterior resembling a fortress rather than a place of worship. In accordance with the notions of church restoration which prevailed in the last century, Giotto's famous frescoes have been covered with a thick coating of whitewash, the sapient official who was responsible for the restoration considering these paintings too dark and gloomy for mural decoration. Now the most noteworthy objects in the church are the Gothic tombs of the Angevin kings.

The two churches of S. Domenico and S. Lorenzo are not far off, and the sightseer in this city of "magnificent distances" is grateful to the providence which has placed 333] the three most interesting churches in Naples within a comparatively circumscribed area. S. Domenico should be visited next, as it contains some of the best examples of Renaissance sculpture in Naples as Sta. Chiara does of Gothic art. It was much altered and repaired in the course of the sixteenth and seventeenth centuries, but still remains one of the handsomest of the Neapolitan churches. Its most important monument is the marble group in relief of the Virgin, with SS. Matthew and John, by Giovanni da Nola, which is considered to be the sculptor's best work. The Gothic church of S. Lorenzo has fortunately escaped in part the disfiguring hands of the seventeenth century restorer. This church is of some literary and historical interest, Petrarch having spent several months in the adjoining monastery; and it was here that Boccaccio saw the beautiful princess immortalized in his tales by the name of Fiammetta.

In order to appreciate the true historical and geographical significance of Naples, we must remember that the whole of this volcanic district is one great palimpsest, and that it is only with the uppermost and least important inscription that we have hitherto concerned ourselves. To form an adequate idea of this unique country we must set ourselves to decipher the earlier-written inscriptions. For this purpose we must visit the National Museum, which contains rich and unique collections of antiquities elsewhere absolutely unrepresented. Here will be found the best treasures from the buried towns of Cumæ, Herculaneum, and Pompeii. The history of nearly a thousand years may be read in this vast necropolis of ancient art.

To many, however, the living present has a deeper interest than the buried past, and to these the innumerable 334] beautiful excursions round Naples will prove more attractive than all the wealth of antiquities in the Museum. Certainly, from a purely æsthetic standpoint, all the best things in Naples are out of it if the bull may be allowed. To reach Pozzuoli and the classic district of Baiæ and Cumæ, we pass along the fine promenade of the Villa Nazionale, which stretches from the Castello dell' Ovo (the Bastille of Naples) to the Posilipo promontory, commanding, from end to end, superb unobstructed views of the Bay. Capri, the central point of the prospect, appears to change its form from day to day, like a fairy island. Sometimes, on a cloudless day, the fantastic outlines of the cliffs stand out clearly defined against the blue sea and the still bluer background of the sky; the houses are plainly distinguished, and you can almost fancy that you can descry the groups of idlers leaning over the parapet of the little piazza, so clear is the atmosphere. Sometimes the island is bathed in a bluish haze, and by a curious atmospheric effect a novel form of Fata Morgana is seen, the island, appearing to be lifted out of the water and suspended between sea and sky.

The grounds of the Villa Nazionale are extensive, and laid out with taste, but are disfigured by inferior plaster copies, colossal in size, of famous antique statues. It is strange that Naples, while possessing some of the greatest masterpieces of ancient sculptors, should be satisfied with these plastic monstrosities for the adornment of its most fashionable promenade. The most interesting feature of the Villa Nazionale is the Aquarium. It is not merely a show place, but an international biological station, and, in fact, the portion open to the public consists only of the spare tanks of the laboratory. This 335] institution is the most important of its kind in Europe, and is supported by the principal European Universities, who each pay for so many "tables."

At the entrance to the tunneled highway known as the Grotto di Posilipo, which burrows through the promontory that forms the western bulwark of Naples, and serves as a barrier to shut out the noise of that overgrown city, is a columbarium known as Virgil's Tomb. The guide-books, with their superior erudition, speak rather contemptuously of this historic spot as the "so-called tomb of Virgil." Yet historical evidence seems to point to the truth of the tradition which has assigned this spot as the place where Virgil's ashes were once placed. A visit to this tomb is a suitable introduction to the neighborhood of which Virgil seems to be the tutelary genius. Along the sunny slopes of Posilipo the poet doubtless occasionally wended his way to the villa of Lucullus, at the extreme end of the peninsula. Leaving the gloomy grotto, the short cut to Pozzuoli, on our right, we begin to mount the far-famed "Corniche" of Posilipo, which skirts the cliffs of the promontory. The road at first passes the fashionable Mergellina suburb, fringed by an almost uninterrupted series of villa gardens. This is, perhaps, one of the most beautiful drives in the South of Europe. Every winding discloses views which are at once the despair and the delight of the painter. At every turn we are tempted to stop and feast the eyes on the glorious prospect. Perhaps of all the fine views in and around Naples, that from the Capo di Posilipo is the most striking, and dwells longest in the memory. At one's feet lies Naples, its whitewashed houses glittering bright in the flood of sunshine. Beyond, 336] across the deep blue waters of the gulf, Vesuvius, the evil genius of this smiling country, arrests the eye, from whose summit, like a halo,

"A wreath of light blue vapor, pure and rare,
Mounts, scarcely seen against the deep blue sky;
....
... It forms, dissolving there,
The dome, as of a palace, hung on high
Over the mountains."

153

Portici, Torre del Greco, and Torre del' Annunziata can hardly be distinguished in this densely populated fringe of coast-line, which extends from Naples to Castellamare. Sometimes at sunset we have a magnificent effect. This sea-wall of continuous towns and villages lights up under the dying rays of the sun like glowing charcoal. The conflagration appears to spread to Naples, and the huge city is "lit up like Sodom, as if fired by some superhuman agency." This atmospheric phenomenon may remind the imaginative spectator of the dread possibilities afforded by the proximity of the ever-threatening volcano towering in terrorem over the thickly populated plain. There is a certain weird charm born of impending danger, which gives the whole district a pre-eminence in the world of imagination. It has passed through its baptism of fire; and who knows how soon "the dim things below" may be preparing a similar fate for a city so rashly situated? These dismal reflections are, however, out of place on the peaceful slopes of Posilipo, whose very name denotes freedom from care.

The shores of this promontory are thickly strewed with Roman ruins, which are seldom explored owing to their comparative inaccessibility. Most of the remains, 337]theaters, temples, baths, porticoes, and other buildings, whose use or nature defies the learning of the antiquary, are thought to be connected with the extensive villa of the notorious epicure Vedius Polio. Traces of the fish-tanks for the eels, which Seneca tells us were fed with the flesh of disobedient slaves, are still visible. Descending the winding gradients of Posilipo, we get the first glimpse of the lovely little Bay of Pozzuoli. The view is curious and striking. So deeply and sharply indented is the coast, and so narrow and tortuous are the channels that separate the islands Ischia, Procida, and Nisida, that it is difficult to distinguish the mainland. We enjoy a unique panorama of land and sea, islands, bays, straits, capes, and peninsulas all inextricably intermingled.

Continuing our journey past the picturesque town of Pozzuoli, its semi-oriental looking houses clustered together on a rocky headland, like Monaco, we reach the hallowed ground of the classical student. No one who has read his Virgil or his Horace at school can help being struck by the constant succession of once familiar names scattered so thickly among the dry bones of the guide-books. The district between Cumæ and Pozzuoli is the sanctum sanctorum of classical Italy, and "there is scarcely a spot which is not identified with the poetical mythology of Greece, or associated with some name familiar in the history of Rome." Leaving Pozzuoli, we skirt the Phlegræan Fields, which, owing to their malaria-haunted situation, still retain something of their ancient sinister character. This tract is, however, now being drained and cultivated a good deal. That huge mound on our right, looking like a Celtic sepulchral barrow, is Monte Nuovo, a volcano, as its name denotes, of recent origin. Geologically speaking, it is a thing of yesterday, 338] being thrown up in the great earthquake of September 30th, 1538, when, as Alexandre Dumas graphically puts it, "One morning Pozzuoli woke up, looked around, and could not recognize its position; where had been the night before a lake was now a mountain." The lake referred to is Avernus, a name familiar to all through the venerable and invariably misquoted classical tag, facilis descensus Averni, etc. This insignificant-looking volcanic molehill is the key to the physical geography of the whole district. Though the upheaval of Monte Nuovo has altered the configuration of the country round, the depopulation of this deserted but fertile country is due, not to the crater, but to the malaria, the scourge of the coast. The scarcity of houses on the western horn of the Bay of Naples is very marked, especially when contrasted with the densely populated sea-board on the Castellamare side. Leaving Monte Nuovo we come to a still more fertile tract of country, and the luxuriant vegetation of these Avernine hills "radiant with vines" contrasts pleasingly with the gloomy land "where the dusky nation of Cimmeria dwells" of the poet. The mythological traditions of the beautiful plain a few miles farther on, covered with vineyards and olive-groves and bright with waving corn-fields, where Virgil has placed the Elysian Fields, seem far more appropriate to the landscape as we see it. Perhaps a sense of the dramatic contrast was present in the poet's mind when he placed the Paradiso and the Inferno of the ancients so near together.

Quite apart from the charm with which ancient fable and poetry have invested this district, the astonishing profusion of ruins makes it especially interesting to the antiquary. A single morning's walk in the environs of 339] Baiæ or Cumæ will reveal countless fragmentary monuments of antiquities quite outside of the stock ruins of the guide-books, which the utilitarian instincts of the country people only partially conceal, Roman tombs serving as granaries or receptacles for garden produce, temples affording stable-room for goats and donkeys, amphitheaters half-concealed by olive-orchards or orange-groves, walls of ancient villas utilized in building up the terraced vineyards; and, in short, the trained eye of an antiquary would, in a day's walk, detect a sufficient quantity of antique material almost to reconstruct another Pompeii. But though every acre of this antiquary's paradise teems with relics of the past, and though every bay and headland is crowded with memories of the greatest names in Roman history, we must not linger in this supremely interesting district, but must get on to the other beautiful features of the Gulf of Naples.

Capri, as viewed from Naples, is the most attractive and striking feature in the Bay. There is a kind of fascination about this rocky island-garden which is felt equally by the callow tourist making his first visit to Italy, and by the seasoned traveller who knew Capri when it was the center of an art colony as well known as is that of Newlyn at the present day. No doubt Capri is now considered by super-sensitive people to be as hopelessly vulgarized and hackneyed as the Isle of Man or the Channel Isles, now that it has become the favorite picknicking ground of shoals of Neapolitan excursionists; but that is the fate of most of the beautiful scenery in the South of Europe, if at all easy of access. These fastidious minds may, however, find consolation in the thought that to the noisy excursionists, daily carried to and from Naples by puffing little cockle-shell steamers, 340] the greater part of the island will always remain an undiscovered country. They may swarm up the famous steps of Anacapri, and even penetrate into the Blue Grotto, but they do not, as a rule, carry the spirit of geographical research farther.

The slight annoyance caused by the great crowds is amply compensated for by the beauties of the extraordinarily grand scenery which is to be found within the island desecrated by memories of that "deified beast Tiberius," as Dickens calls him. What constitutes the chief charm of the natural features of Capri are the sharp contrasts and the astonishing variety in the scenery. Rugged precipices, in height exceeding the cliffs of Tintagel, and in beauty and boldness of outline surpassing the crags of the grandest Norwegian fiords, wall in a green and fertile garden-land covered with orange-orchards, olive-groves, and corn-fields. Cruising round this rock-bound and apparently inaccessible island, it seems a natural impregnable fortress, a sea-girt Gibraltar guarding the entrance of the gulf, girdled round with precipitous crags rising a thousand feet sheer out of the sea, the cliff outline broken by steep ravines and rocky headlands, with outworks of crags, reefs, and Titanic masses of tumbled rocks.

155

These physical contrasts are strikingly paralleled in the history of the island. This little speck on the earth's surface, now given up solely to fishing, pastoral pursuits, and the exploitation of tourists, and as little affected by public affairs as if it were in the midst of the Mediterranean, instead of being almost within cannon-shot of the metropolis of South Italy, has passed through many vicissitudes, conquered in turn by Phœnicians, Greeks, and Romans; under Rome little known and used merely 341] as a lighthouse station for the benefit of the corn-galleys plying from Sicily to Naples, till the old Emperor Augustus took a fancy to it, and used it as a sanatorium for his declining years. Some years later we find this isolated rock in the occupation of the infamous Tiberius, as the seat of government from which he ruled the destinies of the whole empire. Then, to run rapidly through succeeding centuries, we find Capri, after the fall of Rome, sharing in the fortunes and misfortunes of Naples, and losing all historic individuality till the beginning of the present century, when the Neapolitan Gibraltar became a political shuttlecock, tossed about in turn between Naples, England, and France; and now it complacently accepts the destiny Nature evidently marked out for it, and has become the sanatorium of Naples, and the Mecca of artists and lovers of the picturesque.

One cannot be many hours in Capri without being reminded of its tutelary genius Tiberius. In fact as Mr. A. J. Symonds has forcibly expressed it, "the hoof-print of illustrious crime is stamped upon the island." All the religio loci, if such a phrase is permissible in connection with Tiberius, seems centered in this unsavoury personality. We cannot get away from him. His palaces and villas seem to occupy every prominent point in the island. Even the treasure-trove of the antiquary bears undying witness to his vices, and shows that Suetonius, in spite of recent attempts to whitewash the Emperor's memory, did not trust to mere legends and fables for his biography. Even the most ardent students of Roman history would surely be glad to be rid of this forbidding spectre that forces itself so persistently on their attention. To judge by the way in which the simple Capriotes seek to perpetuate the name of their illustrious patron, 342] one might almost suppose that the Emperor, whose name is proverbial as a personification of crime and vice, had gone through some process akin to canonization.

Capri, though still famous for beautiful women, whose classic features, statuesque forms, and graceful carriage, recall the Helens and the Aphrodites of the Capitol and Vatican, and seem to invite transfer to the painter's canvas, can no longer be called the "artist's paradise." The pristine simplicity of these Grecian-featured daughters of the island, which made them invaluable as models, is now to a great extent lost. The march of civilization has imbued them with the commercial instinct, and they now fully appreciate their artistic value. No casual haphazard sketches of a picturesque group of peasant girls, pleased to be of service to a stranger, no impromptu portraiture of a little Capriote fisher-boy, is now possible. It has become a "sitting" for a consideration, just as if it took place in an ordinary Paris atelier or a Rome studio. The idea that the tourist is a gift of Providence, sent for their especial benefit, to be looked at in the same light as are the "kindly fruits of the earth," recalls to our mind the quaint old Indian myth of Mondamin, the beautiful stranger, with his garments green and yellow, from whose dead body sprang up the small green feathers, afterwards to be known as maize. However, the Capriotes turn their visitors to better account than that; in fact, their eminently practical notions on the point appear to gain ground in this once unsophisticated country, while the recognized methods of agriculture remain almost stationary. The appearance of a visitor armed with sketch-book or camera is now the signal for every male and female Capriote within range to pose in forced 343] and would-be graceful attitudes, or to arrange themselves in unnatural conventional groups: aged crones sprout up, as if by magic, on every doorstep; male loungers "lean airily on posts"; while at all points of the compass bashful maidens hover around, each balancing on her head the indispensable water-jar. These vulgarizing tendencies explain why it is that painters are now beginning to desert Capri.

But we are forgetting the great boast of Capri, the Blue Grotto. Everyone has heard of this famous cave, the beauties of which have been described by Mr. A. J. Symonds in the following graphic and glowing picture in prose: Entering the crevice-like portal, "you find yourself transported to a world of wavering, subaqueous sheen. The grotto is domed in many chambers; and the water is so clear that you can see the bottom, silvery, with black-finned fishes diapered upon the blue-white sand. The flesh of a diver in this water showed like the face of children playing at snap-dragon; all around him the spray leaped up with living fire; and when the oars struck the surface, it was as though a phosphorescent sea had been smitten, and the drops ran from the blades in blue pearls." It must, however, be remembered that these marvels can only be perfectly seen on a clear and sunny day, and when, too, the sun is high in the sky. Given these favorable conditions, the least impressionable must feel the magic of the scene, and enjoy the shifting brilliancy of light and color. The spectators seem bathed in liquid sapphire, and the sensation of being enclosed in a gem is strange indeed. But we certainly shall not experience any such sensation if we explore this lovely grotto in the company of the 344] noisy and excited tourists who daily arrive in shoals by the Naples steamer. To appreciate its beauties the cave must be visited alone and at leisure.

Those who complain of the village of Capri being so sadly modernized and tourist-ridden will find at Anacapri some of that Arcadian simplicity they are seeking, for the destroying (æsthetically speaking) fingers of progress and civilization have hardly touched this secluded mountain village, though scarcely an hour's walk from the "capital" of the island.

We will, of course, take the famous steps, and ignore the excellently engineered high-road that winds round the cliffs, green with arbutus and myrtle, in serpentine gradients, looking from the heights above mere loops of white ribbon. Anacapri is delightfully situated in a richly cultivated table-land, at the foot of Monte Solaro. Climbing the slopes of the mountain, we soon reach the Hermitage, where we have a fine bird's-eye view of the island, with Anacapri spread out at our feet, and the town of Capri clinging to the hillsides on our right. But a far grander view rewards our final climb to the summit. We can see clearly outlined every beautiful feature of the Bay of Naples, with its magnificent coast-line from Misenum to Sorrento in prominent relief almost at our feet, and raising our eyes landwards we can see the Campanian Plain till it is merged in the purple haze of the Apennines. To the south the broad expanse of water stretches away to the far horizon, and to the right this incomparable prospect is bounded by that "enchanted land" where

"Sweeps the blue Salernian bay,
With its sickle of white sand."

157

345]and on a very clear day we can faintly discern a purple, jagged outline, which shows where "Pæstum and its ruins lie."

In spite of the undeniable beauties of Capri, it seems so given up to artists and amateur photographers that it is a relief to get away to a district not quite so well known. We have left to the last, as a fitting climax, the most beautiful bit of country, not only in the neighborhood of Naples, but in the whole of South Italy. The coast-road from Castellamare to Sorrento, Positano, and Amalfi offers a delightful alternation and combination of the softest idyllic scenery with the wildest and most magnificent mountain and crag landscape. In fact, it is necessary to exercise some self-restraint in language and to curb a temptation to rhapsodize when describing this beautiful region. The drive from Naples to Castellamare is almost one continuous suburb, and the change from this monotonous succession of streets of commonplace houses to the beautiful country we reach soon after leaving the volcanic district at Castellamare is very marked. In the course of our journey we cannot help noticing the bright yellow patches of color on the beach and the flat house-tops. This is the wheat used for the manufacture of macaroni, of which Torre dell' Annunziata is the great center. All along the road the houses, too, have their loggias and balconies festooned with the strips of finished macaroni spread out to dry. All this lights up the dismal prospect of apparently never-ending buildings, and gives a literally local color to the district. There is not much to delay the traveller in Castellamare, and soon after leaving the overcrowded and rather evil-smelling town we enter upon the beautiful coast-road to Sorrento. For the first few miles the road runs near the 346] shore, sometimes almost overhanging the sea. We soon get a view of Vico, picturesquely situated on a rocky eminence. The scenery gets bolder as we climb the Punta di Scutola. From this promontory we get the first glimpse of the beautiful Piano di Sorrento. It looks like one vast garden, so thickly is it covered with vineyards, olive groves, and orange and lemon orchards, with an occasional aloe and palm tree to give an Oriental touch to the landscape. The bird's-eye view from the promontory gives the spectator a general impression of a carpet, in which the prevailing tones of color are the richest greens and gold. Descending to this fertile plateau, we find a delightful blending of the sterner elements of the picturesque with the pastoral and idyllic. The plain is intersected with romantic, craggy ravines and precipitous, tortuous gorges, resembling the ancient stone quarries of Syracuse, their rugged sides covered with olives, wild vines, aloes, and Indian figs. The road to Amalfi here leaves the sea and is carried through the heart of this rich and fertile region, and about three miles from Sorrento it begins to climb the little mountain range which separates the Sorrento plain from the Bay of Salerno.

We can hardly, however, leave the level little town, consecrated to memories of Tasso, unvisited. Its flowers and its gardens, next to its picturesque situation, constitute the great charm of Sorrento. It seems a kind of garden-picture, its peaceful and smiling aspect contrasting strangely with its bold and stern situation. Cut off, a natural fortress, from the rest of the peninsula by precipitous gorges, like Constantine in Algeria, while its sea-front consists of a precipice descending sheer to the water's edge, no wonder that it invites comparison with 347] such dissimilar towns as Grasse, Monaco, Amalfi and Constantine, according to the aspect which first strikes the visitor. After seeing Sorrento, with its astonishing wealth of flowers, the garden walls overflowing with cataracts of roses, and the scent of acacias, orange and lemon flowers pervading everything, we begin to think that, in comparing the outlying plain of Sorrento to a flower-garden, we have been too precipitate. Compared with Sorrento itself, the plain is but a great orchard or

158

market-garden. Sorrento is the real flower-garden, a miniature Florence, "the village of flowers and the flower of villages."

We leave Sorrento and its gardens and continue our excursion to Amalfi and Salerno. After reaching the point at the summit of the Colline del Piano, whence we get our first view of the famous Isles of the Syrens, looking far more picturesque than inviting, with their sharp, jagged outline, we come in sight of a magnificent stretch of cliff and mountain scenery. The limestone precipices extend uninterruptedly for miles, their outline broken by a series of stupendous pinnacles, turrets, obelisks, and pyramids cutting sharply into the blue sky-line. The scenery, though so wild and bold is not bleak and dismal. The bases of these towering precipices are covered with a wild tangle of myrtle, arbutus, and tamarisk, and wild vines and prickly pears have taken root in the ledges and crevices. The ravines and gorges which relieve the uniformity of this great sea-wall of cliff have their lower slopes covered with terraced and trellised orchards of lemons and oranges, an irregular mass of green and gold. Positano, after Amalfi, is certainly the most picturesque place on these shores, and, being less known, and 348]consequently not so much reproduced in idealized sketches and "touched up" photographs as Amalfi, its first view must come upon the traveller rather as a delightful surprise. Its situation is curious. The town is built along each side of a huge ravine, cut off from access landwards by an immense wall of precipices. The houses climb the craggy slopes in an irregular ampitheater, at every variety of elevation and level, and the views from the heights above give a general effect of a cataract of houses having been poured down each side of the gorge. After a few miles of the grandest cliff and mountain scenery we reach the Capo di Conca, which juts out into the bay, dividing it into two crescents. Looking west, we see a broad stretch of mountainous country, where

"... A few white villages
Scattered above, below, some in the clouds,
Some on the margins of the dark blue sea,
And glittering through their lemon groves, announce
The region of Amalfi."

To attempt to describe Amalfi seems a hopeless task. The churches, towers, and arcaded houses, scattered about in picturesque confusion on each side of the gigantic gorge which cleaves the precipitous mountain, gay with the rich coloring of Italian domestic architecture, make up an indescribably picturesque medley of loggias, arcades, balconies, domes, and cupolas, relieved by flat, whitewashed roofs. The play of color produced by the dazzling glare of the sun and the azure amplitude of sea and sky gives that general effect of light, color, sunshine, and warmth of atmosphere which is so hard to portray, either with the brush or the pen. Every nook of this charming little rock-bound Eden affords tempting 349] material for the artist, and the whole region is rich in scenes suggestive of poetical ideas.

When we look at the isolated position of this once famous city, shut off from the rest of Italy by a bulwark of precipices, in places so overhanging the town that they seem to dispute its possession with the tideless sea which washes the walls of the houses, it is not easy to realize that it was recognized in mediæval times as the first naval Power in Europe, owning factories and trading establishments in all the chief cities of the Levant, and producing a code of maritime laws whose leading principles have been incorporated in modern international law. No traces remain of the city's ancient grandeur, and the visitor is tempted to look upon the history of its former greatness as purely legendary.

The road to Salerno is picturesque, but not so striking as that between Positano and Amalfi. It is not so daringly engineered, and the scenery is tamer. Vietri is the most interesting stopping-place. It is beautifully situated at the entrance to the gorge-like valley which leads to what has been called the "Italian Switzerland," and is surrounded on all sides by lemon and orange orchards. Salerno will not probably detain the visitor long, and, in fact, the town is chiefly known to travellers as the starting-place for the famous ruins of Pæstum.

These temples, after those of Athens, are the best preserved, and certainly the most accessible, of any Greek ruins in Europe, and are a lasting witness to the splendor of the ancient Greek colony of Poseidonia (Pæstum). "Non cuivis homini contingit adire Corinthum," says the poet, and certainly a visit to these beautiful ruins will make one less regret the inability to visit the Athenian Parthenon. Though the situation of the 350] Pæstum Temple lacks the picturesque irregularity of the Acropolis, and the Temple of Girgenti in Sicily, these ruins will probably impress the imaginative spectator more. Their isolated and desolate position in the midst of this wild and abandoned plain, without a vestige of any building near, suggest an almost supernatural origin, and give a weird touch to this scene of lonely and majestic grandeur. There seems a dramatic contrast in bringing to an end at the solemn Temples of Pæstum our excursion in and around Naples. We began with the noise, bustle, and teeming life of a great twentieth-century city, and we have gone back some twenty-five centuries to the long-buried glory of Greek civilization.

Printed in Great Britain
by Amazon

18193449R00098